# BRUTAL

## MY AUTOBIOGRAPHY

### IWAN THOMAS

BLOOMSBURY SPORT
LONDON · OXFORD · NEW YORK · NEW DELHI · SYDNEY

BLOOMSBURY SPORT
Bloomsbury Publishing Plc
50 Bedford Square, London, WC1B 3DP, UK
29 Earlsfort Terrace, Dublin 2, Ireland

BLOOMSBURY, BLOOMSBURY SPORT and the Diana logo are trademarks of
Bloomsbury Publishing Plc

First published in Great Britain 2024

A catalogue record for this book is available from the British Library

Library of Congress Cataloguing-in-Publication data has been applied for

ISBN: HB: 978-1-3994-1364-0; ePUB: 978-1-3994-1366-4; ePDF: 978-1-39941361-9

2 4 6 8 10 9 7 5 3 1

Typeset in Adobe Garamond Pro by Deanta Global Publishing Services, Chennai, India
Printed and bound in Great Britain by CPI Group (UK) Ltd, Croydon, CR0 4YY

To find out more about our authors and books visit www.bloomsbury.com
and sign up for our newsletters

# CONTENTS

# FOREWORD

This is as candid a book as you will find and lays bare the realities of a sporting career with unflinching honesty. But this fascinating sports odyssey is more than just a chronicle of medals won and races run. It delves deep into the heart of the modern athlete's experience, shining a light on the challenges and triumphs that extend far beyond the field of play.

In sharing his story, Iwan opens a dialogue on issues that have long been shrouded in silence. He bravely confronts the hurdles faced by athletes in their everyday lives, breaking down barriers and paving the way for a new era of openness and understanding in sport.

This book will resonate not only with those who have chased their own dreams on the track, but with anyone who has ever faced adversity and emerged stronger on the other side.

Lord Sebastian Coe, May 2024

# PROLOGUE

## 5.00am. 16 June 2021

The pain is unbearable. I've been limping from the start thanks to my still injured foot, but by Mile 10 my good foot hurts so much that I don't even notice the bad one. As miles go by, cramp-like pain grips my whole body. Each tiny stone I step on feels like broken glass.

'He might as well quit. He's not going to make it.' That's what the steward says as I leave the checkpoint.

'Fuck off,' I respond breathlessly. I've avoided the cut-off by four minutes and still have three checkpoints left; that amounts to another 30 miles. I know for sure that I'll make it, though – as long as my body doesn't give out on me. I have a photo of Teddy in my pocket, and on my arm I've marker-penned the words 'For those less fortunate'. Every time it hurts, I look at my arm and my picture and they remind me why I am here . . .

# One

# ENERGY TO BURN

I was one of those kids who ran everywhere. To my mate's house, to the shops, to school. Why would anyone walk? It was too slow, too boring. I wanted speed, action, excitement. I loved running. It made me feel alive, exhilarated and free. 'Iwan's got ants in his pants.' 'He's exuberant.' 'He can't sit still.' These days I might be tested for ADHD. Back then they called me hyperactive. 'He's got too much energy to burn' – to me it sounded like a compliment. I must have been such a handful for my parents.

I was small and a little podgy as a youngster, a redhead with a rather unfetching pudding-bowl haircut. Careering around dressed in my shabby dungarees and scuffed trainers like a Tasmanian devil. I was out all day, every day, with just a 10-pence piece to call home if I got into trouble.

In the muddy fields, gardens, trees and playgrounds of my sleepy town, Godmanchester, I discovered danger. That meant taking on any dare my reckless mates thought me too stupid to refuse. Like taking my life into my own hands by walking across the lock by Portholme Meadow. Traversing the slippery wooden gates, with the pounding River Ouse below willing me to misstep and plummet into her murky depths.

And if there was no obvious jeopardy, I made my own. I bunny-hopped on my bike over five fearful – and, on reflection, foolish – friends; jumped through a bonfire in the back garden; skateboarded along a 3-metre (10-ft) wall; leaped out of my parents' bedroom window (I think I was practising to be a stuntman). It's a miracle I made it to my 10th birthday. I was a kid who just loved danger, that rush of blood – a pre-teen adrenaline junkie. Once, part of the local quarry froze over, and I decided to take to the ice to breakdance (well, it was the 1980s!). To my shame, the police interrupted my backspins and drove me home. That took some explaining to my parents.

*Impressing* – that was my favourite thing. To get a 'Wow!' from a mate, a nod of approval from an older boy or even a tut from an old lady – those were my medals as a kid. I didn't think of it as showing off. I was an entertainer. I got a thrill from having an audience and felt connected to them. It made for a story that my friends and I could talk about for days: 'You've got a massive bruise', 'I thought you were a goner there', 'I heard someone called the police'. If doing mad things made them happy or gave them something to talk about, I was making their lives more exciting. That can only be a good thing. Right?

Like most boys, I loved football. We played on the rec, a big island in the river. Every kid from the area gathered for a match. There was no time to show your skills in those 30-a-side games with kids of all ages and sizes tearing around. We played until someone took his ball home or we lost it in the water or it became impossible to see the ball in the fading light.

In summer, we plunged into the River Ouse. Even when it was a sunny day, the water was freezing enough to put the chill in your body in seconds and leave you shivering. But I was there for hours mucking about, jumping in from heights of 12 metres (40 feet) from the overhanging branches. And it was dangerous: talk of the strong undercurrent or the fact we were miles from help if something went wrong never crossed our minds. All that scared me were the tales of the monstrous pikes. They patrolled the depths and could come up and take a finger or toe at any moment. I never kept my legs still when they were underwater.

In summer we often went to North Wales. We'd stayed with my grandmother, who lived outside Penygroes near Caernarfon and in the foothills of Yr Wyddfa (Snowdon). That was the real outdoors. Whenever I think back to those endless summers, the kind you have as a kid, I have Dexys Midnight Runners' hit 'Come on Eileen' running through my head – it was constantly on the radio – and the film *Stand by Me*. Just like in that film, my brother, a local lad and myself spent hours walking along a disused railway line (though, thankfully, we never found a dead body). We liked exploring: jumping across streams, sometimes getting soaked, climbing the stone walls, making dens and building a fire or charging through the fields of sheep.

My brother, Gareth, was three years older than me. Back when we were very young, we were close, though it gradually became very apparent that we had very different personalities. We shared the same red hair, but that was it. We were chalk and cheese: the serious, studious indoor child and the all-action, fresh air fiend.

I took the annoying brother role usually reserved for older siblings, winding him up to the point where he had to react. I must have been such an annoying little git to have as a younger brother. Gareth went off to boarding school at 11 and we grew apart. We will always be brothers and I'd do anything for him, but as we got older, we took different paths.

My dad was away a lot of the time too. From Monday to Friday, he worked for the MOD and stayed in London. He was a military man, a sharp dresser and he cut a dashing figure – he was mistaken for Michael Caine on a number of occasions. He was also very musical, playing the piano and guitar to a high standard. He played in a rock band in his youth, when he met my mum. He was great fun when I was young and I really looked forward to weekends when we spent time together, and missed him when he wasn't around.

Dad had a dazzling white Alfa Romeo Alfasud Sprint, a car you didn't see much around our way – and it turned heads. A real petrolhead's car; classy, elegant and sophisticated. It was his pride and joy and he made sure it was tuned up and polished so you could see your reflection in it. On Sundays, going for a drive down the country lanes, we might come across some guy in a souped-up Astra or similar, and Dad would say, 'Tighten your seatbelt. Watch this.' Then he'd put his foot down and burn them up.

Dad instilled a lifetime love of fast cars and motorbikes. He started me early. When I was 11, he helped me buy my own 50cc motorbike: a Honda Z50 motocross. It wasn't legal to ride it on the streets, so I took it to the local rec. The speed, power and the noise were intoxicating and I put my foot down and pushed it as fast as it would go. My mates and myself would rip round the field, perfecting skids and jumps and pulling wheelies. We'd dodge kids and dogs and generally be annoying – I loved it. That bike led to a brush with the local police, when I was stopped for wheeling it home. Apparently, wheeling it wasn't legal either. However, the constable pointed out a loophole: if I put the front wheel on a skateboard and pushed it, nobody could touch me.

Dad could be an old-fashioned parent. He came from a working-class background and worked his way up to become an RAF group captain, the equivalent of an army colonel. He had set himself high standards in his life – and met them – and he expected the same of his children. He could be formal and quite strict. I understood and respected that and did my best not to let him down. Pleasing him was my number one aim – from my earliest memories to the present day – maybe because he was away from home so much when I was young, or maybe because it seemed so hard to meet his expectations. When I got it – a nod or a simple 'well done' – it was such a great feeling.

Come Monday, Dad went off to London again. With my brother away at boarding school, it was often just Mum and myself together in the house. Mum was a teacher and she really cared about her pupils. One day I got home from school and there were about 25 kids in the house. They were running riot, screaming and shouting and charging round the house. It was mayhem, in a fun way. It turned out the school's camping trip had been cancelled and so, feeling sorry for them, she invited them to pitch their tents in the garden. I don't think Dad was too happy about it when he came home, though. Later she taught at the roughest school in the area, where the kids who had been expelled from every other school ended up. They responded to her kindness and good nature and she loved it there.

Life with Mum was so easy-going. With just the two of us in the house we got along so well and were so close. She was happy to give me the freedom I wanted and I didn't take advantage. If she said to be home by eight, I'd make sure I was back at five to. Mind you, she was a terrible cook. (She admits to being the world's worst in the kitchen.) She could muster a spaghetti bolognaise at a push, but that was about it. I lived off packaged microwave meals that looked like a glorified prison tray with compartments for potatoes, meat and veg. I sat eating them in front of the TV while watching *Junior Kick Start* or *The A-Team* – and I'm not complaining, it was most kids' dream.

Mum was slim and glamorous with a warm smile that made people instantly like her. (In her younger days, she'd won Miss Personality Girl Dolgellau.) She constantly had a cigarette in her mouth. It probably seemed elegant back then, but as a 10-year-old I hated the smell. She spoke Welsh as her first language and rang her mum every Sunday evening to chat away in Welsh. It would infuriate me that I couldn't understand what she was saying about me. With a name like Iwan Gwyn, I never had any doubt that I was Welsh too. She had met my dad at University in Aberystwyth. He, however, was a proud Englishman. Watching England play rugby against Wales on TV was like World War III in our house.

We had great family holidays, and Dad tells me he first noticed on one in Spain, when I was about eight, how fast I could run. Every morning, we walked or jogged back from the shops to our villa and this soon developed into a competition between us. It was about 3 km (2 miles) home and quite a climb, so it wasn't an easy run. Around the third day of racing, he recalls, I was beating both my brother and him – then in his late 30s and a reasonably fit man.

That desire for acceptance from Dad wasn't going quite so well on the academic front, though. I wasn't a star pupil. I had a lot to live up to because my brother was exactly that. Dad's oldest son was ticking all the boxes; he was super-intelligent, studious and academically successful. While I was out tearing around, he was playing Dungeons & Dragons; when I was building bonfires, he was making model aircraft. While he was getting 'A's for every subject, I was unexceptional. I was successful on the sports field, but whatever helped me succeed there left me at the classroom door. With a ball at my feet, I was self-confident; when it was my turn to read in class, just nervous and breaking out in a cold sweat.

All this came to a head when it was time for me to go to secondary school. My brother had gone to boarding school when he was 11. He was really happy there and was excelling in his studies. Dad was keen that I should follow him, but I knew it wasn't for me. I didn't want to leave my friends and adventures and my life at home. And I felt intimidated by the idea of being among posh kids and facing academic expectations that seemed beyond me.

Fortunately, I had an ally in Mum. I can still hear them arguing:

'Iwan's going to be fine, don't worry about him,' she'd say.

'Fine isn't enough. The third set isn't fine. Just getting by isn't excelling in life.'

While Mum was concerned about me as a person – that I was happy, had good friends and tried my best – Dad was more concerned about my academic progress. For him, exam results were everything. That was how he had made his way to the top and there was no other route to success in life. OK, his younger son was good at sport, but there was no future in that!

Mum and I won that battle (I would later discover the war was not over) and I went to Hinchingbrooke School, a comprehensive on the edge of Huntingdon. I was terrified of this new school. I was prepared to suffer the awful school uniform – the shirt and tie with a terrible green blazer made of some disgusting material (in Chemistry lessons, I'd stay clear of the Bunsen burners for fear of going up in a ball of fire) – but the rumoured fate of first years put the fear of God into me.

The talk was of an initiation ceremony where they pushed first years into a holly bush. I was petrified and cried my eyes out to Mum, whose words 'I'm sure they won't – and if they do, it won't be so bad' didn't seem reassuring enough. The thought caused nightmares in that last week of summer holidays. Of course, Mum was right. When I saw the tree, it looked pathetic. *Bring it on*, I thought; I'd jumped through bigger bushes than that deliberately!

I loved school. I liked being with my mates, the fun with the teachers and most of the classes. I was hyperactive, but it didn't affect my concentration in class. I settled down, did my homework and never once got a detention. For all my energy, I was never in trouble at school. Not real trouble. I was a bit of a class clown, a cheeky chappie who liked to make people laugh – and that included the teachers as well as my schoolmates. I loved a prank; I was that kid letting off stink bombs in the playground and squirting fart spray into teachers' lockers.

Once, when I was 14, I wrote on the board in a classroom in the upper school that after lunch, the History class should go to the lower school, a 10-minute walk away. The teacher arrived back from lunch to find the classroom empty and had a long walk fetching them all back. She wasn't happy, but the other teachers laughed and when I was sent to see the head, Mr Whiteside, he just smirked and called me a bloody idiot.

Mischievous and cheeky, I like to think I was – and I seemed to get away with it. I'd usually be up to something, but it was all harmless. I was a bit of a wheeler-dealer too. I remember once buying a box of knock-off Mars Bars at the back of the garage. I was selling them for 20p each, until someone complained the chocolate had gone white and that the sell-by date was long past.

Hinchingbrooke was such a good school for sport. We had a PE lesson every day; every lunchtime we kicked a ball around and if there wasn't a school match, I'd organise some kind of after-school game. Mr McGrady, our PE teacher, was enthusiastic and encouraging. He reminded us of the 'tough but fair' PE teacher Geoff 'Bullet' Baxter in *Grange Hill*. A tough Northerner, he wore shorts all year round and joined in every game he could.

I was the classic all-round sporty kid; good at football, rugby, athletics and cross-country. Some of the kids there even called me 'County' because I was county standard for all those sports. I came second in the 1500 metres in the County Championships in 1988. I ran it in 4 minutes 45 – pretty handy for a 13-year-old. Roger McGrady was the first to spot that I had athletic talent and tried to push me further. I remember him quoting *Chariots of Fire* – 'You can't put in what God left out' – when I spurned athletics for other sports. He was a good sportsman himself and he recognised my potential. He followed my career closely and we continued to stay in touch. Maybe I should have taken what he said more seriously.

Sport became part of my identity. Kids in the school knew me and I got smiles and nods in the corridor. Even the sixth-formers knew who I was. Of course, I liked being good at sport, but that connection with people really made me feel good. I chatted to kids I'd never met before and made new friends. I really enjoyed it, but that was as far as it went. There was no idea of sport as a career; that would be ridiculous.

I played rugby for the county as a right winger, but cross-country was a big focus at school. The school was set in a large park and there was a great course through forest, fields and mud. I was good at the long distance and I'd literally lap many of the other kids. I had speed and stamina and never minded the cold and rain. Cross-country was where I first discovered that pain didn't have to be a hindrance. Rather than slow you down, it can drive you on. Don't give in to it and it becomes exhilarating, like some kind of superpower. On those muddy fields of Hinchingbrooke, I learned a lot about pushing my body more when it wanted to slow down and stop.

When I was 14, I ran the cross-country in the County Championships. We were running round Ferry Meadows in Peterborough. A tough race, but I thought I had a decent chance of finishing in the top three and qualifying for the English Schools Athletics Championships. I noticed one boy I passed because he was running in football boots. It just looked a bit odd. I passed, left him and thought nothing more of it. I came into the last lap in second place; I wasn't going to win but runner-up would be good enough. Suddenly a boy comes sprinting past me. *Hang on!* I thought. *I recognise that lad. Where have his football boots gone, though?* I finished third and secured my place in the English Schools competition, but was suspicious. Eventually, the mystery was solved. It turned out there were identical twins and one had hidden behind a tree and emerged to take the last lap!

English Schools was another level, though: I finished 365th. Maybe cross-country wasn't my game after all. No big deal. By that time, I was deep in a new sport; one that suited me down to a T.

# Two

# ON TWO WHEELS

'They're opening a BMX circuit on the Roman Way Industrial Estate,' Mark said one night. 'You should ask your parents for a bike for Christmas.'

In December 1984, I was only 10 years old and still needed looking after when my parents were out. My babysitter, Mark, was 16. He was a cool teenager, and I looked up to and listened to him. Mark knew me pretty well, and knew what kind of boy I was. If I wasn't out playing football, I was out on my bike or swimming. And I didn't scare easily. A few jumps and crashes were never going to put me off.

The bike I got for Christmas was a second-hand Mongoose – an iconic BMX bike of the 1980s. It wasn't a surprise, but that didn't stop me from bursting with anticipation and excitement as I took off the wrapping. I hit the quiet streets of Godmanchester on Christmas morning – and here was a quality bike; lighter than anything I'd ridden before. With a bit of effort you could be flying in a few seconds. That feeling of flying grabbed me and didn't let go.

The bike and myself were inseparable. I rode to the shops, to school, around town; all day, every day. They just couldn't get me off it. One day, I was taking a breather at the Chinese Bridge, Godmanchester's biggest tourist attraction. The next thing I knew, someone saw the bike and me on the front cover of a book in a shop in Huntingdon. I was famous!

I'd excelled at different sports for a few years, but this was something else: I felt different from the other bikers. I was strong, determined and really, really hated losing. At the track it was rough and ready: no helmet, no pads, you came off and got back on again or you went home. No one there could live with a boy who could go fast and knew no fear. In no time, I felt like I was king of that track, beating boys who were bigger and older. Still, I never imagined that within a year I'd be racing against the best riders in the country.

There are two types of BMX competition. Freestyling, out on your own, choreographing moves on the bike to impress the judges. I wasn't really interested in stunts and tricks. I just wanted to go as fast as I could and pit myself against others, so I took the other option: racing. Myself against a handful of others. One lap of a circuit of dips, bumps and berms (corners). No holds barred; simply first across the line wins.

The thrill of the race was everything and I couldn't wait to get on the track. (It had been built by local parents, and 35 years later, Dad, now mayor, would instigate the building of a new pump track in its place.) Like the hundreds that had appeared in towns and cities across Britain in the 1980s, this was a dirt track that weaved around sharp corners and hit ridges at which the bikes would literally take off.

BMX racing is hard, fast and dangerous. Each track and each race is never the same, the risk levels are high; and broken bones, gashes and bruises are an accepted hazard of the sport. From the starting gate to the finish line was one massive adrenaline rush and I was wired. And still buzzing by the time the next race came around. It was so addictive, and I couldn't wait for the weekend.

From the very first day I hit that track, it was clear that BMX and I were going to get along just fine. The chemistry was perfect. I had a certain combination of bravery, stupidity, stamina and maybe natural talent that the other kids were missing. If they had designed a sport specifically for me back then, it would have been BMX. I wanted speed, laced with a little danger, and I craved competition; rivals who pushed me, but (hopefully) were left in my wake. Scoring a goal or taking on my mates in a race to the rec might be fun, but BMX was more than that: it was serious, adrenaline-pumping, heart-stopping, all out do-or-die battle.

It wasn't long before I had tired of racing the kids of my own age and was taking on the older lads. When I started beating the bigger boys, people began to take notice of the little upstart. My mates become my cheerleaders as I jumped the doubles – the successive mounds which you could either ride through or get enough air on the first to fly onto the descent of the second. Jumping was faster and looked great, but it was risky with a big chance of crashing. Of course, I always jumped.

Word gets around fast in a small town, and Dave Hudson, who ran Spoke Cycles in Huntingdon, soon found out about the lad who was tearing up the track in Godmanchester. He already ran a small team comprising his son, daughter and another lad and now he offered to sponsor me. By the mid-'80s the BMX scene was at its peak and there were tracks up and down the land, with regional leagues and open races for every age group. Kit, bike repairs, transport and entry fees were not cheap and riders relied on either bike manufacturer teams or enthusiastic local shops like Spokes Cycles for support. Dave was my gateway into BMX racing; he knew the set-up, how to enter the races and, crucially, he had a van and a caravan and was prepared to give up his weekends to take us racing.

That was my life as a teenager. Fast and busy, weekdays at school with whatever sport was happening and weekends driving up and down the country. Every Friday afternoon, Dave drove the van and caravan to wherever the meeting was taking place. I'd be in the back of the van, often with one of the others. There were no windows, just a bench seat on one side with the bikes on the other. It was my job to hold the bikes upright when we went around corners.

There were two organisations running BMXing in Britain then – NBMXA and UK BMX – so there were races going on all over the country. The BMX track and its surroundings was our home for the weekend. One week it could be Nottingham, the next Felixstowe, then Slough or Hillingdon. The journeys could be long, especially on the way back if you'd lost. I still remember those Smokey Robinson songs word for word; I think it was the only tape Dave had!

By this point, the BMX scene had been going nearly a decade but it was still a backwater sport. Meetings were on recreation parks or scrap ground or industrial parks in hidden corners of town. Competitors' caravans – including Dave's – often surrounded the track, which resembled a makeshift travellers' camp for the weekend. On race day, the fly-tipping and dogs picking at discarded boxes of fried chicken gave up the space to a hot dog and ice cream van doing good business.

The sounds of a scratchy tannoy with a local commentator doing his best Murray Walker impersonation filled the air and the local Red Cross stood ready for the opportunity to practise their first aid. They were rarely disappointed: cuts, grazes and sprains were guaranteed, bones were regularly broken and the flashing lights of a real ambulance were not an uncommon sight. It all served to raise the excitement levels – you knew there was a good chance you wouldn't leave there unscathed.

These were big events, with races in age groups from age 7 to adult, and there were often more than 100 riders attending. Saturday was practice day when you battled for a chance to ride the track, watched the older riders to pick up any tips, or checked out your rivals (if they weren't already staring you out). Sunday was race day; three motos (heats with accumulated points) and a final. It wasn't until late in the afternoon that we set off for home again and I'd still have my homework to do.

Often I turned up for school on Monday bruised and battered from a crash. 'I'll have to take it easy today,' I told the PE teacher as I lifted my trouser leg to reveal a huge gash. The school seemed to take pride in my BMX exploits and was always supportive. Mum often wrote a note to get me off Friday afternoon lessons, and I never remember it being a problem. It was what I did.

There was little in the way of BMX coaching. I picked it up as I went along, copying the older riders and sometimes getting the odd bit of advice from Dave or my dad. I never trained for racing; that never occurred to me. I got fitter and stronger just from riding and I was immediately winning trophies across the country. Within six months I was East Anglia champion (I'd retain that title every year until I stopped riding) and I was ranked as high as number two in the country.

The racing was intense. Often chaotic. A minute's kamikaze dash around the track with no thought other than getting to the finish line as soon as possible. You knew it could be carnage, but if you had any fear you'd already lost. Now an Olympic sport, it is recognised as one of the most dangerous events in the Games. Crashing happens in a hundred different ways: losing grip on a corner, getting knocked off by another rider, catching wheels or pedals, crashing out on a jump or just losing control of the bike. Hopefully it's only a scrape and you get straight back on for the next race, but a broken bone and that's it – sometimes for a few weeks until you've recovered just enough to hit the starting gate again.

The worst break I had was when I fractured my wrist in a fall. It was agony. Worse still, we were going to set off for a family skiing holiday the next day. I was sitting in the hospital with Dad and asked him: 'Are we still going to be able to go skiing tomorrow?'

'Shhhh!'

'What?'

'Don't mention the skiing.'

They bandaged and set my wrist in plaster and no more was said. Off we went on holiday. Of course, 'go careful' wasn't in my vocabulary. I was skiing down those black slopes one-handed. By the third day of the holiday, the bandages were soaking and the plaster cast had broken. Dad wasn't going to let that stop me. Somehow he found a local shop selling plaster of Paris and did a bit of DIY surgery. It was a mess but it did the job. When we went back to the hospital, though, they were not impressed. It was a job to get the new cast off.

'This is awful. Who did the cast?' they said, scanning my notes. Some poor doctor got the blame, and it was all Dad and myself could do not to burst out laughing. *When the gate drops, the bullshit stops*, was the BMX motto. The start was crucial. Not so much in gaining fractions of a second, but in getting clear of the other riders who could block you in or obstruct your run-up to the first berm. At elite levels, BMX has a starting gate, a platform that snaps open as the race begins. Focus and technique are everything. Forget how your rivals are looking, who's watching you or what you are having for tea – as soon as that gate drops, you need to be away. Then it's all about the holeshot; being the first rider through the first corner and defending your ground.

I enjoyed the life: making friends – and some enemies – at the race; receiving the trophies which were beginning to pile high at home; telling my mates at school on Mondays how I'd got on and wearing my countless bruises, scars and casts protecting broken bones with pride. Mostly, I loved the challenge. Walking to the starting gate and eyeing up my opponents. We were all in the same age group, and some boys looked massive, some were riders I'd raced before and some were unknown, but they were all rivals. At the starting gate, I knew that man to man I could beat any of them.

I was always super-confident, but victory was never assured. Crashes happened all the time, blocking you or bringing you down. In my first nationals at Derby Greyhound Stadium in 1985 I had a good chance of winning – until I hit the deck in a massive pile-up. I was also in an age group where I was competing against the best riders the sport has seen. I had many battles against Lee Ives, Nathan Bash, Paul Flavin, CJ Butler and the astonishingly good Dylan Clayton (a rider so stylish they called him Doctor Smooth). They were great rivals and all became BMX legends.

Every track was different and there were some really tough ones. The Peterborough Pirates had a longer track than most, and that's where I first encountered lactic acid – which would later become very familiar. Poole had two big jumps called the Dollys (named after Dolly Parton for obvious reasons), while the doubles at Wigan were impossible to jump. Wigan was home to Doctor Smooth and his dad had helped to design it. He made it so difficult that only the Doctor was good enough to jump them.

BMX was a real father-and-son sport and the tracksides were full of guys cheering on their sons. My dad was no exception. I was always grateful for his support even if it could be a bit embarrassing. For one big race he made me a T-shirt that read: *I've smashed Bash and slayed CJ, Dylan Who get out of my way!* He was my biggest supporter and came along to all of my big races. He believed in my ability to beat anyone and drove me to push myself as far as I could. In return, I desperately sought his approval by winning every race I entered. I felt I was riding that bike for the both of us.

Dad took great pride in my success and, of course, I loved that. However, the other side of the coin was that this became a burden. He would be massively disappointed if I came third in a race where I was one of the favourites. It didn't seem to matter that I had made the podium. By not winning, I felt that I let him down. I could always cope with my own frustrations and disappointment and bounce back, but having to deal with his too was much more difficult to bear. Maybe I was growing up, but I went from being carefree to feeling immense pressure to win.

I had to toughen up pretty quickly. BMX was a working-class sport. Polite middle-class kids like me who weren't prepared to scrap from the off had no chance. Your rivals would elbow you, cut you up, ride you off the berms. I remember Paul Flavin ('Dirty Flav' to his mates), who was one of the best riders around, and also one of the toughest. He'd knock you right off if you gave him half a chance. I wasn't a fighter at school or a dirty footballer and I played on the wing at rugby, as far away from the mauls as I could, but BMX taught me to be aggressive on the track. You don't survive long on those tracks if you let yourself be bullied, you had to give as good as you got. It was on those dirt tracks that I learned to be a sporting animal. *You can ride a Scorpion or you can be a nice guy. Never both.* So ran an advert for Scorpion, one of the biggest BMX bike manufacturers. After a year or so riding, I joined the Scorpion team, which Dave Hudson was now running. To take your place on the starting line in team livery with a factory bike put you among the elite. From now on I proudly wore my full yellow and red Scorpion gear: helmet, gloves, padded trousers and a top with 'Scorpion USA Factory' and a red scorpion emblazoned across the front.

In 1987, I went to Orlando to compete in the World Championships. My mum, dad and brother and some family friends who lived in the States all came out to support me. It was a long and expensive trip. Most of the riders I knew from home didn't have that kind of money. They were with one parent, if that. Here I was with a whole team. Now, I was at the age when I could get a little self-conscious about such things, and seeing them all lined up trackside in their matching blue T-shirts that carried the legend *Iwan's Team* was something I just had to bear.

The 1987 World Championships were a huge step up for me. At home, I had got to know my rivals. Looking along the starting gate, I knew what they could do and that I could match them. This was something different. These were the best kids in the world. I might have heard one or two names bandied about, but they were all strangers. Then there were the crowds. The venue was packed out and noisy with a cacophony of cowbells ringing almost constantly. They created a gladiatorial atmosphere and this 13-year-old was petrified.

The immensity of what I was facing hit home with the sight of one particular jump on the track. It was a massive 9-metre (30-foot) leap from one jump to another. I went and looked at it and immediately thought: *No, I can't do it*. It wasn't fear, I just knew it was way beyond my capabilities. I was thinking, *I'm just going to have to push through* [ride over both jumps] *rather than do the jump. It will be slower, but I'll still be in the race.*

Dad had other ideas. 'I've seen other kids jumping it. If you are going to make the final – and then win it – you're going to have to jump it. The others are all going to do it.'

'But they're all big kids,' I argued. 'They're all older than me.'

Deep down I knew Dad was right; if I wanted to win I'd have to do it. He was always so full of positive reinforcement: *'You can do it'*, *'You're better than all of them'*, *'Believe in yourself, you can win this.'* Maybe he knew I was right too, knew I just wasn't quite at that level, but he wasn't prepared to accept it. One of us had to back down, and my need to please him was always going to be the deciding factor.

This was a jump I had never taken on before – and with good reason. But I didn't think I had a choice. At these events, you don't get allocated much practice time, so it was now or never. I rode through twice and on the third time round went for it. I hit the take-off as hard as I could. I got over, but my back wheel caught the lip of the jump. I crashed down and smashed my back wheel. I'd tried and failed.

When I came to the actual heats, with a new wheel and a little more practice, I tried again. This time I managed to clear it. It was enough to see me through to the semi, but then a fall put me out of the race. My family had come so far to cheer me on, and I felt terrible. I was learning that with defeat came not only disappointment but something that cut even deeper: guilt.

Defeat always hurt. That's the downer of having a competitive spirit. The upside is that you are back up again, more determined than ever. The following year, I was at the 1988 European Championships in Slagharen, Holland. Once again, I crashed out. I was gutted; I was so desperate to prove myself.

This time, though, I had another chance. I also had a Cruiser class bike. They had 24-inch wheels rather than 20-inch wheels (60cm versus 50cm), so were bigger and heavier. These were ridden mainly by older riders but some competitive youngsters, like me, rode both classes to give themselves more chances of racing. I didn't really like riding Cruiser, but when you're fired by a desire to win, that doesn't matter and I rode myself into fourth place. As it wasn't my preferred class, I felt pretty chuffed with that result. It was a bonus I hadn't expected.

In 1989, I was back at the World Championships, this time in Brisbane, Australia. It was a big trip for me – and Dad. We were out there for three weeks, plenty of time for me to acclimatise and enough for Dad to ramp up my expectations without Mum's calming influence to diffuse things. It was the longest time we had spent together and we did have a great time. I took part in some local competitions to warm up for the finals and did pretty well. Things were looking good. On the outside.

I was 15 now and my mindset was changing. I was beginning to fall out of love with BMX. I wasn't enjoying the racing quite as much as I did. The sport had moved on and the jumps had got bigger and scarier. Physically I was quite a late developer and most of the other boys had begun to look like men to me. The track in Brisbane looked huge and dangerous. The starting gate was set really high with a steep drop to the first jump, so the race was going to be really rapid from the off. This was a feeling that was unfamiliar. Where before I had only a fear of failure rather than a fear of getting hurt, now I had become more self-aware.

When I lined up at the starting gate, there must have been 1000 spectators filling the air with their yells, but for me there was only one person out there I could hear, even if it was just in my head. Dad's opinion of me was the only thing that really mattered. That wasn't enough, though. I crashed out in the heats and didn't even make it to the semi-finals.

It was a bad crash and though I wasn't hurt, my pride was smashed to bits. In addition to the anger and frustration, there was something worse. Dad had put so much money, time and emotion into backing me, had travelled to the other side of the world, all for us to go home empty-handed and downhearted. I'd been the boy who always bounced back – but was I still? On the long flight back home my mind was whirring. *What's the point? Do I even want to do this any more?*

Now I somehow had to find a way of telling him that I'd had enough.

As it happened, my BMX racing ended with that crash and not much whimpering. Events took over. First, Dave Hudson, who had done so much to enable me to compete in the sport and ran my sponsorship, revealed he was moving to Scotland. Then Dad told me that his job was taking him to the NATO Allied Air Command headquarters at Ramstein Air Base in south-western Germany for three years. He and Mum would soon be relocating to Landstuhl, a town outside Kaiserslautern.

BMX had dominated four years of my teenage life and I had loved nearly every minute. I'd lapped up the travelling, the friendships, the rivalries and the thrill of the race and there is not one day of it I regret. When I started athletics, I realised just how much I had learned about racing from BMX; how important the start is, how to deal with the pressure, how to pace a race and how to deal with defeat. It gave me life lessons too; about the value of hard work, about being tough and not being trodden on and about dealing with disappointment. And I would continue to chase that adrenaline rush all my life. Would I let my own boys risk broken bones and bruises on the track? You bet. I can't wait until they are old enough so I can buy them their own bikes.

I was now a different boy from the podgy, pudding-bowl-haired lad who had climbed onto that Mongoose five years previously. I'd grown and was a tall, slim 16-year old. I was into hip-hop, especially the *Street Sounds Electro* albums and dressed the part. I wore British Knights trainers or Kickers, baggy jeans, tracksuits, and a Naf Naf top from London that was the envy of my mates. I'd practise my breakdancing and fancy myself as a b-boy and upset my mum by playing NWA's 'Fuck Tha Police' when she gave me lifts around town.

My hair was still ginger but it was now spikey. I went in to get the back and sides shaved and the barber said, 'Your mum has been in and told me that if you ask, not to give you tramlines.' She'd been to all the hairdressers in Godmanchester and even Huntingdon, but I got them done anyway!

As I spent the summer holidays in Germany with my best mate Steve, I faced a dilemma. It seemed I had two options: Steve's parents had kindly offered to let me live with them so I could do my A levels at Hinchingbrooke School, or I could go to Stamford, the boarding school that my brother had just left. Stay with my friends in a school I liked or go off to a new school where I knew no one and was convinced they were all posh snobs? It wasn't a difficult decision to make . . .

Except, there wasn't actually a choice. Once again I had Mum on my side, who thought my staying local sounded a nice idea, but this time we did not prevail. Dad was adamant that I was off to boarding school. And even that relied on me getting good GCSE results. If I failed to get five, then I was set to live with them in Germany and find myself a job. Results day was tense. My parents asked my gran to go into school to collect them and ring them through. When the phone rang my heart was in my mouth: three Bs, two Cs and an A. I'd done it! Even then, my academic success was slightly tainted: I had failed Maths and would have to retake it in the autumn.

Life had caught up with the kid who just loved running around in the open air without a care in the world. I was being sent away from my friends and family to a school I didn't want to go to and felt a deep resentment that Dad had made the choice for me. Oh well. It had been a good 15 years . . .

# 5.00am. 15 June 2021

What am I doing? At five in the morning, this seems such a ridiculous idea. Who do I think I am? No one is holding me to this. No one is going to think less of me if I back out.

*But it's non-negotiable. This is like a dark cloud hanging over me. Goading me. Blocking every other ambition and plan I have. I just can't move on until I've done it. There are too many promises I've made in my head, too many people to let down. It's become that mountain I have to climb.* I am not going to let myself fail.

*I've been limping from the start thanks to my already injured foot immediately radiating pain. I've no idea if it will last a mile, three miles or whatever. There is nothing I can do about it, so I put the pain in a box, put it to the back of my mind and say: 'Get fucked! I don't care. I'm doing this . . .'*

# Three

# LEARNING FAST

*It will be OK*, I'd told myself, going over it in my mind all morning. *I'll explain the situation; how desperately unhappy I am and that I've tried really hard, but I know for certain that I will never fit in here. They'll understand and give me a hug. I'll collect my things and I'll never have to come back here again.*

Except it didn't happen like that . . .

We'd spent a couple of hours looking at the dorm and wandering the grounds. Mum asked me how I was getting on with the other boys and showed concern about my arm (now in a plaster cast and sling). Dad asked practical questions about my timetable and the sets in which I'd been placed. I was quiet and downcast. No way was I going to give the impression that there was anything here that made me happy.

'I've given it a good go, honest,' I pleaded. 'It's just I'm not comfortable here. It's not for me. It's not like Hinchingbrooke. It's all . . . '

I could feel my words falling on stony ground. I tried again. Maybe I could win over Mum.

'I could come and live in Germany with you?'

If Mum looked concerned, Dad just looked disappointed by my lack of mettle.

'Your education is far too important,' he said, fixing me with that disappointed look.

He was right. I was a mummy's boy. And I knew it. I could do tough. I had proved I could look out for myself on the BMX track, shoulder to shoulder with pretty rough kids. I had gone off in the caravan every weekend to far-flung towns across the country. But I had never been away from home on my own for more than a couple of days. Like one of those chocolates, I had a soft centre. I couldn't believe I wouldn't be able to get a hug from my mum when I wanted. There was no softness here. No kind smiles. No female company at all. Even the thought punched me hard in the gut.

Back at my old school there would be 1200 kids who knew my name. Teachers who I could have a little fun and mischief with and knew what I was about; kids I'd stop and chat to and mates who I'd been friends with for years. Here I was on my own. I'd skipped through life, taking it for granted that there would always be a friendly face around. Now I was getting a crash course in loneliness, and I wasn't ready.

As I walked with Mum and Dad across the car park, I gave it one last go. I made every promise I could think of to reassure them that I would be fine in Germany. *I'll knuckle down, I'll get a job.* Was it cutting through? Maybe. One last push. My eyes filled. I pleaded to be allowed to leave and looked at them desperately.

I could sense Mum struggling. I recognised that glimmer in her eye. She turned to Dad with a questioning look. That moment of hope was dashed immediately. Dad was just looking at me. 'You'll be fine,' he said. 'It'll be the making of you.' He turned to Mum and just uttered, 'Annie, get in the car.'

That was the end of the matter. The car door slammed shut and so did my chance of escape. The car wound its way down the long drive out of the school with the tail lights growing fainter and fainter. When I'd seen Mum looking back at me in the mirror, the tears began to stream down my face. All my hopes, my reasoning, my clumsy attempts at emotional blackmail had come to nothing. I had nothing left but self-pity. I was a strapping 16-year-old; a rugby-playing, BMX-riding teenager who'd taken hundreds of knocks and broken a few bones, crying my eyes out in an empty car park because what else could I do?

Standing in the drizzling rain in the car park, I was glued to the spot as I watched until the car disappeared from view. I'd pinned everything on my parents' visit to the school and it had all been in vain.

I waited a long time before I trudged back to the boarding house; long enough for the signs that I had been crying to wear off. Being laughed at would have made the pain even worse. I looked at the place I now realised I was going to have to call home. A massive building, all stone, with massive doors and stained glass everywhere. A square with flower beds and a perfectly tended lawn complete with Wimbledon stripes. It might have been only 50 km (30 miles) from my old home, but it seemed like millions to me. It was imposing and scary and just added to my insecurity.

Talk about being taken out of your comfort zone! Just a few weeks previously, in one fell swoop, I had found myself away from my mum and my mates, thrown into a world that seemed old-fashioned and bizarre. A weird world with toffee-nosed kids, ancient echoing corridors and teachers wearing gowns and mortar boards. Among the Old Stamfordians were MPs, bishops, authors, a few famous sportsmen – and Gareth Thomas, my high-achieving brother who had left the previous summer to study at Leeds University. A lot to live up to, and it was all too much.

'Have you done your homework?' Mum used to shout at home. 'Yeah, Mum,' I'd lie. Then I'd bash out a paragraph for English 10 minutes before tea or draw a graph while I was watching *EastEnders*. Failing that, I would get Mum to 'help' (I always knew she'd do it for me eventually) or find someone on the bus in the morning who had done their maths so I could copy their answers.

Now I discovered I had to endure a thing called 'prep'. We were shut away in our rooms after school for two hours and expected to work in total silence. No talking, no TV or music; it was torture and so boring. There was no getting out of it because masters came and checked up on us regularly, poking their heads through the door and making some encouraging or sharp words.

I was also now expected to attend a religious service twice a week. The school had its own chapel which was hundreds of years old. When I first entered, I felt just like I was walking into St Paul's Cathedral. It was massive and eerie and I had no idea what was going on. I followed along with everyone else, hoping they didn't notice that I knew none of the hymns, couldn't make head nor tail of the sermons, and that the whole praying thing left me cold. If my old friends had seen me singing and mumbling, they'd have been amazed.

I missed them. I missed everything about my old life. I felt like I had never been away from home before. Of course, I'd been away BMXing nearly every weekend, but that was different. I loved that, I was engrossed in the competition. Here, I had too much time to think, and found out what 'homesick' meant.

My home was now my house. The school was divided into houses. This was where you boarded but was also the focus of your school life. I was in Byard House, situated right on the town's high street which cut through the centre of the school. It was a short row of large Victorian houses with large bay windows looking out onto the road, but inside was pokey and dark. I soon discovered that your house became part of your identity, and representing it, especially in sport, was a big part of school life.

Once a week we joined the other houses for assembly, led by the headmaster, Mr Timm, not at all affectionately referred to by all the boys as the Pig. I still have no idea why they called him that; maybe because he'd lumber around with his head down. I never asked. As I was new to the school in the sixth year, there were so many school conventions I never really understood.

This was all a big culture shock, but nothing was weirder than the tradition of fags. All through their lower school days, the boys now in my year had fagged – or run errands for – an assigned sixth-former. At every break the fag had to attend the sixth-former and attend to his demands: a cup of tea or maybe Marmite on toast. After dinner the older boy would say something like: 'Here's a couple of pounds, go to the shops. I want two cans of Coke, a packet of Quavers and a magazine,' and the fag would have to run off and get them. Sometimes the relationship could get mean.

Now was payback time as the former fags themselves became sixth-formers and were given fags of their own to collect sweets and crisps or clean their shoes. I was no rebel and I don't pretend I tried to buck the system, but I did feel incredibly guilty when I was given my own fag, having never had to run around after anyone through my school days. To assuage my guilt, I tried to be fair on my fag. I never asked him to clean my shoes or iron my shirt, and if he went to the shop for me, I'd give him a little extra cash to keep. Fagging was the one thing I never could get used to.

So here I was. At the lowest of lows. Dumped in a strange world and my parents far away in a foreign country. Everything used to be so free and easy and now I was told when to get up, where to go, when and what to eat. It was incredibly strict. I was making new friends, but I hadn't grown up with them like my old mates. I just couldn't be myself.

I told myself that it was like a prison sentence, albeit in a very posh Young Offenders Institution. *You've got two years to survive and then you're out of here – free again.*

Stamford was an odd place to do some quick growing up, but that was where I was and what I had to do. It didn't take me long to realise what being alone meant. It dug down into your soul and mercilessly and continually reminded you that it was just down to you now, there's no one else.

I did a reckoning, a mental audit of my situation. I was facing a strange culture with new traditions, rules, behaviours and even a language I didn't always understand. I felt bereft of any support, and I was homesick – I missed my mum and my mates.

On the other hand, I did have some cards to play. I could cope with the work; I was never going to excel like my brother but I'd get by. I could get along with people; I was fine at making friends and never had a problem with teachers. And I was good at sport. Give me a ball to kick or hold or a race to run and I was happy. The gym and playing field were my safe places.

Stamford took pride in its sporting reputation. The facilities were impressive, from the gym to the changing rooms, the pool to the playing fields. They read out the results in assembly and wrote up match reports for the school magazine. School sporting heroes – especially rugby players and cricketers – were celebrated. I knew that I could find appreciation and value as a sportsman. I immediately put myself forward for the rugby team. They had seen I was quick in PE lessons and threw me in to the fourth team as a winger.

It started well. Just three weeks into term, I was picked for the match against a Nottingham public school and was determined to make my mark. I stepped out on that pitch in a freshly laundered maroon shirt (and remembered I was used to digging my smelly unwashed Hinchingbrooke one out of the laundry basket). It felt like being at Twickenham. There was none of that having to keep one eye out for dog crap and avoiding muddy puddles and divots when playing (unlike my last school). Here every blade of grass glistened in the autumn sun and gently cushioned each step I took (again, unlike my last school).

I took one look at the full back, a tall, lumbering boy, and knew I had the beating of him. Sure enough, early in the game I was fed the ball and went for it. I burst past him and he barely got a hand on me. My first try. It's amazing how much better that can make you feel. By half time I had notched up two more. I was alive and kicking. I was at home here on the pitch.

As the second half got underway, a fourth was on the cards when I picked up the ball and headed for the line from 30 metres (100 feet) out. Suddenly out of nowhere I was hit. Not a tap tackle or a smother but a roughhouse clattering that sent me flying.

It happened in slow motion. Off balance and taken by surprise, I flew sideways through the air. With my left arm instinctively trying to cushion my fall, I hit the concrete path running parallel to the pitch. It was immediate agony. I tried to lift my arm, but even the slightest movement sent bolts of pain through my body. I gave it a minute. Maybe it was just a bruise and the pain would die down? I was desperate to play. This was my route to acceptance at the school. I went to lift it again, but it was seizing up and even the slightest movement was torture.

And so, even as the game carried on, a teacher picked me up to take me to hospital. Instead of being lauded as a hero at full time, I was having a broken arm set. All through the journey home I sat in the back seat of the teacher's car, with my arm throbbing with pain.

It was just a few days later when Mum and Dad arrived to visit, but the sympathy that I hoped for when they saw my sling counted for nothing. Standing in the drizzling rain in the car park, I was glued to the spot as I watched them slowly disappear from view. I'd pinned everything on their visit to the school.

And now that sport had been taken out of the equation until my arm healed, life at Stamford looked even more grim.

Most of the boys had been living and studying at the school together for five years. They knew each other so well and had their cliques. They were not bullies or even unfriendly, but this was a tough social challenge. First of all was sharing a room, a concept that filled me with dread. I'd never shared with anyone except my brother, and that was when I was really young. To spend every evening and night with another boy, one I had never met, seemed so wrong, so unnatural. He'd know the ropes and what was expected, but I had no idea. I was shaking when I approached the noticeboard where details of who was in which room were posted.

A crowd hustled around the board. I could hear a couple of them saying 'Oh my God, who's got Rob?' *What was this guy?* I thought. *A sociopath? Did he have strange habits? Was he some kind of sexual deviant?* I scoured the board for my name and eventually found it. Of course, next to my name was written: Robert Freer.

I feared the worst as I entered the small two-bunk bedroom we would share for the next year. It turned out none of those things were true. He was a really nice lad, just a bit different. Rob wasn't rich or privileged like most of the other boys (one was dropped off and picked up from school in a helicopter). He was a local lad and in boarding school because his mum had died, leaving him an orphan.

Rob wasn't bullied, but he was different to the others. He was a bit of a loner; he was really bright, but he didn't join in. He'd listen to his heavy metal and keep himself to himself. He didn't invite attention, but one night he couldn't help it. He was seen coming into the house shaking and with blood all over his hand. Everyone charged out of the TV room to find out what had happened.

After prep we always had some free time and sometimes people would nip into town, especially to the chippie. On this evening Rob had gone off on his own and been attacked by three townies down an alley. The Stamford locals didn't like us posh boys and never shied away from letting us know. Rob, though, wasn't one to back down even when outnumbered. He'd fought back and had given them a hiding.

It was a big talking point for days after at the school. 'Don't fuck with Freer!' they said. He wasn't big or strong, but he was mentally tough. He'd taken smacks to the face and carried on fighting. It didn't help his image, though. In fact, boys gave him an even wider berth as they were a bit scared of him now. I was his roommate, though, and he was alright. I felt pretty proud of him.

Rob had no interest in sport and we had little in common. However, thrown together in a room just four by four, we found we were kindred spirits. Neither of us were there from choice or privilege; we were both outsiders finding our own way to survive and we got on just fine. In fact, I grew to really like him and we have stayed in touch ever since.

I got through that first year, helped by Rob – and, it turned out, sport.

'There's that new kid who broke his arm playing rugby.'

'He was going for his fourth try – he was so quick!'

Having your arm in a sling – especially after a rugby game – gave me some kudos. A badge of honour. I was recognisable, I had an identity. I even looked a bit tough. The injury actually helped me adapt quicker to the school than I might have – although I wouldn't recommend it as a strategy!

As predicted I wasn't thriving academically at the school, but that was down to me. My heart wasn't in it. The only class I really looked forward to was PE. The school had plenty of good sportsmen and I loved pitting myself against them.

The Burghley Run was another of the school's big traditions. The whole school took part in a mass run through the Burghley Estate, the site of the famous horse trials. It was long, muddy and gruelling, a real endurance test, and a lot of the kids hated it. It was another step towards recognition for me and winning it was a big deal in the school. Having my name read out as the Run winner added to my growing reputation as a sportsman. When my arm fully recovered, I became part of the basketball team and also enjoyed a meteoric rise up the ranks from the rugby fourths to the first team.

In the summer term, not ever have been the slightest bit interested in cricket, I chose athletics. This was still just another sport for me. I was good, but despite some encouragement from the PE staff to concentrate a bit more, I thought athletics was just running. Don't get me wrong, I still wanted to win every race I entered and I was faster than most of the boys. It just wasn't my focus.

Half of my two-year sentence had now been completed. Sport had saved me, bringing me back from the darkest place I had been. After a summer in Germany back with my parents, I returned to school. A year older, with friends and making my mark in the rugby firsts – a huge deal at Stamford, where the rugby stars had the status of heroes. Various mentions in assembly meant that even some of the girls at the girls' school knew who I was. Things were a whole lot easier.

As the sixth form progressed, school rules became much more lenient and the boys, given an inch, took a mile. We made trips into town where there were pubs which we knew would serve us. Or we would go to the off-licence for cans of beer. There was a thriving drinking culture. Even my brother had been suspended once, getting caught for climbing down the drainpipe and going into town to the offie. For this, he was still considered a legend.

I was now feeling altogether more comfortable. In the second year, Rob opted for a single room and I was able to pick a new roommate. I chose to share a room with a new friend named Stuart Hobkirk or, more commonly, Mini (he was a small guy).

Also, I didn't push it with any of the *lovable rogue* antics that I'd played at Hinchingbrooke; I kept it straight and did my talking on the sports field. The school was good to me too. I'd bought myself a Yamaha TZR 125, which they let me keep in the shed. And I rode back to Godmanchester after school on Saturdays to see my childhood sweetheart, Nicole – a really freezing ride down the A1 when the winter months kicked in.

Friday afternoons at school were put aside for training with the CCF (Combined Cadet Force). Despite having a dad in the military, I couldn't think of anything worse. So I opted for community work. I'd go and sit with an elderly couple and chat for a couple of hours over tea and biscuits. It was the same couple my brother had spent time with, so there was some nice continuity there.

I really enjoyed chatting with them and doing any chores around the house. There was only one problem. They had the heating turned up so high, I found myself dropping off. More than once I woke up to find they'd left me sleeping on the sofa for hours! I became really fond of them.

I took my driving test in Stamford. Mid-test an old bloke pulls out on a push bike right in front of me. It was the fella I'd been chatting to every Friday afternoon.

I'd like to say I knew that Stamford Sports Day 1992 would be a turning point in my life. But that would be miles from the truth. However, as my time at Stamford came to a close, that day did loom large. School Sports Day at Stamford was a big event in the school calendar. The playing fields were busy with athletes and all the kids who brought picnics and cheered on their house representatives. There was even a PA giving out updates and commentary on the races. Records were kept, medals awarded and house points totted up. It was proper racing and those in with a shout of winning took it very seriously. That was me.

I'd spent only two years at the school, but I still wanted to leave my mark. I still felt I had something to prove. Perhaps to show Dad how strong I'd been and how well I had adapted or maybe to make up for not being the outgoing, cheerful lad I knew I could be. Whatever. It was time to show myself.

I didn't have the balls to pull off one of the final assembly pranks that were part of the school tradition. (Our final assembly would see massive banners unfurled from the air conditioning pipes proclaiming: *Long Live the Pig – We're out of here*, and led to the expulsion of the organiser on the final day of school.) Nor was I was ever going to get the grades for Oxford or Cambridge or be accepted at the Royal College of Music. I desperately wanted to do something no one else could do.

That was only ever going to happen through sport. On Sports Day the whole focus was on the sports field. I'd won the 100 metres and the long jump the previous year, but now I was in the top year and knew what I was up against. No one who scared me.

As the Summer Term came around, I wondered how many events I could win. Had anyone ever won three, four or even five? It was an idea, but I needed help.

I approached Kevin Johnstone, a Housemaster at my boarding house. He and his wife lived in Byard House and could be pretty strict with the kids, especially around lights out, but he was well liked. He was slim, tall and moustachioed, and his similarities to *Top Gun's* Goose hadn't gone unnoticed. I had a great relationship with him, partly because he was also Head of PE. He had seen how sport, especially rugby, basketball and cross-country, had helped me get through my time at the school and I knew he'd be keen to help me.

I told him I wanted to run in all five track events at the forthcoming Sports Day. He smiled as if he'd been expecting this but shook his head. 'No one's ever tried five,' he said. 'Besides, the timetable won't allow it.' He was right. It was a tightly scheduled event and it just wasn't physically possible to do all five.

I wasn't going to be put off easily. 'Nah! I've got to do five. What events can I do?' I was prepared to be flexible and look for events that didn't overlap. 'What about field?' I suggested. The shot-put? How difficult could it be? As I said, Kevin was a good bloke and happy to look for a solution.

We sat down and looked at the timetable in detail and worked out a plan. Events were staggered through the afternoon, so with careful choice I could move from one to another. There were some events that overlapped, so it wasn't possible to do everything I wanted. I was really keen to run the 1500 metres which I thought was a nailed-on win, but that just didn't fit the schedule.

If I was going to fit five in, everything would have to go like clockwork. I would be rushing from one event to another, and if anything overran I could easily miss the next. I would have little time for recovery and could forget about preparation. But we agreed, it might just work.

'It'll be quite a day!' he said, as I thanked him and walked out with a grin that stretched from ear to ear. He wasn't wrong.

I built this day up so much in my head. It was just a school sports day but somehow in my mind it was an Olympic pentathlon. Why? I wasn't really sure. I'm not even sure I thought about it. Was I doing it because I could? Because I enjoyed putting my abilities on trial? Because I wanted the congratulations, even adulation of others? Winning mattered to me far too much, far more than it should have done. I might have had A levels coming up, but this was my test. That *must win* sap was rising.

My day started with an event I'd never really tried before: the high jump. I wasn't completely sure what I was doing, but I'd had a go in practice and got myself a bit of technique. I did my best impression of a Fosbury Flop – jumping, twisting and throwing myself backwards over the bar, kicking my legs up behind me. It wasn't elegant, but turned out to be pretty effective. I ended up recording 1.74 metres. I thought I could have gone higher, but it was a decent effort and I slowly realised it was going to be enough to win the event. One down, four to go.

That felt good, but it was the 100 metres I really had my eye on. The record holder for that event was a certain G. Thomas, my brother, who had run the distance at just over 11 seconds two years before. It was all very well running for house pride, but family pride, that was something different.

My main rival was a boy named Richard Hawkins. He was 1.93m (6' 4") and well known as one of the quickest boys in the school. As we lined up, the nerves settled in. Everything I had learned at the BMX starting gate came back to me. I had no idea how to prepare myself and focus at that point. I looked across at him and those long legs. I'd beaten him a year ago and even taken his position in the rugby team, but now he was bigger and quicker. I palmed the doubts away and readied myself. The gun went; there were no blocks just a grass track, and instead of a smooth start, I immediately had a slight stumble.

I steadied myself and without being aware of it, I was in that zone. Utterly calm and determined, stretching every sinew to be as fast as I could. I was single-minded, this race was mine; he wasn't going to get it. Second by second, stride by stride I got closer to him, clawing myself level as we approached the line. I just wanted it more. That was enough for a lurch for the line to take me over in first place. Eleven seconds exactly! The Thomas name would be still be against the 100 metres in the school record book – but now preceded by an 'I' and not a 'G'.

Two out of two. For the first time, I had a few minutes to catch my breath. The adrenaline, the sprint, the way I had built up the day had all taken their toll and I was already feeling shattered. There were still another three events to go. I had some friendly encouragement from my friends and a pat on the back from some younger Byard house boarders supporting me, and I set off for the 200 metres start, where Richard Hawkins was waiting for Part Two.

I was learning fast. This time I didn't look at him. I don't know if he was frowning, plotting revenge or giving me a *Here we are again* smile – I didn't want to know. I took my place on the starting line and looked forward. *Just don't stumble this time*, I told myself.

I didn't.

I took off and there was no stopping me. This time I crossed the line alone. I had posted a time of 22.3. Another school record and I could hear murmurs of 'Wow, that is so fast!' Now people were beginning to talk about whether I could do the unthinkable and win all five. They knew that my fourth event was the long jump, the other event I had done well in the previous year. Surely that one was in the bag.

I wasn't so sure. The timetable had caught up with me. The 400 metres was due to start any minute and there was talk that I would have to skip the long jump or the 400 metres. Neither was an option. I hurried over to the jump. A little negotiation and it was agreed that I would be able to fit in just a single attempt. I didn't even have time to measure my run-up. I watched the boy before me jump a good distance and thought, *That will do, I'll steal his run-up.* There was no time to think it out, I just got my head down and sprinted as fast as I could on the runway. I hit the board and then bang, just took off. I landed, got to my feet and jogged off to the 400 metres start. They were still measuring it as I left, but as I went, I thought I heard someone say, 'He's only gone and jumped 6.64.' I was pretty sure that was going to be enough to win, but I put it to the back of my mind. There was still one event to go.

I hurried along to the 400 metres start and saw Kevin Johnstone with a big grin on his face. He was deep in conversation with the Head. The two of them were watching me as I came over to the start. I caught the end of the conversation.

'Look at him. He's knackered,' said the Head. 'There's no way that boy can win this. He's done far too much already.' Then he shook Johnstone's hand.

I don't know what that was about, but I had a good guess. I was convinced that he was betting against me. A tenner? Fifty quid? And even if it was a sportsman's bet, I was incensed. How dare he write me off like that. I looked at him with contempt, thinking, *Yeah, go on then, bet against me!* I'd make him pay.

He was right, I was knackered. But I was also pretty pumped, and now I had something more to prove. Hungry and fired up; that's the way to start a race.

Quite a crowd had gathered around the track. It was one of the last events of the day and word had got around that I'd already won a hatful. The boys from my house had all turned out to support me, but there was a swell of teachers and boys from the rest of the school who were curious to see what would happen. I could hear the hum of conversation and the sense of expectation as I readied myself at the start.

The 400 metres wasn't my event. It was a similar distance to the BMX tracks I'd ridden countless times, but that was where the similarity ended. I had no technique, no strategy, just the desire to run faster than anyone else. I got my head down and sprinted, telling myself, *This is the last event of the day, just hang on. You have to win.* I was completely focused and unaware of any of the other runners, but convinced they would pass me if I let up. When I crossed the finish line, I couldn't see anyone to the left or right of me. I looked around, and still there was no one in sight. I had run the lap in 49.4 seconds.

I was still trying to catch the Head's eye with a smirk when Kevin Johnstone came over. I thought he was going to hug me, but he didn't. Instead, he cuffed me around the head. 'Do you realise what you've done, boy?' he barked, as if I'd broken the chapel window.

'What do you mean, Sir?' I had wanted this so much and now I seemed to have done it, but I needed to hear him say as much. Even then I was gobsmacked by his response.

Calmly but very seriously, he spelled it out: 'Not only have you won five out of five events, you've now smashed every single school record.

'The last time I saw raw talent like that, they went on to win an Olympic medal.'

As I walked off I was bursting with pride. Proud that I had shown what I was made of, proud that that I had broken all of the school records (four of which still stand today) and proud that I had finally made my mark at that school.

I was awarded the Victor Ludorum Shield (the Latin means 'the winner of the games'). This was an award that had been around for almost a century. I'd now become part of the tradition that I had scorned and which had made me feel so overawed less than two years earlier. I called my parents and talked them through the day. It felt good to be able to show I had made some success of my time there. There was a way to go, but I had grown up a lot.

It was an end and a beginning.

I had little time to bask in my glory. As well as being Head of PE, Kevin Johnstone's speciality was athletics. He knew what he was talking about and knew raw talent when he saw it. He'd seen enough that day to push me further, to make me take athletics seriously as 'my' sport. He wanted to see just how good I was and how much further I could be pushed. In a fortunate twist of fate, the County Championships were being staged the following weekend. Without telling me, he entered me into the 400 metres.

It could have been any of the events (although I would never do the long or high jump ever again). I'd have picked the 200 metres myself, but the margin of my win in the longer distance persuaded him that was my best event.

When I turned up to the County Championships, it was the first time I had run on a synthetic track rather than grass. Once again, the naysayers were out in force. 'Yeah, you're pretty good at our school but look at that lad.' They were pointing to a tall, muscular boy. Everything about him – his physicality, his self-confidence, his aura – was intimidating. He looked like an athlete. I felt like someone pretending to be one.

We took to the starting line. I was in Lane 8. I would soon discover that Lanes 1 and 8, the outside and inside, are the least favourable, but that meant nothing to me at the time. I still had no strategy apart from just going all out from the starting gun. I felt good, though. I had a smooth start – again a standing start, no blocks – and by the time I was in the back straight, I knew I was leading.

I had a good advantage from the off, but was convinced that the big guy, who was in Lane 4, was going to go past me at any minute. I kept looking across for him. *Where is he? Where is he?* With 100 metres to go, the stagger had unwound, surely I'd see him now? I still waited, but eventually looked back and there he was, yards behind me. I won easily and had taken over a second off the time that I'd run the previous week with a personal best (PB) of 48.2.

On that rainy day back in autumn 1990, when Dad had insisted I stayed at the school, he had told me that the experience would be good for me. The 16-year-old me couldn't see what he meant. But I saw now he had been right. In less than two years I'd gone from a pampered mummy's boy to an independent soul, from a daunted newbie to a confident student, from a boy to a man. If he thought it would also see me prove myself academically, well, he was wrong on that count. But his words 'It will be the making of you' did prove prophetic: Stamford had made me an athlete.

# Four

# NEW WORLDS

'What's your name again?'

   'Iwan . . . Iwan Thomas.'

   'Who's your coach, Iwan?'

   'I don't have one.'

   'So, who do you race for?'

   'Sorry?'

   'Which club do you belong to?'

   'I don't. I've just left school.'

It was a conversation that must have taken place a dozen times as I met up with the rest of the Under-20 British contingent to travel to the World Athletics U20 Championships in Seoul in September 1992. I'd heard a few of the names before. I'd already encountered Carl Southam and Guy Bullock and had seen Darren Campbell and Jamie Baulch. They didn't know me, but they seemed to be pretty familiar with each other. They had their friendship groups and knew one another from race meetings.

Most of the team had been at athletics clubs for five or even ten years; receiving proper coaching and regularly racing at the highest level. I was a fish out of water. I wasn't an athlete. I was just someone who had run fast in a couple of races. They seemed to know so much about the sport – the set-up, the training, the competition. I had never trained at all. Was I even good enough to be in this company? Imposter syndrome doesn't even begin to describe it, but it was too late: I was on the plane to Seoul.

As a result of the victory at the County Championships, I had gone on to represent Lincolnshire in the English Schools Championship in Hull. On the way there, I sat in an increasingly packed minibus that was calling in on every little village in the county. And stared out of the window, not knowing anyone and too shy to talk to any of the others, although I do remember briefly looking up when a couple of pretty blonde girls got on. They turned out to be sisters – the heptathletes Julie and Anne Hollman.

I was allocated a host family in Hull. That night, I lay in bed like a French exchange student wondering quite what I was doing there. Once again, I felt alone and like a fish out of water. This time, though, there was an element of excitement and jeopardy too. Was I going to get found out now, come last and go home with my tail between my legs? Or was there any truth in what Kevin Johnstone had said about 'raw talent'? I fell asleep trying to make sense of it all.

At the English Schools I came second to Carl Southam from Leicester. Being beaten was a new sensation for me! But I felt OK: Carl was massive. I looked at him and thought, *I'm just a boy really, but he's a man.* He was huge with muscles bulging everywhere. He would have the better of me all through the junior years. It wasn't until around 1994 that I was beating him.

Next up was the Independent Schools Athletics Championships. That was fun. The politician and author Jeffrey Archer, himself a former Great Britain sprinter, was there to see his son race in the 400 metres. His son was highly rated. In fact, he was the hot favourite – which made it all the more fun when I came in first. I didn't see his famous dad's reaction, but Archer Jr did not look like he had taken defeat well, and looked annoyed.

Things were snowballing. I had been invited to take part in the following week's AAA Junior Championships at Stoke-on-Trent. This was the foremost competition in the country and I'd be competing against the best Under-20s in the country. This was proper athletics. I remember watching Darren Campbell and Jamie Baulch warm up for the 200 metres in their sponsored kit and club vests and thinking, *These guys look the business – they know just what they're doing.*

Once again Carl Southam beat me and I was shaded into fourth place by Guy Bullock and Adrian Patrick. But that was still an achievement. These boys were all expected to feature in the places. Southam had already won three other junior national titles that year; Guy Bullock had topped the boys 400 metres rankings for two years and trained with the soon-to-be British record holder David Grindley; and Adrian Patrick had been on the radar since he won the Under-17 AAAs in 1988. I was the odd one out, the one who had everyone scratching their heads. I had come from nowhere; literally no one knew who I was. I had been racing for only three weeks and was still wearing the spikes borrowed for Sports Day.

After the race, the guy who had been fancied to win but had finished behind me was devastated. He was kicking off, angry with himself for missing out on a podium place. He pointed a finger at me and I heard him say, 'Fucking 'ell bruv, I've even been beaten by this kid!' I smiled to myself. I'd run 47.6, my best time yet.

I was sure I could run even faster, but had no idea. I had no training and no coach. I really had no clue how to run the 400 metres apart from roaring out of the blocks and carrying on as fast and for as long as I could. All I did know was that when I got onto the starting line, I felt different. All the nerves and the self-doubt vanished. This bit I knew I could do.

People were beginning to notice me. After the event, Adrian Thomas, one of the British Athletics coaches came over and took down my phone number and address in his notebook. 'There's a World Junior Championships in Seoul at the end of the summer,' he mentioned. 'You've got a chance of being selected.' I didn't get too excited or think too much of it, except . . . when I had won at the County Championships just a couple of weeks earlier, Dad had done his bit to make me focus on my running by betting me £200 that I wouldn't run for Britain within two years. Might he have to pay up a lot sooner than he thought?

Sure enough, the letter with its British Athletics letterhead arrived inviting me to join the team for the World Junior Championships in Seoul. I read it with my mouth wide open. It was one thing talking to a coach after the AAAs, but another reading an official letter saying I had been selected. I felt numb with excitement and nerves. It was just three months since Sports Day, I was going to a world championships and, what's more, I would be running the 4 × 400 metres relay – an event in which I had never previously competed. *Whoa!* Shit had got real. *Maybe*, I thought, *I should be doing some training?*

In Germany for the summer with my parents, I found that the little village of Landstuhl had a running track, a gravelly, cinder affair in the local park. I went down there on my own two or three times a week and, with absolutely no idea what I was doing, set out to train. I would be there, timing myself with my little stopwatch as I did 200m or 300m reps. It wasn't much to watch. Just me sprinting, checking my watch, recovering and sprinting again on a desolate track in a small, tree-lined park. However, at one point I looked up and saw a few lads who had been playing football pausing to watch me run. Suddenly, I became aware of dog walkers, parents with pushchairs and passers-by taking an interest in this lanky, ginger-haired teenager doing his best impression of being a proper athlete.

Come mid-September 1992, here I was, getting off a plane in South Korea alongside the cream of young British athletics – one of the strongest teams we ever sent. It included future stars like Darren Campbell, Paula Radcliffe, high jumper Steve Smith and pole vaulter Nick Buckfield.

Some would become friends for life. This was when I first got to know Jamie Baulch. He ran the 200 metres then and finished fourth in Korea, but he would soon swap to 400 metres. I was a little star-struck sitting down to breakfast with this really cool dreadlocked guy. He was small but had a big presence. I'd never have dreamed we would be rivals, roommates and friends throughout our careers and beyond.

I also met the 400 metres runner Katharine Merry in Seoul. She would take a bronze medal in Sydney and become the fastest woman in the world over that distance in 2001. I really liked Katharine , but never imagined we would become lifelong friends; I went to her wedding and we work together all the time.

My first international competition was a tough moment. I felt out of the loop. I was a wide-eyed boy who had run a few races and who was now rubbing shoulders with the future elite of the sport. Some – like the London Rude Boys or the North West crew – had been mates for years; others had trained together or competed in countless events. But they were friendly towards me and I enjoyed being part of it.

I took to Darren Campbell right from the start. I instantly knew our worlds were miles apart. He'd grown up in the notorious Moss Side in Manchester, while I was the son of a group captain and until a few months ago had been in a posh boarding school. I hadn't ever mixed with people like him before. Darren was charismatic, tough, funny, mature beyond his years and a bit of a cheeky rascal to boot. He was a born leader, everyone loved him and looked up to him – including me.

Being set free in Seoul was overwhelming. The city was buzzing. I tagged along with the others as they hit the stores for the knock-off games, electronics and trainers. Someone told me they ate cats and dogs there. I wasn't sure, but the only dog I saw was when our taxi driver swerved suddenly in an attempt to hit it. He missed but turned round to us with a massive grin.

I was awestruck at the track too. I'd stand there watching athletes warm up and race. The Trinidad and Tobago 100 metres runner Ato Boldon, a future four-time Olympic medal winner, was there. But it was the Africans who really left me gobsmacked. Benson Keoch and the other Kenyans, and the soon-to-be Ethiopian legend Haile Gebrselassie left me thinking, *Wow, there are so many good athletes here.*

I was in the 4 × 400 metres relay team with Guy, Carl and Adrian Patrick. I'd never run a relay before, but everyone was chilled about it, so it all seemed routine. The coaches took me through the zones and the handover rules and put me on first leg; with one handover, it's the easiest to do. We had a few run-throughs and there I was: a relay runner.

We came second in our heat, which qualified us for the final on the next day. Adrian was replaced in the final by Allyn Condon. Usually a 100 or 200 metres runner, Allyn already had a gold medal from the 4 × 100 metres relay, but couldn't help us finish better than fifth.

It wasn't a lightbulb *Oh God, I'm going to be an athlete* moment. I'd only made the relay team after all, but I came home from Seoul with renewed confidence in my running. I had proved that this kid that no one had ever heard of could mix it with athletes who had been coached at club level for years. Yeah, that felt pretty good. And Dad now owed me £200.

My immediate future was already plotted. I had been rejected by Loughborough University and had turned down a place at Leeds Carnegie in order to study Sports Science and Leisure Management at the West London Institute of Higher Education (soon to become Brunel University). It wasn't that I'd set my heart on a career running a fitness centre or being a hotel manager; I had absolutely no idea what I wanted to do, but I had to choose a course and this seemed the closest fit to my interests.

There was a feeling of déjà vu as my parents dropped me off at the Stockwell Hall halls of residence in Osterley. I had a sixth-floor room in a grim tower block that always reminded me of Nelson Mandela House in *Only Fools and Horses*. It was a small room, but all I needed. I even had my own sink – which of course, doubled up when I needed a middle-of-the-night pee.

I was being left to make my way on my own again, but now I was older, more confident and mentally prepared for what was in store. Though I could never have guessed what great people I'd meet and what a laugh I'd have while I 'worked' for my degree.

British athletics is a small world. Word gets around fast and a new kid on the block always gets tongues wagging. I realised now that after my performances and times in the English Schools and the Junior AAAs people were talking about me. Going to Seoul had confirmed that I had promise. That I had something special – those words 'raw talent' echoed in my mind again.

'Iwan Thomas (Unattached)' – that was how my name had appeared in the programme or schedules at the World Junior Championships. The other athletes had their club name listed next to their names. It was clear that I wasn't signed up to anyone and pretty soon after I arrived at uni the phone began to ring with clubs asking me to join. First out of the blocks was the Greek shipping magnate Eddie Kulukundis. He was a great patron of athletics and supported many great British athletes, but rang me as Chairman of Belgrave Harriers. He said, 'Come and join us, boy, and I'll buy you a Ford Fiesta.' A brand-new car? I felt like I'd hit the jackpot, but it wasn't over yet.

While I was mulling over the offer, word got around that I was thinking of joining Belgrave. I had a call from Tony Shiret of Newham and Essex Beagles. 'What have they offered you?'

'A Fiesta,' I told them a bit sheepishly.

'Meet me tomorrow. I'll buy you a Ford Escort, whatever colour you want, if you sign for us.'

It was unbelievable. I was 18, had won one race at county level and here were club owners bidding to sign me. I accepted Tony's offer and went to meet him at Putney Ford Dealers – eventually; I got off at the wrong stop, twice. I ended up being bought a white 1.6 GL Ford Escort just for joining their athletics club. I was no longer unattached. Now I was representing Newham and Essex Beagles and, when I ran, I would be wearing the black vest with a gold hoop just like Daley Thompson before me. It was, I supposed, time I started training.

The university track wasn't a great help. Due to some listed trees, the track was egg-shaped. It had one normal bend, but the other was so tight you needed to slow down to get round it – and it wasn't even 400m long. As long as you were doing 200m reps it was OK, but nothing further than that.

Being a member of the Beagles just meant that I represented them in races, especially British League meetings against other clubs. As a student I ran the 200m, 4 × 100m, 4 × 400m, sometimes a 400m and, on one occasion, the triple jump for them. Despite offers, I never left the Beagles, and although as my career progressed I mainly ran in international meetings, like other elite athletes, I would run in British League fixtures when I wanted a no-pressure race without the world watching.

The Beagles trained in Plaistow, East London, which was a bit of a trek. So once or twice a week, I joined a couple of other students who trained with Thames Valley Harriers just by the Wormwood Scrubs prison in Shepherd's Bush.

This was my first experience of proper training.

Situated right next to the White City estates, the club was full of the kind of inner-city boys I had met in Seoul. These were older than me. They were streetwise, exuding toughness and attitude. I'd knocked about with tough kids back in Huntingdon, but this had a different feel, an edge that made me cautious and reserved. Among these London boys was Linford Christie, who had just won gold in the 100 metres in Barcelona. I really had to pinch myself, thinking, *Here I am, training with an Olympic champion.*

You can't get better than working with one of the most respected coaches in athletics as your first coach. Thames Valley Harriers' Ron Roddan was a legend in British Athletics, having guided over 30 athletes to international status – Linford being the most celebrated of them. Ron was very tall with grey hair. A quiet father figure, he was very approachable and kind and he welcomed me to the sessions. Ron didn't speak much and when he did, it was short and to the point. He wanted to take his sprinters to levels that were real only in their dreams.

I was doing the winter training with the guys, running 200m and 300m reps and not feeling out of place. More than that; my speed endurance was very good. After reps, a lot of the guys would be on their backs gasping for air and I'd still be on my feet walking around. For the first time I realised I had a real appetite for training. I was not afraid of hard work, actually enjoyed putting myself through the pain, and seemed to recover very quickly.

Still, I was a student and there was more to life than training. Stockwell Hall was another eye-opener. There were students there from different backgrounds – all kinds of ethnicities, rich and poor and from all over the country – all finding their feet and mucking in together.

Like students everywhere we were on the beers most nights; Mondays out clubbing in Ritzy's or Options in Kingston, Wednesdays in the Student Union. I was very much a student before I was any kind of athlete; beers and laughs first, training way down the list.

As well as the freedom, I enjoyed my independence. I learned to structure my days, get to lectures and carefully tracked how I spent my allowance (I was laughed at for carrying a notepad where I'd record every expense – even a bar of chocolate). Most people there seemed to have a career route mapped out. They might be going to go into teaching or banking. Me? I had no idea where my degree would take me and zero plans for my future. I was living for the moment, and it was great fun. Studying was a necessity rather than a passion. I would have rather not been there. The truth is, I chose to go to university, just as my brother had, to please my parents. The only other option was living in Germany with them – and that was far too much outside my comfort zone.

There was one man who helped make the difference throughout my days at university. Charles Lipton, always ready with to greet me in his own style.

'Oh, you blighter. Only your mother could love you. Come and sit here!'

It was a request I never tired of hearing. Charles was a retired history lecturer who had been visiting the university every day since the late 1960s. He loved athletics and rugby and acted as a scout for the university, recruiting prospective students and encouraging them to join us and not Loughborough. He was well respected up and down the country in athletics stadia, instantly recognisable in his flat cap and knee-length tweed coat.

A legend at Brunel, he held court in the university refectory. I had lunch with him every single day throughout my time there. He was eternally good-humoured, had an endless supply of fabulous stories and was always ready to listen. Whether it was an academic or personal issue or to do with athletics, his advice was kind, considered and invariably spot-on. I'd spend time with him whenever I could, and liked to drive him back to Osterley station so he could get home to North London. I loved him like the grandad I never had.

Encouraged by Charles and enthused by my weekly sessions at Thames Valley Harriers, I was still running. I won the 400 metres at the 1993 British Universities Indoor Championships in Birmingham (I always took great pleasure beating Loughborough boys – it was my revenge for their rejection!). I couldn't kid myself, though; I was a good-time guy getting by on Big Macs®, beans on toast and pasta with tuna and drinking too many Mad Dog 20/20s or snakebite and blacks.

I was also back to being the cheeky chappie I'd been at Hinchingbrooke. The practical jokes returned. I broke into a fellow student's food cupboard and changed the labels on her tin cans; I put up an 'official' notice for a morning STD Clinic in the Nurse's office which our rooms overlooked; and I sent my mate a letter headed 'Hounslow Police', telling him his old Vauxhall was not roadworthy and to report to the station. They got me back. They put up a poster announcing a breakdancing competition, knowing I fancied myself as a bit of a b-boy. We all went along and I did my bit, only to find it was all a set-up – even the DJ was in on it. I heard the whole room laughing.

My first year at university had been pretty special. I'd had fun, hadn't been thrown off the course and, although I'd only run a few races, I was making steady progress. I looked to finish on a high in Spain, taking part in my last competition as a Junior: the European Junior Championships in San Sebastian. Once again I was running for Great Britain in the 4 × 400 relay, this time in a team with Paul Slythe, Nick Budden and Guy Bullock. We won the heat easily and our only threat in the final were the other heat winners, the Germans, and we were confident we could beat them.

It was all going so well. We were winning golds all over the place and spirits were high in the camp. Then, on the eve of the final, team manager Max Jones called me to his room. He told me I was being replaced in the team for the final by the sprinter Allyn Condon. 'We need some fresh legs,' he said. 'Besides, this race is nothing for you,' Max said. 'You've got a huge future ahead of you.' Those words meant diddly-squat to me. It was the first time I'd had to face up to real disappointment, and it hurt. I tried not to show it, but inside I was a mess. I was gutted, confused and seething with anger.

My blood was still boiling as I watched them go on to win the gold. I suppose I must have got a medal, but I have no memory of it. It counted for nothing. I could have packed the whole thing in there and then, but that sense of pride kicked in. They couldn't doubt me like that. I so wanted to make them regret it.

I had made enough of an impact to receive £3000 from the Ron Pickering Memorial Fund. It was supposed to help young athletes reach their potential, to support warm weather training and travel. What did I do? I returned my Escort to the Beagles and bought myself a Peugeot 205 GTI, the hot hatch of the moment. There weren't many students driving around in one of those!

I obviously still wasn't fully committed to being an athlete. I'd moved out of the halls and into a house with my mate Dan and his fellow geographers Roger, Neal and Leigh and carried on with student life. I'd train at Wormwood Scrubs, but that was it – the rest was just about having as much fun as I could.

I'm sure Dad had his own opinions about how I was approaching athletics, but he let me make my own way. If he had been a little pushy when I was younger, he was nothing but supportive in my running. He made sure I had rent and spending money at uni and was there to support me at race meetings whenever he could. I particularly remember his pride when I ran in the British University Championships at Crystal Palace in 1993. It was a tough field and, as always, the Loughbrough contingent looked to dominate. Not only did I win, but my time of 46.93 matched Seb Coe's British University record. It was a great night with all my uni friends coming down to support me and Dad forked out the cash for me to buy them all a few drinks.

With hindsight it was perhaps one of the most important races I ever ran. It seemed even at the time like a turning point. My housemates realised that I had something. They really started to believe in me and pushed me to take running more seriously. That made it really sink home. *Just how far I could take it? What more could I be doing?*

As the winter approached, I had a big decision to make. Dan Donovan, a lad in the year above (who would run for GB), said I should think about going to train with Mike Smith in Southampton. Mike was a specialist 400 metres coach who had trained Donna Hartley, Todd Bennett, Roger Black and Kriss Akabusi. I'd been training with Rod Roddan for a year now and as much as I loved it, this was an opportunity I just couldn't turn down. So every Thursday afternoon I'd climb in Dan's mum's car, give him a fiver petrol money and we'd drive down to Southampton.

Here the training was different. It was tough, brutal even. The intensity was nothing like I'd ever been put through before. We'd train all evening and be dead on our feet. I was in my element. By the time we'd done the obligatory trip to McDonald's and driven home, we'd often missed last orders at the Student Union bar.

England or Wales? That was my next decision and an easy one. I was eligible for either as Mum was Welsh and Dad was English. 'Nain [Welsh for Gran] would love to see you run in a Welsh vest,' said Mum, not holding back with the emotional blackmail. She needn't have worried. There wasn't ever any doubt in my mind. I sound English, I'd been brought up in England, but I was always Welsh through and through: I was running for Wales.

In the early summer of 1994, I ran in the Welsh Championship in Wrexham, my first competition as a senior runner. I'd met Jamie Baulch before at the Junior

Championships, but I'd never run against him. He had only just swapped from the 200 metres to the 400 metres. It was a tough race and I had to battle really hard against him on the home straight, neck-and-neck right up to the finish line. This was a case of mental strength – and I was just that little bit stronger. I came through, winning in 47.09, a record for the Championship. Dad drove me home and I could tell he was really pleased. Maybe it was the BMX spirit that had prepared me, but I had shown him what I was made of.

The 1994 Commonwealth Games in Victoria, Canada was just an amazing trip. To this day, it is the competition I enjoyed the most. I was representing my country in one of the biggest athletics events in the world. You might think the pressure and nerves would be agonising, but there was none of that. I was still a student, no one outside the British Athletics world knew me, there were no expectations. I was just there to get some experience and to do my best.

I soaked up the atmosphere and the whole fantastic circus. I'd been to the Junior Championships with track and field athletes, but this was something else. There were synchronised swimmers, boxers, cyclists, weightlifters, divers – it was huge. The Commonwealths are often known as the Friendly Games and that's exactly what they were. Everyone mingled.

Jamie Baulch and myself shared a room. Although we were competing against each other on the track, we got along really well. While we were in Canada, Jamie got a phone call from his girlfriend, who told him they were expecting their first child. It dawned on me that though we were a similar age, our lives were at different stages. Jamie was already a serious, professional athlete and had to be even more committed now he had responsibilities. It was one element of the trip that opened my eyes to how my own future might look.

People thought it was odd that we shared, but I would choose to share a room with him over anyone else. We were very similar in many ways; he trained hard and raced hard but he was always good for a laugh. From the get-go I have really liked and respected Jamie; he's more like a brother than a rival and was my best friend in athletics, ever. He won't like me saying this, but I never saw him as a real rival – he was a fantastic athlete, but he only ever beat me a few times. I was never able to race him indoors, I didn't want to run a relay against him but, throughout my career, every time we lined up against each other outdoors, I was sure I had the beating of him.

We went down for breakfast on the first morning – and couldn't believe the buffet spread. There was even steak for breakfast! I put on about half a stone during the Games. At home, I was still a student eating out of tins. I didn't even have steak at weekends. Here I was having a great time. I had nothing to prove, they were feeding me like a king and I was rubbing shoulders with Linford Christie and Sally Gunnell, and a teammate of Colin Jackson.

I was feeling good on the track too. I was in competition against top athletes and performing in front of decent crowds. The training with Mike, even if it was only one night a week, seemed to be paying off. I was running faster than ever. I won my heat in 46.37, beating Jamie's Welsh record, and knew I had plenty more left. In the semi-final, I went even faster: 45.98. It wasn't quite enough to get me into the final, but I'd run under 46 seconds for the first time. It was a milestone which announced my arrival on the international scene. Unfortunately we had a disaster in the 4 × 400m, where I was running the last leg. As Paul Gray approached the changeover another runner cut past him and Paul hit the deck, dropping the baton. I can still see his big eyes looking up at me from the track. I picked up the baton and gave it all I was worth, but any faint chance of a podium place had already passed.

Sometimes you can be disappointed with the way things turn out, but I really wasn't. I'd made an impression and people had started talking about me. I sat in the stands watching the final. I fixed my eyes on Du'aine Ladejo, who had beaten me in the semi-final. He was running nearly a second faster than me, but suddenly that seemed achievable. As I watched him, I couldn't stop myself thinking, *I wanna beat you . . . I wanna beat you so bad*. I'd had a taste of it and I wanted more.

I didn't want to just share the track with the best; I wanted to be the best.

## 12.30pm. 15 June 2021

*Where has everyone gone? There's not a runner in sight. No run markers either. We are lost. We've strayed off the route. On top of every other fucking thing that had already been sent to try us. We'd run up that hill in the midday sun when I already felt I was on my last legs. I'm dripping sweat like a human Niagara and being roasted alive. For absolutely nothing.*

*We've added miles to the already ridiculous total. I'm spitting angry. My face is pumping crimson – is it sunburn, exertion or fury? It's impossible to tell. With every thought I can still muster, I blame everyone and anyone – the marshals, the course, the signing – except the idiots who took it on themselves to run the wrong way.*

# Five

# THE REAL WORLD

I beat Du'aine Ladejo in the first race of the 1995 season. He was the European champion and a motormouth of the sport. He'd come down to breakfast that morning in Ljubljana, Slovenia, wearing a tight T-shirt that showed off his ripped body and read *No one trains to come second*. I had the greatest respect for him as an athlete and maybe it was just a joke, but it got to me. It really did.

I felt something extra kick in – a determination to make him eat those words. He came second. A big moment for me. The first race of the year and I'd run 45.72 – a personal best. A week later, in Switzerland, on my second race I ran 45.58. I was in such good shape and had the whole season in front of me.

When I'd arrived back from the Commonwealth Games for my final year at uni, things had changed. Around campus, people recognised me from the TV and shook my hand. The rugby guys gave me respect; I was no longer that bloke who was always having a joke and mucking about. I began to feel more like an athlete than someone who happened to be able to run fast. My housemates knew

I was onto something and were really encouraging and supportive. I was going to Southampton once a week to train with Mike, and I'd now added circuit training on a Monday to my routine; but hey, I was still a student and there was plenty of partying to be done.

There was still a degree to finish, too. Fortunately Tony Shiret, the Chair of Newham and Essex Beagles, had my back. Tony was a suave, high-rolling City boy – with something of James Bond about him. He had a big wallet and a big heart and was really supportive and generous to me. When I had to do a work placement for my business studies, he found me a place with an analyst at a City bank. Of course, I rarely turned up. On one occasion the lecturer rang him to see how I was getting on. Tony gave me a sparkling report, but the lecturer was really calling to say she was on her way in to see me. I had a panicky phone call, saying: 'You've got to get here, now!' and I made it just in time for her to find me at my desk.

Tony even wrote one of my papers for me. When I was called into the office for an assessment, they went through my work. 'You got 53 per cent for this one, 48 per cent, 64 and a 93!'

'Oh yes,' I said. 'I really enjoyed doing that one.'

They knew, of course, but were happy to let it go. I put it down to my cheeky smile.

In the summer, I left university with a 2.2 (otherwise known, appropriately enough, as a 'drinker's degree'). I'd effectively left home at 16 and never gone back. University was never about the education for me, it was about growing up. Now there were more decisions to be made. One that required me sitting down with my parents in their living room with my serious face on.

Dad was always keen that his boys had an eye on their future. My brother had left Leeds University and had got his first job. Now it was my turn.

'What are your plans now?' he asked.

I really didn't have a clue. Not a scooby. 'Well, I know what I don't want to do,' I told him. 'I'm through with education.' I kept shtum for the next bit – that I wasn't ready for a career either and I didn't want a proper job.

'Maybe,' I suggested vaguely. 'I might give the running a serious go?'

The Commonwealth Games had shown I might make a go of it and Dad wasn't stupid. I knew he'd seen what I was capable of on minimal training. It wasn't a complete punt in the dark. But athletics? As a career? I wasn't completely sure how he would react.

He looked me in the eye and nodded thoughtfully. 'Working with Mike seems to be making a real difference,' he admitted. 'How about moving to Southampton to train regularly with him? I'll pay your rent for a year and you'll have to get a job to pay for your living expenses.'

It was exactly what I wanted – well, maybe the *getting a job* bit wasn't, but I wasn't going to worry about that for now.

Looking back, that moment was the springboard for the rest of my life. Without his generous offer, I just couldn't have done it. It was still a gamble. I was still the best part of a second behind the best British 400 metres runners, Roger Black and Du'aine Ladejo, and another half-second behind the world's best like Michael Johnson and Butch Reynolds. My thoughts went something like this: *If I can be a second slower than them when I'm training once a week, how quickly might I close that gap if I'm out there every day?* I wasn't mega-confident this approach would work but was willing to put everything into trying.

Before I moved, there was a small issue to sort out. I had torn a hamstring and hadn't raced since that second race in Switzerland. I'd missed the whole season and couldn't afford to miss winter as well. As time went on and I was getting a bit frustrated with my lack of progress, I got talking to Callum Taylor, a New Zealand 400 metres runner, about the injury.

'You should go and see Torben Hersborg, this Danish osteopath who's in London,' he told me. 'He's fucking crazy –' those were his exact words – 'but he'll fix you in one treatment.'

I thought, *Impossible, I've torn a hamstring*. But he did. I couldn't explain how, it seemed he just had a magic touch.

---

By the end of the year, I was living in Southampton. Mike and his wife found me the ideal place. Ideal in that it was cheap – and not far from his house so he could keep an eye on me. Not so great was that it was a cramped, dingy bedsit. Just one room with a tiny kitchen in the corner, a toilet and a shower and a bed that pulled down from the wall. It was in Bursledon Green, a suburb of Southampton now referred to by estate agents as a sought-after location, but back then, less so. It was lonely – and horrible.

After I was dropped off in my new home, I sat on my bed. All I knew of Southampton was the track, the McDonald's at Hedge End and how to get to the M3. Memories of being dumped at boarding school and of arriving at university flashed through my mind. Here I was, alone in a new place again. Everything was alien and I was living on my own for the first time. I was nervous and excited; unsure of just what I had taken on. I remember checking the door was locked three times before I went to sleep that night.

The next day I wandered into town. Dad had been so good in supporting my move and backing me financially. It seemed the least I could do was to keep my side of the bargain and get a job. Well, try to get a job. *I'll ask around a bit*, I thought. *I won't get anything, but at least I can call him and say I'd given it a go.* The first shop I tried was the clothes shop, Next. Things did not go to plan. The manager took an immediate shine to me (I wasn't a bad-looking lad!) and said I could start that day. Just my luck!

For the next six months, this would be my life. I'd work from eight until four at Next, taking in the deliveries and working in the shop. I never really minded going in. They were a good crowd and we had plenty of laughs. We had secret codes like putting an empty coat hanger on the left end of the rack if there was an attractive girl in the shop, and the 'Flash on Menswear' announcement that there was a shoplifter in the store always brought a frisson of excitement. We weren't allowed to chase them if they left the shop, but anyway no one knew – or if they did know, no one cared – that I was an athlete.

I'd be on my feet all day, get home and have time for a rest and something to eat before training. I'd been used to training one evening a week with Mike and his group, but now I was going six times a week. Tough, but I threw myself into it. I soon learned not to complain; some of the lads were sacrificing more than me. I remember telling Paul Sanders, one of the guys in the training group, that I'd had a hard day at the shop – and he looked at me in disbelief. He was a travelling sales rep and had driven up from Devon that day, on the road since five in the morning. I never complained again.

This was my life now, and I settled into it. As the newcomer to the training group, the last thing I wanted to do was put anyone's nose out of joint by being brash, loud or too competitive. I couldn't hold back, though; it wasn't in my nature. I loved training and threw myself into it, but they were a great set of blokes and welcomed me as one of them.

The group had a settled hierarchy, but after a month, I was moving up the pecking order. I was there to run as fast as I could and the truth – one that I think they all accepted pretty quickly and decently – was that good as they were, none of them had the same mix of desire and talent that I had to make it at the highest level. There was a definite changing of the guard. Paul Sanders, probably the fastest there, soon retired, but I'd like to think I didn't demotivate anyone or cause anyone to drop out.

The only person I really knew from my Thursday night sessions when I arrived was Tim Odell. Tim was a naturally gifted athlete and a beautiful flowing runner. He ran the 400 metres in 46.3 and was truly talented. Talented, but his body couldn't take the volume of 400m training. He could have run at least a second faster, but he'd give up after two reps when the rest of us went on to do five. He later told me: 'I wasn't as tough as others, I remember saying to Mike, "I wish I could just race and not train!"'

Simon Ciaravella, who was known to all as Gumbo, followed me to Southampton to train with Mike. He was a similar age to me and had finished third to my second in the English Schools three years earlier. Gumbo was a strong athlete, and especially good at the longer runs. Then there was Peter Brend, a tough and reliable runner and great company too, and Martin Blade. Martin was a soldier and running in the Army team. He had seen active service and was superfit. Even though he was only able to come to training three times a week, he was a real character with endless incredible stories and was a great bloke to have around.

Lee Fairclough was an interesting case. A great athlete and as strong as an ox. In training he gave anyone a run for their money. But I felt he never really realised his potential. When they called: 'On your marks!', I'd grow ten feet tall. Lee, though, seemed to do the opposite. Racing isn't for everyone. You can train hard and ooze with talent, but still not be a winner.

We were at different levels but we all trained hard.

Chris Lawton was doing a degree in astronomy, so naturally got called Space Cadet. Chris was an average athlete, but he gave his all at training. Mike could see that. He valued commitment and gave Space Cadet as much attention as any of the others. If you were serious about the sport, whatever your level, he gave you his time.

This was my crew, and I wouldn't have swapped any of them. I continued to train with them even as my career took off. Other athletes didn't understand. They regularly asked me what I was getting out of it when there was no one to challenge me. I told them that I had found the perfect training partners, and I meant it. The thing about 400 metres is that it's not about sprinting or power or stamina, it's about all three combined and that crew challenged me on all fronts.

I used each of their talents to push me. In the gym I set myself against Martin Blade. He was rock hard and no one else could stay with him on the circuit training. On the forest runs or over the dunes, I stuck with Gumbo, knowing he'd be the one making the running. And on the track, I arranged it that I had to chase down Space Cadet in Lane 8, way ahead of me on the stagger; catch Lee Fairclough in Lane 6; and then go past Tim, if he hadn't given up by then!

Tim was a lifesaver when I arrived in Southampton and has remained a true friend. Even now, I know I can call on him day or night. He was a bit older than me and took me under his wing: picking me up from the bedsit, taking me to wherever we were training that night and getting me home afterwards (it seems fitting that he is now a taxi driver!). I had no idea of how to get around town. The first time I drove home from work, just a 10-minute journey, I got lost and had to ring Tim, who told me that I'd somehow ended up the wrong side of town. We were soon great mates and went out together most evenings after training for beers or something to eat. On Mondays and Wednesdays, I'd go back to his parents for dinner because they knew I wasn't eating properly. We were inseparable.

Just because I was a serious athlete didn't mean I wasn't still juggling work, training and having a good time. McCluskey's was the biggest nightclub in town and a frequent destination. Especially because they had a barmaid who seemed to take a real shine to me. The first time I got a round in she served me and said:

'One pound, please.' Every time I went to the bar after that, no matter how many pints I ordered, she only ever charged me a pound. It was always my turn to get the drinks in!

The fact I'd missed most of the previous season didn't bother me too much. People were talking about me as a prospect now. I was on the radar – I was mentioned in the same bracket as Roger, Du'aine, Mark Richardson and Jamie Baulch – and I knew I'd come back even stronger. I had beaten Du'aine then, and I could do it again now I was committed. Through Mike's winter training, I was becoming superfit, my body getting stronger and stronger, and I couldn't wait for the season to begin.

Not long after the Commonwealth Games, I was signed up by a race agent. These are the guys who enter you in races around the world and negotiate your fees. I got an agent through Mike. There wasn't a process or a conversation, it just happened. Mike knew this guy, Andy Norman, who organised the Solent Games and he arranged for Andy to be my race agent. I'd actually already met Andy after the University Indoor Championships when he came up to chat and I remembered he told me he had been impressed and that I had real potential. That race in Slovenia in July 1995 was the first race he'd got me.

Andy had been a major figure in the athletics scene since the 1980s, when he managed Steve Ovett, Linford Christie and Jonathan Edwards – he was also married to Fatima Whitbread. Andy, who died in 2007, had great experience and contacts and worked with World Athletics (then known as the IAAF) and the British Athletics Federation (the predecessor to UK Athletics) and regularly set up athletics events in South Africa and Eastern Europe.

He was a controversial figure. His methods and business style would eventually land him in big trouble. It was said that you never cross Andy. He was like the Godfather of Athletics. I was told of a young athlete, running the 110 metres hurdles, who got a late call from Andy telling him that someone had dropped out and there was now a lane free for him at Crystal Palace.

'You're running tomorrow evening,' Andy told him.

'I can't. I'm not prepared. I've got training tomorrow,' the guy replied.

'You're running tomorrow evening,' Andy repeated sternly.

'I'm not doing it.'

That guy never ran again. He never got an invitation to run anywhere. Andy Norman was that powerful: he could make or break you.

I have to say I never had a problem with Andy. He was on my side from day one – the kind of wingman everyone wants. I wasn't savvy, so the money wasn't great – I started on about $1500 for a race in Eastern Europe, but it would get a lot better. Andy was smart, though. He'd put me in races where my opponents were just good enough to push me, but where he knew I'd win. That way, he built up my confidence. I know I could have earned more money with another agent, but he looked after me in other ways. He paid for me to bring training partners along with me on trips to South Africa and, even when he was driving around in a rubbish little hire car, he'd make sure I had something decent to drive. I really liked him.

When I was with him, he was also looking after many star athletes, including Steve Backley, Jonathan Edwards and Tony Jarrett. He remained a powerful man in the sport despite conflicts with the British Athletics Federation. In 1998 he was in charge of the European Championships in Budapest. He sat me down in the hotel before the competition began and said: 'What's your favourite lane?' I told him I liked to run in Lane 3. I thought nothing of it until years later because everyone knows that the lanes are always drawn at random. However, as I said, Andy was a powerful man. In the heats I ran in Lane 3, in the semi-final I was 'drawn' in Lane 3 and in the final? Lane 3! That's quite a coincidence.

In January 1996, Andy rang Mike Smith to tell him that there was an opportunity for me to go to South Africa to race in their Grand Prix series. It was a fabulous opportunity; warm weather training and a few races featuring the best South Africans and whatever top international athletes they could attract in the winter season. Andy knew I could be fast enough, but he wanted Mike to confirm that I was in good enough shape to compete out there.

I went along to the track one Thursday evening with just Mike and another athlete he coached, Carol Dawkins.

'There's a chance to go to South Africa, but I need to you run a 300 metres,' Mike said. 'Just one run, don't think about it. Don't try to run too quick and tighten up, just be relaxed.'

Now, it might have been summer out in South Africa, but it was the depths of winter in Southampton. The track was covered in snow. Together Carol,

Mike and I swept one 400-metre lane clear. I bet Michael Johnson never had to do that.

So, there I was, alone at the start line on a chilly evening with snow lying all around, just waiting for Mike to say '3, 2, 1, Go'. I ran. He might have told me not to think about it and to be relaxed, but I was only too aware that I had to impress him. I could feel the cold burning on my lungs as I tried to suck air in, but I willed myself on: *Come on! Give it fucking everything*, I screamed inside. As I crossed the finish line, I looked back to see Mike grinning as he showed Carol the stopwatch.

I shouted, 'Was it fast?'

Never one to compliment, Mike just smiled and said, 'You're going to South Africa, boy!'

It turned out I'd run 32.8, which is pretty fast for 300 metres on a freezing winter night.

Two weeks later, I was out in Pretoria. Andy Norman was always generous and had paid for Tim and Peter Brend to come out to train with me. He booked for us to stay in Bentley's Country Lodge about 80 km (50 miles) north of Johannesburg. In the middle of nowhere, but beautiful; complete luxury. We had individual thatched huts and our own chef. That was Andy Norman looking after us to the max.

We were out jogging the first day and I felt lousy. My lungs were burning and I was struggling to find any energy. I couldn't finish a training session. I was so pissed off, thinking I was going to miss out on such a great opportunity.

I rang Mike and said, 'Something's wrong, Mike. I'm not feeling good out there.'

He said, 'You're 2000 feet up, you're training at altitude. Of course, you're not going to feel right, you bloody idiot.'

I clearly had a lot to learn.

There were all kinds of athletes at Bentley's Country Lodge and we had some fun. Early in the trip, after a BBQ, I got into drinking Flaming Sambucas with Virgilijus Alekna, the World Champion discus thrower who was 1.99m (6' 7") tall and 114 kg (18 stone), as well as some other giant Lithuanian athletes. They would just put their hand on the glass to extinguish the flame, tip it twice and down it in one.

It was a Friday night. Andy Norman had already gone to bed and, by now, I'd had at least six Sambucas. I'd come back from the loo and one of the Lithuanians turned to me and said in booming English, 'Drink mine!' I didn't know it had been alight for ages. I put my hand on it and straightaway could smell the burning flesh on my hand. It was agony, but not wanting to seem soft, I carried on anyway. I threw it down and immediately felt my lip blister.

When I came out of A & E with my hand bandaged, I thought, *Oh no. Andy's going to kill me when he finds out. There's no way he's going to let me run next week.* So we made up a story that I'd tripped and sprained my hand. I even trained with a bandaged hand to hide the burn. I carried on wearing it for a few days until, after I had done a good training session, Andy sidled up next to me and said in my ear, 'I know you did that drinking, you bloody fool.' He'd known all the time.

Pretoria was something else. One night Tim and I went to a nightclub. At the entrance they stopped us and asked, 'Are you carrying guns?' What! We looked around and it was like a scene from a film; people were handing in guns and bullets like coats in a cloakroom to pick up later. It was scary and I never really felt safe when I was out and about.

The training was brutal, it was so hot and hard to breathe, but after a couple weeks or so I acclimatised. I was running well and was entered in a race at Roodepoort. Now, my PB was still 45.5 from that race early in the '95 season, but here, in my first race of 1996 I ran 45.2. Training with Mike and the altitude work had already made a difference.

I was sitting on the track recovering when a camera crew came over and the South African reporter said, 'Ivan Thomas, very fast, track record. You must be very pleased.'

I was still suffering and said, 'Sorry, can you just give me a minute.'

A few seconds later he returned and stuck a microphone in my face.

I said, 'Listen, I'm going to throw up, give me a minute.'

Then he came back for a third attempt. I'd had it and snapped, 'Look mate, just fuck off!'

Now, back at the hotel, Tim who had stayed behind feeling unwell, was watching TV. When I returned, he greeted me with 'Iwan, you're a legend!'

I looked puzzled. I hadn't realised that it had all been broadcast live.

Tim thought it was hilarious: 'A PB, puking up and swearing – all live on TV! What a guy!'

The following week I was back in Pretoria and ran 44.98. This was a massive deal. For 400 metre runners, the 45 seconds is a marker, like the four-minute mile. I had crossed the line into Olympic class. Tim, my other training partners and even Du'aine Ladejo, who was out there training, were all watching. It felt great. Andy Norman said, 'Wow. You're on your way now!'

I just couldn't wait to ring Mike to tell him I'd broken 45 seconds. It was so great to hear him speak with real pride: 'That's my boy!' I was buzzing. I rang everyone I knew back home. When I got back, my Vodafone bill for just that one month was £1200 – that's how thrilled I was to have reached that point.

My next race, the third in as many weeks, was in Johannesburg. I had Lane 7. Andy had chosen that lane for me because, like Mike, he didn't want me to think about it too much. In an outside lane you are ahead in the stagger and can't worry about your rivals, you just run. And in the lane near me, there was an athlete who I'm sure had been promised an extra $500 by Andy if I ran a PB. This guy flew over the first 300 metres and was the perfect pacemaker. I felt so good. Charging down the back straight, everything felt right – and I ran 44.66. I'd gone from 45.2 to 44.9 to 44.6 in three weeks – unheard of.

It was a Welsh record and I had become the fourth fastest British 400 metres runner ever. You know you've done something special when the drug testers come knocking. Three times they came to my hotel that week. Better still was when I got word from America. Roger Black was training out there at the time and, so I was told, was approached by Michael Johnson. He'd seen the result and, mispronouncing my name, asked Roger: 'Who the hell is this Iwon Thomas kid?'

Andy, being a seasoned agent, naturally thought it was time to make some money out of this kid. Back in Britain, he arranged for me to run in a meeting at Birmingham. The only problem was that it was indoor running. I didn't run indoors. The last time I ran indoors was the AAAs in 1993, when I came in fourth with a time of 47.94. Being tall and rangy, I wasn't suited to indoor running: the tracks are 200 metres long, so you do two laps with the tight bends, which is better suited to athletes with a low centre of gravity like Jamie Baulch or Todd Bennett.

I was now, after my South African heroics, ranked number one in the world. And I was taking on the World Indoor Champion Darnell Hall while the world was watching. The gun went and off we went. After a lap I was already thinking, *What the hell am I doing here?* I finished in 46.55 and came in fifth out of six runners. Tim Odell was laughing as he watched me puking up in the corridor and I said to myself, *Listen, mate, I am never, ever chasing the dollar again.* And I never have.

As Olympic year season started back home, I had nevertheless made an impressive start. I went out with Mike and the boys to Portugal for preseason training and was running really well. Out there, I noticed that I was being watched by a man with a stopwatch: Thomas Schönlebe, a great 400 metres runner in the 1980s whose European record of 44.33 seconds still stood. My times in South Africa had put me in the spotlight and I was being talked up. There were still doubters, though. 'He did those times at altitude,' they said. 'That's a lot easier. I bet he can't do it when it really matters.' Ahh . . . there was nothing I liked better than people betting against me.

The AAA Championships in Birmingham (thankfully, outdoors) in June were effectively the trials for the Olympic Games in Atlanta six weeks later. The first two across the line would be selected automatically and another seat on the plane decided by the selectors. I had a chance, but it wasn't a given. The field was really strong with Roger, Du'aine, Jamie and Mark Richardson as well as Guy Bullock, Adrian Patrick and Mark Hylton.

They called the race one of the greatest 400 metres in the history of British athletics. It was definitely the fastest ever – and quicker than that year's US trials. Roger won the race in 44.37, regaining the British record that David Grindley had set at the Barcelona Olympics four years earlier. Du'aine came in second in 44.66 and I crossed in third place in 44.69. Jamie was just a couple of hundredths of a second behind me, making it the first time in the world that four runners crossed the line inside 45 seconds in one race.

I was on the podium next to Du'aine and Roger, who had a well-publicised squabble when Du'aine bet Roger a grand that he would smash his record by the end of the season. I let them get on with it. I stood there thinking to myself that I'd run a really good time and that surely I had to be selected. But it wasn't nailed on; Jamie and Mark had both run fast times too. I wouldn't be at ease until they told me for sure.

As one of the four fastest, I knew I was going to Atlanta as one of the 4 × 400m relay team, but whether I'd get to run in the individual race was down to the selectors – one of whom was Max Jones, the very same guy who had dropped me for the relay team in the 1993 Junior European Championships. It's funny how things come full circle: he was the guy who told me I'd been picked. He gave me a nod and a wink as if he too remembered telling me my time would come.

The morning after the trials, I was still at the hotel in Birmingham when I got the call to go and get kitted out in my official clothing at the Adidas factory. It was really happening! I was going to the Olympics! I found myself in a massive warehouse, looking like a kid in a sweet shop as I was shown around, my mouth hanging open at all the gear with that shiny Great Britain Atlanta 1996 logo. It was a cool kit too. The vests incorporated the red, white and blue with a bit of style, while the tracksuit tops were a real statement, splashed with a large roaring Union Jack motif.

It was just four years since Kevin Johnstone, my PE teacher had said, 'Last time I saw raw talent like that, he went on to win an Olympic medal.' I was on the way to fulfilling that prophesy.

# Six

# THE HARD YARDS

My heart pounded like it was trying to escape my shaking body, sweat ran down my face and my head throbbed. I desperately tried to catch a breath, gasping for more air. From the pit of my stomach, I felt a stirring. I braced myself with my hands on knees, powerless as it rose and I threw up on the ground next to me. *This*, I thought to myself as I grinned, *this is what I came here for*.

When I arrived in Southampton, I had no idea what I was letting myself in for. I'd done Thursday evening sessions, but had little idea of what would happen on the other five days we trained. All I knew was I was going to put my heart and soul into it. I'd made a promise to Dad and was determined to be true to my word. I wasn't going to let him down. He was going to be proud of me even if I ultimately failed. That picture of him in my head, gently nodding with a half-smile as he watched me, was a recurrent image in those early days as, cold and wet, I flogged myself through the winter runs.

Soon a real life image took its place. My coach Mike Smith. Above all else, Mike believed in hard work and that's what he judged you on. With every extra effort I put in, every time I came in five metres ahead of the others, every fraction of a second I took off my time, I'd look at his face. He looked impassive, neutral, as if it was nothing more than he expected. I'd go again.

Mike was of an older generation; his silence was his power. He didn't give much away and always seemed slightly irritated not just with me, but with everyone. In fact, with life. But I came to realise that deep down he cared deeply about me – and I would go through anything to make him proud. Somehow, I'd managed to find a father figure who was just like my father!

Mike Smith was the best in the business. A tall, grey-haired man in his early sixties, he was usually turned out in a shirt, tie and a V-neck jumper, slacks and sometimes an anorak. You really couldn't imagine he'd ever worn a pair of shorts and a running vest. He'd played a massive part in building the golden age of British 400 metres running. I remember watching the 1991 World Championships in Tokyo, when GB's 4 × 400m team famously won gold. And I knew that Mike had coached the man who ran first leg, Roger Black, and anchorman Kriss Akabusi.

I knew if I was ever going to make it to those heights, it was Mike who would help me get there.

Mike was no-nonsense, authoritarian and hard-to-please – to be frank, on the surface, a difficult person. When he spoke he demanded respect and you had no reason not to give it. Athletics was Mike's life. He had been coaching for decades. His son Bob was heavily involved in my club, Newham and Essex Beagles, and his daughter, Janet, trained with us. But at the point that I joined him, the zip had gone out of his life.

Both Roger and Kriss, coached by Mike to become world-class athletes, decided to move on. They both had their reasons, but I know that he felt betrayed and hurt. He had finally got to the point where he was working with world-class athletes – and they'd left. Mike knew that the group of athletes in front of him were talented, but ultimately limited. It hit him hard – and many thought he might give up coaching at that point.

Then this lanky, red-headed kid turns up for training. I was far from the finished article, but even from those Thursday evening sessions, I was showing enough that Mike could see I definitely had something worth working with. Here was a runner who attacked every training session with an animal passion and was already a match for his best runners.

Mike never gave any sign to me that he thought I could be something special. It just wasn't his style. I can only remember one time that he ever complimented me directly. At home, though, he must have been talking. If I rang him and his wife, Jo, answered, she'd call out: 'It's Wonder Boy' and hand him the phone. Then he'd sometimes stretch to a sentence in reply: 'Yes, seven o'clock at the hall' and that would be it. He saved his words for what was essential.

We made for an odd couple. The morose, mostly silent coach in his 60s who just wanted everyone to get on with the session without a fuss and this ball of energy who never stopped answering back, mucking around, chatting, joking. He didn't stop me. He knew that when we got down to it, I took training more seriously than any of the others.

Mike knew exactly how to press my buttons. He'd just drop a comment here or there about being slower on a run or that one of the others in the group was catching me. Being a daft youngster, I didn't realise it at the time, but later I clicked that he had another ploy. He would wait until I was in earshot and then say to one of the others something like: 'Yeah, Iwan's going all right, but I heard last night that Mark [Richardson] is averaging 34.2 for this 300 metre session.' It was total BS, he had no idea what Ricco was doing, but he knew exactly how I would react. I'd be irritated, riled and pumped, thinking, *Yeah? Well, you can go and tell him what I'm running.* I can still picture him smirking when I then did go and run 33 seconds.

Mike used mind games to let you know he was in charge. He could sulk for England. If we talked too much during circuits, he would storm out and we wouldn't see him for five minutes. You never knew what mood he would be in. Some days he'd arrive OK, even almost cheery, then others he wouldn't speak a word to you. I'd get back to the bedsit thinking: *Have I done something wrong? I averaged 22.5. That's alright – maybe it isn't?*

I developed one get-out card, but used it sparingly. West Ham United was his kryptonite. Say we were doing something like six 300m reps with four minutes recovery. If I was having a bad day and still feeling tired as the recovery time ran down, I'd say: 'How are things looking for West Ham this year, Mike? Signed any good players?' I knew I'd get an extra minute as he'd forget about training and go off on one. 'Bloody West Ham, don't talk to me about that bunch of . . . ' I'd make sure I always kept some snippet of West Ham conversation in my locker just in case I needed a break.

Mike trained us for the love of the sport. He wasn't well off, but he never took a penny for all his time, even though I offered. When I broke through as an athlete, I spoke to his daughter saying, 'I've got to pay him something. I wouldn't have done this if it wasn't for him.' She said, 'He'd be so offended. But his TV broke yesterday, so you could get him a new one.' I went to Currys and bought him a state-of-the-art new television and the look on his face when it was delivered; he was so pleased.

Mike expected nothing but graft and I was more than happy to deliver. He was the perfect coach for me at the time. I was young, a bit cocky, a bit too eager to be a Jack the Lad, but I was also ambitious, willing to listen and learn and always gave 100 per cent effort. I enjoyed the circuits, the hill and sand dune runs as much as the track sprints. I threw myself into every training routine with enthusiasm and a smile, even if sometimes I didn't feel like smiling.

I became an absolute beast in training; something had been unleashed. Everyday I'd bust my gut. In the gym, on the track, out in the fields, I gave it everything. Turns out that we came into each other's life at exactly the right time. People have said that when I moved to Southampton to train with him, it gave Mike a massive boost. 'You were the last throw of the dice for Mike,' Tim told me later. Mike got a new lease of life, and he gave me the key to mine. Fair exchange.

The desire to please Dad and Mike might have been the impulse and was certainly still there, but something else took over when I got out there. I developed a compulsion to push my body to or even beyond its limits. Beyond anything else – the effect on my performance, the competition with the other guys, the feeling of being superfit – I relished both the physical and mental feeling. I embraced – no, I welcomed – the pain. Rather than drag me down, it pushed me on. In driving, freezing sleet or amid an energy-sapping heatwave, I didn't stop until my body gave up; when I could no longer stand, when my heart and lungs waved the white flag or my stomach decided it was time to expel anything it had left.

Most athletes will agree that training for the 400 metres is the toughest of all the track events. Usain Bolt shied away from trying the 400 metres at the end of his career even though it would have made him an even bigger legend: 'Nah,' he said, 'the training is too hard.' They call the 400 metres the 'death race' for a reason. It requires the speed of a 100 metres runner and the endurance of an 800 metres runner. You are effectively running 100 metres in 11 seconds, four times – which takes power, endurance and metal strength. And that doesn't just *happen*. It takes a whole lot of effort and pain, every day. Not that anyone told me that when I started.

Mike's training schedule followed the same routine that he had been putting his athletes through for probably 20 years or more. It was mostly based within a few miles of his house in the Southampton suburbs. Mike was great at making do. Sometimes the training felt like it was all based on a sequence from *Rocky*. We'd be hauling medicine balls, running through woods or sprinting through the streets. It certainly wasn't glamorous. There was the musty-smelling Boys' Club, where we'd do circuits or run up and down planks leaning up against the wall; Southampton athletics track, where the changing room was smelly and cramped, the toilets always locked and the running track cold, windswept and soul-wrenchingly bleak; and the school hall where we did intense shuttle run drills after the pupils had been let out of detention.

The type of training depended on the time of year. From September to January would be conditioning, getting mega-fit. It was often bitterly cold: the ground might be frozen solid, the wind cutting right through you, and every breath you were taking visible, but we'd be out there regardless. Sometimes, I'd need two pairs of gloves and three shirts just to keep warm.

We spent a lot of time running through the local woods, when the runs were long and the recovery times brief. It was great to be out in the open air and so much more interesting weaving through trees, jumping over branches and avoiding the muddy puddles than running endless laps of the playing fields. But it had its pitfalls. The woods were also a favourite destination for dog walkers and you had to keep one eye open for a charging whippet or a carefree dachshund cutting you up. Or worse. On one occasion I was chased and bitten by a Jack Russell and had to get a jab in Southampton Hospital.

Our hill running took place just by Mike's house – on the next street. It was a long gruelling hill and we ran 12 × 200m reps, walking back down for recovery and going again. On Sundays we headed out to the dunes at Lyndhurst, 16 km (10 miles) out of Southampton. They had some killer hills. Running on sand is really energy-sapping. Running fast uphill on sand is instantly knackering. It's all short strides, pumping arms and knowing the hurt is going to get worse until you hit the top. We did 20 runs, which varied from 10-second sprints to taking more than 2 minutes.

When I was running up those dunes, I blanked out everything my body was telling me; the pain, the exhaustion, the thumping heart and the gasps for air. I was fixated on getting to the top as quick as I could. Everything else could wait. But when I finished . . . it hurt so much. I was temporarily paralysed by an agonising charge that radiated through my head and chest to my legs, which quivered and threatened to give way. Undercutting all of that, though, was a sense of achievement, of victory over pain and of physical power.

For an indoor session, we were in the Boys' Club. There we'd do circuit training, plyometrics – jumping over the old wooden chairs – and Mike, being old school, got out the medicine ball. They were classic sprinter's workouts: repeated chest throws against the wall, side passes and twisting and lifting exercises for the core. The weights were only 5 kg (11 lb), but my whole body ached all night after a session.

As spring came around, the emphasis changed to speed endurance. No more long runs, but the shorter stuff, over and over. This is speed endurance where the recovery times are a little longer, but you are running flat out. We were still flogging ourselves into the ground, but in a different way. We ran eight 200 metres with two minutes' recovery time, then six with four minutes, and four with eight.

The early days of winter training are sheer hell. Sooner or later, your legs somehow manage to feel like jelly but burn like acid, and there's no way you can stop yourself throwing up. I went home to my bedsit shattered. It was the world's most uncomfortable bed ever, but that didn't matter. By then, I was so knackered that I lay down and fell straight asleep every time; often I didn't even have the energy to take a shower. In the morning I ached so much I struggled to get out of bed to go to work, but by the evening, somehow I'd be ready to go again.

At Easter, we headed out to Portugal for warm weather training. This was a week to concentrate on finessing strength with weight training and track work; timed 200 metres and 300 metres runs, strategic work concentrating on different parts of the 400 metres and short bursts of 30 metres.

We might have been holed up in a holiday resort, but we were here for a purpose. No all-day breakfasts, Union Jack shorts or Jägerbombs for us. At least, that was the theory. But we were group of young men in our twenties, all good friends, and we had plenty of time to kill in the evenings and the bars and clubs were right there. It didn't get out of hand – apart from the time Gumbo disappeared for 48 hours, finally appearing like a ghost during a session at the track dressed in a hospital nightshirt, having first had his stomach pumped due to heavy alcohol consumption and then hitched back from the hospital. For athletes on an intense training week, starting the day with a hangover wasn't ideal, and at least once in the week we found ourselves sitting down for a lecture from Mike on our priorities.

Out in Portugal, you discovered whether all that winter work had paid off, via a 3 × 300 metres test with 10 minutes recovery between each run. After a week's hard work, the real litmus test came in a gruelling sequence known as the 5-4-3-2-1. This was sprinting 500 metres with a ten-minute rest, 400 metres with eight minutes, 300 metres with six minutes, 200 metres with just a minute break, then the final 100 metres. It was a killer, but left you in no doubt as to your condition.

When we got home, the season was nearly underway. No more hills, no circuits, just sheer speed sessions on the track.

The sessions were usually short and absolutely brutal. For an hour or so, we warmed up – jog two laps of the track, a lot of static stretches and running drills – and then put on our spikes, do some strides and it was time to train. It was then that I started working out what times I needed to do in the sprint training. *What are Mark (Richardson) or Roger (Black) doing?* I asked myself. *I need to match that – or preferably go faster. If we're doing 3 × 300 with 15 minutes recovery* – my mind began whirring as I went into maths overdrive (and I'd failed my Maths GCSE first time round!) – *that means I should run the first one in 33 flat* . . . I was a right old Carol Vorderman.

The sprint sessions lasted 20 minutes or 30, but they killed us off. Dragging yourself to your feet after draining every ounce of energy in a run and then doing it all over again is a form of self-torture. We pushed ourselves to the very limits of what we could bear. We ran 150 metres pure, full-on sprinting, or we ran 200 metres at full pace with 20 minutes recovery in between. There was no let-up. It was intense, full-on racing and these were guys who could really push me. Todd Bennett and Paul Sanders were quality 400 metres runners with PBs sub 46 – and part of the group when I arrived.

The end of most sessions looked like the aftermath of a battle. Bodies were strewn all around, most lying on their backs, still, others bent double, some puking where they stood – accompanied by a soundtrack of grunting, groaning and gasping. All the while, Mike stood there in his Marks and Spencer V-neck and cagoule, watching calmly. I usually spent 20 minutes throwing up, another 15 waiting for the dizziness to stop, and more before my legs felt like they could take my weight. It could be an hour until I was able to walk back to the car. Just brilliant. I loved it.

I've no idea how he did it, but Mike was just amazing at getting me to peak as the summer came along. You can maintain the very top levels for only a limited time and, come those vital racing months, I needed to be in the shape of my life. Through the winter and spring, I tended to be thinking there was no way I was going to get under 45 seconds, but Mike always knew. I stayed training with him for as long as I could, always putting everything I had into it, always seeking his approval.

I never had a stopwatch on me, but each time I ran through the line I knew to within a tenth of a second how I'd done. Crossing the line, I'd call out to Mike: '22.6' and he'd reply: 'Yep, 22.62.' When it was two minutes recovery, I'd shout, 'How long 'til next rep, Mike? Twenty seconds?' 'Yes,' would come the reply. '19 seconds to go.' I was so in tune with my body. If I ran slightly slowly, I'd finish saying, 'That wasn't a good one'. I was a human stopwatch.

I was a man possessed – training like an animal, passing through the beautiful Hampshire fields until they were just a green blur in my vision. The slush soaked my socks as I ran through snow-covered hills in midwinter and fought my way through gales and driving rain. That agony, the pounding heart, the pools of vomit; they all became second nature to me. The tougher it got, the better I felt.

I respected all my rivals, but they lived rent-free in my head when I trained. I'd be on my haunches throwing up and thinking, *Jamie Baulch in Cardiff trains pretty hard, but no way is he heaving his guts up like this.* Or there was Mark Richardson down in Windsor. *He might be in a great training group, but I'm 100 per cent sure he's not running until he drops, day after day.* I remember climbing over the fence at the track near my parent's house so I could train on Christmas Day and picturing Roger Black all cosy, sitting by the fire in his cardigan and slippers. It made me feel good.

I often thought of them working out in their high-tech gyms or athletics stadiums with all mod cons. I used them to drive me on. I bet they didn't have to pee against the wall because the toilets were locked, they didn't spend winters freezing their bollocks off and there was no way they were running through housing estates dodging pushchairs, crackheads and lairy kids spoiling for a fight. But I never minded. It was toughening me up.

I often thought of Michael Johnson too. He was always the king, the gold standard, the man that ultimately I had to beat. I knew he'd be basking in the Texas sun when I was facing another rainy, boring day in England. After training, he'd be slipping into the ice bath in a pristine training complex, while I drove home to the cramped, grimy shower in my bedsit. He'd have his physical therapists, masseurs and all the state-of-the-art university facilities, while I had a grumpy pensioner shouting: 'C'mon, boy, one more rep', a bunch of mates on their last legs and training in halls with no heating. I regularly found myself daydreaming about our contrasting lives; picturing myself as Rocky Balboa and Johnson as Ivan Drago and imagining how the story would unfold.

I took to training so naturally; I was fearsome. I can say with my hand on my heart that no one, even Michael Johnson, could have lived with me in training. Motivation was never an issue for me. I was desperate to be the best and was prepared to put myself through anything. I honestly liked the pain, convinced it was getting me closer to my goal. That mentality crossed over until I wasn't happy unless it hurt, which meant I just wasn't pushing myself enough. I still am proud of the way I trained. There was no other athlete I knew of at the time (with the possible exception of David Grindley up in Wigan) who trained as hard as I did – and there is no way current athletes train like I did. With all their lottery funding and sports psychologists, it was 25 years before someone broke my British record.

Hindsight, however, offers a slightly different perspective. If I had my time again, would I do things differently? Well, yes possibly. That obsessive training helped me make enormous improvements in my times in my early twenties. I took almost 3 seconds off my PB in just three years. It took most elite 400 metres runners twice as long or even a decade to do that.

I came from nowhere like a man on a mission and that was down to a combination of natural talent and hard graft. I would pay the price, though.

Training was what made me and, ultimately, what broke me.

The effort I was putting in was fine when I was 21 and 22, but as I got older it began to take its toll. I didn't listen to my body. I continued to try to please Mike (and my dad a bit too). I didn't want to contradict him or say I was only doing 3 × 300m reps today – he'd be in a mood with me for days. His way was *push, push, push*: 'C'mon, boy, one more rep. Don't stop 'til you're sick.' Roger Black even warned me: 'Mike's an amazing coach while you are healthy, but he won't understand injury.'

I nodded, but I wasn't really listening. I was strong and fast and would only get stronger and faster . . .

# 4.30pm. 15 June 2021

*I knew where I was in a race. It was always reliably the same. I had my own little lane; no one could push me or get in my way. I'd be on the blocks, the gun would go, and I was totally in control of what happened. Just one lap of the perfectly surfaced track, finish ahead of the others and I was done. There were no hills to run up, no rocks blocking the way, no puddles of muddy water to leap or overhanging branches to clear.*

*Now, the insufferable heat; the terrain, up and down those fucking hills; the constant requirement to eat and drink; the need to stop and pee – all are alien concepts to me on a run. And there are no opponents, no rivals to spur me on; it's just about getting to the end – somehow. I'm so far out of my comfort zone I might as well be on another planet.*

# Seven

# THE GREATEST SHOW ON EARTH

The niggling injuries, the exhaustion, the loneliness of the bland hotel rooms, the stultifying repetition of training and the disappointments – they all fade to nothing faced with the possibility of appearing at an Olympics. Some athletes wait years for the opportunity to compete in the Games, but I was 22 years old. I had been training properly for only a year, was still to pay the price – and I was going to be an Olympian.

I might not have been one of those athletes who grew up dreaming of winning the gold or even competing at the Olympics, but memories of watching them on TV were etched in my mind. Especially Linford Christie and Sally Gunnell taking gold at the 1992 games in Barcelona. That I was going to be someone cheered on by millions at home, watching their TVs just as I had, wasn't lost on me.

I looked at that pristine, neatly folded GB kit constantly. Every piece of it – and I had the full set, running gear, tracksuit, jacket, tie . . . – had a Union Jack on it. I just couldn't wait to put it on. I had a few weeks before setting off for the States to represent my country in the greatest sporting competition in the world, and it couldn't come soon enough. I was so excited that I had to do something.

So I went down to Tattoo Magic in Shirley in Southampton for my first tattoo.

'Can I get the Olympic rings on my lower abdomen,' I told the tattooist.

'Yes, sure,' he said. 'Why do you want them? You a big fan?'

'No, I'm running. I'm doing the 400 metres.'

He stopped what he was doing and looked at me. Then he said, 'I'm not going to tattoo you.'

'Why?'

'Come back once you've been,' he said. 'If it's everything you expect it to be, I'll do it. You're a young guy, and you're excited, but hold back. See how it goes, eh?'

I rang in sick at Next the day before I left for America. Not that I had any intention of ever going back. For the past couple of weeks, I'd carried on as usual, shifting boxes to the stock room, serving customers, hanging up clothes – all the time picturing my own unopened kit at home. I hadn't told anyone there that I was setting off on the biggest adventure of my life. I wasn't sure if anyone would be bothered and I didn't need the attention. I had all the hype I needed going on in my head.

Everything had happened so fast it was difficult to take it all in. It didn't take much to appreciate that this was all a step up from anything I'd experienced before. The headed letters from the British Olympic Association (BOA), the interviews with local press, the flight and accommodation details – all said this is the big time. And I felt ready. There was no imposter syndrome now. Not only did I feel I deserved to be there in Atlanta, I fancied myself surprising a few people.

I was so full of optimism. Roger and Du'aine had been running well, but they didn't scare me. OK, there were the Americans. Butch Reynolds had run 43.91 in the US Olympics trials – and was still beaten by Michael Johnson. I was ranked 16th in the world at that point, which in theory meant I should scrape into the semi-finals, but I was sure I was better than that. I had been improving race by race.

I was desperate to get through the heats and pitch myself against the best in the world, especially Johnson, who was attempting to be the first ever male athlete to win both the 200 metres and 400 metres gold medal. I had even more incentive when I discovered my parents had bought tickets only for the semi-final and the final. I had to be racing when they were there.

Within a couple of weeks of the AAAs we flew out to our holding camp in Tallahassee, Florida for training and acclimatisation. There had been more than a few grumbles after athletes said they were not prepared for the heat in Barcelona '92, so the BOA had gone to great lengths to find somewhere in the same time zone as Atlanta with the same level of heat and humidity. And, in Florida, they found it – temperatures over 30°C (86°F) and humidity over 90 per cent. You left the air-conditioned buildings and immediately felt like you were in a sauna.

The athletes' team was based at Florida State University, where we trained and then basically chilled, conserving our energy. I'd have been impressed by virtually anything after training at Southampton's decrepit athletics track with its locked toilets, smelly changing rooms and windswept stadium, but this was a different world. A state-of-the-art track and massage therapists on hand. And the sun always shining.

Training sessions were self-led. Mike had provided set sessions for me, and although the team management did keep track of what you were doing, they left you to it. Roger, Du'aine and I kept clear of each other, though. We might be in the same GB kit but we were still rivals and none of us were going to help someone who might end up doing us out of a medal.

Towards the end of our time in Talahassee, I watched Steve Smith's high jump session. We had come through the Juniors together and he had been our captain in Seoul. Here we were, four years down the line, preparing for the Olympic Games together. He was looking good and jumped a super-impressive 2.34m (7 feet 10 inches). We were all there to get on with our own training, but everyone, including me, paused to give him a cheer.

Then it was my turn. As part of the session, I ran a split 400 – a run of 200 metres with 60 seconds for recovery and then another 200 metres. I was with my roommate, the 400 metres hurdler Gary Jennings (who I called 'Joe 90', after the bespectacled cartoon character). We were both Newham Beagles athletes and had always got along well. Joe 90 took the stopwatch and I ran the first 200. It felt pretty good.

'What was that?' I asked Gary as I gasped for air.

'21 seconds flat,' he replied.

'That's bloody great,' I said excitedly. 'I only . . . '

'Yeah, alright,' he said, shutting me up. 'You've only got 30 seconds recovery left now.'

I ran the second 200 and walked back to Gary.

'Stone me!' he said with a smile. '22.8!'

43.8 for the two legs. The idea of the split 400 metres was that you should be able to match or beat your PB. 43.8 was getting on for a second better than my best. The other athletes still there were all looking on. I looked at Steve Smith and he gave me a nod of approval. I'd set out my stall; I wasn't just along for the ride.

After a couple of weeks, it was time to head for the host city. I'd missed the World Championships in 1995 due to injury, so my only experience of a major competition was the Commonwealth Games in Canada two years previously. The Friendly Games were exactly that, a group of athletes mostly there for the fun of it. As soon as I arrived in Atlanta, I realised this was altogether different. I was blown away by the size of the set-up, the number of people milling around, the press and TV cameras and the buzz of excitement. People here meant business.

There was so much to take in and it was a relief to get to my apartment in the Olympic Village. It was an imposing, massive quadrant of redbrick towers, some smaller at just 4 storeys, some up to 12 storeys. Only just built, it housed 10,000 athletes, coaches and officials and double that number of Olympic workers, media people and VIPs. It was like a student campus, but with the most cosmopolitan, multicultural inhabitants ever.

Great Britain's athletes were given one of the smaller blocks – easy to find because of the red phone kiosk outside. Each floor had a number of three-bedroom apartments, making it seem like student accommodation. But these were luxurious compared to Stockwell Halls. There were six people to each apartment, sharing a bathroom, lounge (with a massive TV) and a small kitchen. The only downside was the tiny bedrooms, in which the two beds took up virtually all the space. I chose to share a room with Ian Mackie, a gritty Scottish sprinter I'd got friendly with at the Commonwealth Games. Ian was a very good 100 metres runner who went on to make the semi-finals. A year younger than me, he was tipped to be the successor to Linford, until his career was derailed by injuries.

Our apartment also housed Jamie Baulch and Darren Campbell, all three of us having been in Seoul at the World Junior Championships four years earlier. Keeping us youngsters in order were Colin Jackson and Linford Christie. In two years I'd gone from being star-struck as I watched Linford train to sharing an apartment with him. He was the reigning Olympic 100 metres champion, and at 36 years old he was here for his swansong.

He carried such an aura that you listened to Linford. He made sense. It was down to him that I wasn't one of the athletes at Atlanta's Centennial Olympic Stadium for the Games' opening ceremony. When we were all sitting around the apartment, I brought up the subject. 'Any of you guys going to the Opening Ceremony?'

Linford was no nonsense. 'Real athletes don't go.'

'What d'you mean?'

'You're here to win medals. Not ponce around with wannabe athletes who'll be lucky to get out of the heats.'

I took it in. He was right. This wasn't like the Commonwealth Games; I wasn't here for the show. I'd come to make a name for myself. I'd do better to stay in and conserve my energy.

Turned out to be a good move. The heat, crowds and the long periods of waiting around led to a number of people fainting. Worse still, one Polish official died from a heart attack. I took Linford's advice and for the rest of my career never went to an opening or closing ceremony.

I was no longer the quiet boy I'd been back then, either. I knew I'd earned my place in the squad and was ready to come out of my shell. Atlanta 96 became notorious for its transportation issues: spectators were often left for hours on buses because drivers unfamiliar with the road system constantly got lost.

The athletes received no better service. Our training facility was in Phoenix Park, a few blocks from the Olympic Stadium but 8 km (5 miles) from the Village, and it could take forever to get there or back. One evening we were returning from the training park to the Olympic Village and somehow the driver had got us lost. The coach was full of tired and hungry athletes from every continent all saying the same thing in different languages: 'Oh not again. For fuck's sake!'

The mood on board the coach was getting worse and worse with every wrong turn we made. This was not how Olympic athletes expected to be treated – especially in America. After a fourth stop to check the directions, the anger level was rising. The German athletes on the seats behind me sounded off. Even with my basic German (I only understood the expletives) I got the gist.

I stepped out of my seat and found myself walking to the front of the coach. Seconds later, there I was standing in front of a coachload of bemused Olympians looking at me. For a second I too thought, *What am I doing? Should I go back and sit down?*

I didn't. I took the driver's microphone and began. 'There was an Englishman, a Welshman and a Scotsman . . . ' I got to the punchline to hear a couple of groans as plenty of tumbleweed blew past. Undeterred, I began telling any and every joke I could think of – rude jokes, doctor jokes, gags I remembered from school. Most of the athletes had no idea who I was, and a lot of people were mouthing 'Who is this guy?' to each other, but I gradually I got enough people laughing. And laughter is contagious. Eventually the athletes – even the foreign ones who were still figuring out what was going on – the coaches and team manager Max Jones were all in hysterics. I took my bow to a raucous round of applause and returned to my seat as we struggled through another traffic jam.

I was having the time of my life. How could I not? I was part of the greatest show on Earth. One of the best 10,000 sportspeople on the entire planet. For the rest of my life, I would be able to call myself an Olympian. It was such an honour – and an experience I had never imagined I would get to enjoy, even four years ago when watching the action from Barcelona on TV.

I'd loved the Commonwealth Games in Canada with the free steaks and party atmosphere, but the Olympic Village was something else. For a start, the Village was huge. You had to get on a little train to go to the various zones and the security guys drove around in golf buggies. The main restaurant was the size of two football pitches and was open 24/7. And the food was all free. Not just buffet breakfasts and proper meals, either; the Village had a huge McDonald's where you could help yourself to as much as you wanted any time of day. This was so different to sitting with Gumbo and Taxi Tim after a night out in Southampton discussing who could eat three Big Macs and, more importantly, who was going to pay.

This was a McDonald's of Excellence. It was like a freak show at times. I didn't know who these people sitting next to me were, but at what they did they were the best in the world. It was just amazing. I'd be sitting opposite a Chinese volleyball player 2.1m (7') tall and then a Russian gymnast only 1.2m (4') tall would come and sit next to me. I'd look down the table and see superstars like Magic Johnson. As well as free McDonald's and all the Coke I could drink (it wasn't the heathiest diet, but I was young and figured I needed all the calories I could get), there was the biggest outdoor film screen in the world and a massive dedicated games room sponsored by Sega. There were the most up-to-date games around – driving, baseball, shooting, everything – and it was all free. For a 22-year-old from Godmanchester, this was the Best. Holiday. Ever. And the racing hadn't even started.

Ian Mackie and I knocked around together when we got time. In the Village there was a hairdresser. I persuaded Ian that it would look really cool to have the Olympic rings dyed into his hair. They cut it pretty short and then dyed the rings into the fade at the back. I thought it looked pretty cool.

The next morning I was woken by loud, guttural, unfathomable Scottish cursing. The dye had come off on his pillow and all that was left in his hair was a messy blur of colour. I didn't have my tattoo rings and Ian lost his logo. It just wasn't meant to be.

---

Training at the Games was just about keeping things ticking over until you raced. If you weren't at peak form by this time, it was too late, but nor would you lose fitness. I did a few track sessions, running 120 metres off the bend, but nothing to get the lactic acid going. I became a bit like a boxer desperate to get into the ring. I couldn't wait to race, and was eager to keep sharp, but at the same time I felt the constant worry of getting injured before I even got started.

After I had been there for four days (and three days from my first heat), I did develop a problem. Not something I can be delicate about either: I was shitting green. I couldn't believe my bad luck. Here I was, at a crucial time in my life, and I'd picked up some bug that could now ruin my chances. Jamie and Darren weren't used to me having nothing to say for myself.

'What's the matter? Something up, Iwan?'

'I must have eaten something dodgy, I'm not good.'

'Well, you look alright. What's the matter?'

'My shit's all green.'

They both fell about laughing. Not the reaction I expected. Then the two medical geniuses explained. Just outside our apartment was a free vending machine. I'd been helping myself liberally – too liberally, as it turned out – to the Powerade. I'd drank so much blue and green fluid that it was colouring everything that went through my digestive system.

I was still so much a kid in so many ways. But my naïvety was also good in that it made me fearless. The crowds, the sense of occasion, Michael Johnson in his custom-made golden shoes. I took it in my stride.

I'd also been sent new spikes, by Asics. They weren't golden but they were CYBERBLADES, state-of-the-art running shoe with three Velcro straps and cutaways instead of a tongue so you could see your feet. They looked so cool. The only problem was they were a little too small for me. I thought they looked the business, so I squeezed into them, desperately convincing myself they were OK. It was only when Jamie noticed and said: 'That's ridiculous, you can't wear those' that I changed into my old lace-up Asics, middle-distance spikes. I thought, *If I come back with a medal, there's no way I'm ever tying laces again.*

The 400 metres competition took place over four days at the end of July with heats, quarter-finals, semi-finals and the final taking place on consecutive days. There were 62 competitors at the outset in 8 heats, and the first 3 of each heat and the 8 next fastest finishers across all the heats went through to the quarters. After that, it was the top four from each race who advanced to the next round.

Going all the way to the final – as I was assuming I would – would be a pretty gruelling four days.

My first Olympic race took place on 26 July 1996, the last of the heats. I felt some pressure on my shoulders because Roger and Du'aine had already made it through. I'd drawn Lane 7 and was feeling pretty confident even though a plethora of false starts by some jittery athletes ramped up the tension. I needed to finish in the top three to be sure of progressing.

On paper I knew I should finish in the top three with some ease, but this was the Olympics, where athletes often find something extra and it's easy to get caught out. The heat line-up included some talented athletes. Nigeria's Sunday Bada, Uganda's Davis Kamoga and Jamaica's Roxbert Martin were all capable of running sub-45 seconds, so my place in the next round wasn't guaranteed.

With such a draining schedule my aim was to qualify without taking too much out of myself. In Lane 7 you can't see those running in lanes on the inside until after the stagger unwinds, but I knew I was doing OK when I closed down the Australian Mark Ladbrook after 200 metres. As I went into the final 100, I looked across the track and only saw Bada ahead of me and Kamoga trailing us by nearly a second. At that point I didn't need to go flat out, I just ran within myself and checked my position. I was in the quarters. 'We hope he survives several rounds,' said the BBC. 'He certainly has the ability.'

The next day – a Saturday – wasn't a great one for the GB team. Things had started to unravel. Linford's attempt to retain his title at the age of 36 had come to a frustrating end after he was disqualified after two false starts, a sad way for such a great athlete to bow out. Elsewhere, world record holder Jonathan Edwards had missed out on an expected gold medal and Du'aine had been squeezed out of a tough quarter-final that included Johnson, Kamoga and Martin. Roger, however, had looked really strong as he won his heat.

Once again, I ran in the final race of the round, this time moving to Lane 6, a slight improvement but not ideal. On the starting line alongside me was Alvin Harrison of the United States, who had run 44.09 in the US trials, and Jamaica's Michael McDonald, a former World Junior Champion who had been getting faster all year. I went out pretty fast and stayed shoulder to shoulder with McDonald until going past him early in the sprint. Harrison came through to win, but that was fine. Job done. I had made the semi-finals and knew I had more in me. Increasingly I felt, *I can do this, I can get to the final* – and even getting a medal didn't seem beyond my hopes.

That evening, just after midnight, tragedy hit the Games. A bomb in Centennial Olympic Park in downtown Atlanta, the 'town square' of the Olympics, killed two people and injured over a hundred others. No athletes were among those hurt, but it had been a destination for many. Mark Richardson had even been down there earlier. I had the semi-final the next day and the team managers checked in on me to make sure I was OK – or so I was told; I was fast asleep.

The bombing was headline news all over the world and there was a sombre and tense atmosphere in the Village and stadium. And yet, I was pretty much oblivious. I had a semi-final to run, and that was my focus.

The semi-final was my third race in three days. Roger had already made the final, winning his semi in some style after Butch Reynolds pulled out injured in the first 100 metres. The pressure might have been off in terms of GB having a finalist, but that just made me more desperate to join him. And this time, I was going to be running in front of Mum and Dad; that was a big deal for me.

I knew this was no formality, though. I was up against Michael Johnson, who was so far ahead of every other 400 metres (and 200 metres) runner that they could have given him the gold to match his shoes there and then. That left three other places for the final. Also in the running were Sunday Bada, who had won my first heat, Kamoga, Martin (just beaten in the last race by me), and Michael McDonald, so two of us were going to be disappointed.

I was in Lane 3, two lanes inside the great man. As I waited to get set at the start, I reminded myself that I had to put him out of my mind and race the others for the final places. I just couldn't allow them to get away from me. The racing had already been tougher than I'd imagined, but this was the toughest so far. They all went away so fast and I found myself battling with Jamaican Michael McDonald in the lane next to me. As we hit the first bend, I was swept along by the roar of the crowd as they reacted to Johnson upping the pace and striding ahead with that unmistakable upright, duck-like running style.

I relaxed down the back straight, trying to not let the occasion get to me, but as I came off the final bend I was full of lactic. I wasn't going to give up this chance. I battled with everything I had to make the top four. It was so close, and in the end it was me and the big, strong Nigerian, Sunday Bada.

He wasn't strong enough. I was in dreamland. Ecstatic, raising my clenched fists in delight. It was a feeling of relief, utter exhaustion and pride. That was such a tough race and I'd had to summon every last drop of energy. The result, and the determination and strength I had shown, surprised many people who hadn't seen me run before Atlanta. The pundits had given me only an outside chance of making the final.

As soon as I could, I went in search of Mum and Dad. I'd arranged to meet them in the concourse outside the block where they had been sitting, which had seemed straightforward enough. But I'd underestimated quite how many people there would be milling around the tunnels. I hung around for a while, but just couldn't spot them. It was the one disappointment on a great day and I'd have loved to share my excitement with them, but it wasn't to be.

The first person to congratulate me was Roger Black. He had stayed to watch my semi-final after his and was there with a huge smile and a warm hug. It would be the first time since 1964 that Britain had two athletes in the Olympic 400 metres final.

I came to really appreciate the support Roger gave me as I developed from a promising athlete to his rival as the top UK quarter-miler (although 400m is 2⅓ metres shorter than the old quarter mile race, the original term is still used).

We are so different in many ways. He is serious and quiet. I never take anything too seriously (until I was on the blocks) and am always looking to have a laugh. He turns up to events in a blazer and slacks while I'll be in a cut-off vest and jeans. We are from the same place, well-educated and middle-class – quite a novelty among top athletes. He is kind and supportive, and for all our differences, we shared the same attitude to training and racing.

Back home, Roger and I were a rare success story in an Olympics which was proving disappointing for the Great Britain team. The fact that few people outside the sport had heard of me before meant I was now creating a bit of a buzz. 'His strength is his strength and he's paced the race exactly right . . . marvellous, marvellous,' said David Coleman in the BBC commentary of the semi-final.

Roger took a lot of the pressure off me back home. The talk was of whether he had any chance of beating Johnson. I was a bonus. I had already overachieved in getting to the final. I was the future, not the present. Did I have any chance of getting a medal? Most thought it unlikely, but the odd pundit echoed my own thoughts and admitted there was a slim chance. When I spoke to Mike on the phone, his customary minimal response hit the nail on the head.

'You just run, boy! You might end up getting a medal.'

# 10.30pm. 15 June 2021

*They had warned me that night-time was something else, but I really am not ready for what's going on. Alone in the pitch black with just a headlamp lighting my way, the dark begins to play tricks on my exhausted mind.*

*Shadows cast monstrous shapes, sticks take the form of snakes reaching out for me, axe-wielding maniacs lurk behind every bush. I'm having a nightmare while awake and running through a field in God-knows-where in the dead of night.*

*Then come the screams. Screeching demons that howl with torment or snarl cruel, sadistic laughter. It's like a terrifying soundtrack from a horror film or one of those visions of hell made real. The yelps and screeches hurt my ears and I can't get away fast enough.*

*Only miles later, with the sounds still tormenting my head, am I told I've run past a pig farm.*

*For fuck's sake . . .*

# Eight

# FINAL STRETCH

I was so excited, which masked quite how much those three races in three days had taken out of me. Running 400 metres at that level might last only 45 seconds (less if you want the chance of a medal), but the physical toll it takes is brutal. Added to that is a rollercoaster of stress. Each day begins with excitement, nervous energy and adrenaline – and is followed by relief and exhaustion. These days the qualifying rounds are run faster, but athletes have two or three days' rest between races. Back then, I was going to bed knackered and waking up to a new day and another race.

I had also been carrying a hip flexor injury, which was getting progressively worse. Unfortunately, it came to a head as I warmed up an hour before the final, the biggest race of my life. There was a sharp pain where the thigh meets the hip – and no ignoring it. It was going to be impossible to race against the world's best. I was distraught and desperate.

I called the British team doctor over to me. Yes, he could give me a cortisone jab that would mask the pain and enable me to run. But, there was a chance I could rupture the tendon and that would be the end of my season.

It was a no-brainer. 'Inject me, now!' I cried. I went over to the GB team marquee with the doctor, and 45 minutes before the Olympic final, he administered my first-ever cortisone injection.

The final started at the call room at the Phoenix Park, the warm-up track. You have your number, your kit is checked and you sign in. Then you are on your own. No mates, medics or coaches.

We all signed in and now boarded the bus for the 10-minute drive to the stadium. It was just us and some competitors for a later race. We sat in silence, all concentrating on mentally preparing for the race ahead.

I sat looking out the window. I'd done this journey a few times already, but it dawned on me that something was different. These were streets I hadn't seen before. No one else seemed to have noticed yet, but the coach driver was lost again. With 85,000 people waiting for one of the Games' biggest events, the protagonists were being taken on a tour of Atlanta's roughest neighbourhoods.

The athletes gradually realised. Some looked stressed, others took it in their stride. I was calm about it all; they couldn't have the race without us. Michael Johnson, however, looked flustered. He had his specially made golden shoes ready, and for millions watching, this was the Michael Johnson Show. The rest of us athletes were supporting actors as he attempted Part One of an historic double: the first athlete in Olympic history to win gold in the 400 metres *and* 200 metres.

By the time we got there, we were 20 minutes behind schedule, so were sent straight into the starting blocks with no time for a final warm-up on the track. Understandably, I was more nervous than I had ever been before a race, so the less time to think about it, the better.

Finishing fourth in my semi-final meant I would be running in Lane 1 or 8. I had been drawn in Lane 8 – the most unfavourable because it's difficult to see the other athletes and judge your pace, but it was my preference of the two lanes on offer. For a tall athlete, the inside bends for Lane 1 can be really tight. As difficult tactically as running in Lane 8 is, I was thankful.

Taking my place on the starting line in the outside lane, I had a flashback to the County Championships race four years earlier. Just as on that day, I had been drawn in Lane 8 and now, just as then, I looked across the line to Lane 4 and saw a tall, muscular guy readying himself for the race. *Maybe it was a good omen?* A frisson of hope passed through my mind. *Back then, I'd won against all the odds, I could do it again. Maybe.* But here, there were 85,000 spectators in the stadium and millions more watching around the world on TV. And that tall, muscular guy readying himself for the race was no teenage county runner, it was Michael Johnson . . .

I was relaxed, though. I'd already exceeded expectations, and if the race went my way and I managed to get a medal, what a bonus that would be! There was no reason not to approach the race with confidence. I'd run 44.69 in the AAAs and only Johnson had beaten that in Atlanta (although Roger had equalled it in his semi-final). Kamoga, Harrison and Martin had all beaten me on the way to the final, but they didn't scare me.

*I'll probably need to run a PB, but if I can just get near 44.66, I'll be in with a shout.*

With Michael Johnson attempting to bag the first of his double golds, the crowd is even more hyped. You can feel the buzz all around as we take our starting positions. The silence that then falls over the stadium is eerie. I'm in the zone at that point, trying to freeze everything out, ignoring everything outside that track, that lane.

As soon as the starting gun fires, that becomes impossible. In Lane 8, I am so close to the crowd, I can smell them and feel this wave of energy as a wall of sound erupts. All at once, 85,000 people come roaring to life. Afterwards, it sinks in. It's like being a rock star at a stadium concert. A roar like nothing I've ever heard before and bursts of camera flashbulbs lighting up the stadium.

At the front of the stagger, I go off well but have no idea what is happening behind me and am only vaguely aware of the Qatari athlete in Lane 7 pulling out early. When I come off the top bend no one has come past me. A thought flashes through my mind: *Hey! I'm winning the Olympic final!* Then with 150 metres to go, I feel Johnson's presence, and curse to myself as he sails past me. Then I'm in third place behind Roger. I just have to hold on.

'Well, that was one of the great races, not only in Olympic history but in track and field history,' concluded David Coleman after the final. I didn't think so at the time. I was devastated, having finished fifth.

At one point as we went down the home straight, I thought I could repeat the semi-final finish, stay strong and take a bronze. Unfortunately, although I kept going, so did Harrison and Kamoga. I ran 44.7, just outside of my PB, but needed 44.5 to get a medal. Still, to this day, whenever I rewatch that race I seem to get closer and closer to getting a bronze.

I was disappointed I didn't get a medal, but before the Games, I could only dream of competing in the final and running 44.7. What more could I have done? It is so difficult to get in the top three from Lane 8. By the time I came off the top bend and saw where everyone else was, it was too late to do anything about it. If only I'd finished third and not fourth in the semi-final, I could have secured a better lane. Having other runners to pace myself against – especially in the opening 200 metres when I went off hard – might have made a difference.

The truth was that the effort I made in that semi, in addition to having run three times in three days, had taken too much out of me. I'd had one year of training, and this was my first top-level competition. I was bitterly disappointed, but at the same time, knew I had to be proud of what I had achieved so far.

These were the mixed feelings going through my mind as I climbed the stadium stairs to try once more to find Mum and Dad. It proved even harder than last time. The concourse was full of people who had just watched me run and it seemed every single one of them wanted to shake my hand. There were only minutes before the team bus left for the Village. As time ticked by, I thanked people for their comments while desperately looking out for my parents. It was futile. Once again, I'd missed them. It only added to the disappointment.

The world's focus was on Michael Johnson, and at home Roger was rightly getting accolades for his silver medal – the first Briton to win a medal in the men's 400 metres since 1936.

Roger ran a brilliant race and must have been feeling elated when he gave his post-race interview, so he was really generous to mention me. He said he was pleased to have won the silver since it was only a matter of time before I challenged him 'because this boy next to me is something special'.

And it's true, I had set out my stall – making the final in my first major competition, coming a respectable fifth. There was no social media then and we had little access to what was happening back home, but I could tell from my calls to Mike that I had given a good account of myself. Friends were telling me that I was getting plenty of mentions in the media. 'Mate, you're a hero. Wait 'til you get home – you won't believe it.'

Back home, they were looking for a silver lining to an underwhelming performance by the GB team in Atlanta. In the absence of much good news in the present they were looking for any sign of hope. I was being feted as the future of British athletics. The *Daily Telegraph* wrote: 'Iwan Thomas's fifth place was a remarkable achievement given his youth – he is 22 – and inexperienced.' The *Daily Mirror* suggested that 'Welsh discovery Thomas is clearly earmarked as Black's successor.'

That kind of response diluted my initial disappointment. Everyone was saying the same thing: *This is just the beginning. You are so young, you've got two or even three more Olympics in you.*

In the meantime, I wasn't even finished with this Olympics. I still had another chance of glory in the relay competition.

The 4 × 400 metres relay event began three days later. Still recovering from the exertions of the individual race, I was pleased to be rested along with Roger for the heat. Du'aine and Mark Hylton, who was still only 19 years old, were brought in to join Jamie Baulch and Mark Richardson. They won their heat and recorded the second fastest time next to the USA.

I came back for the semi-final to replace Mark. We were pushed hard by Senegal and Kenya but led them home and qualified for the final in 3:01.36 with plenty left in the tank. We had real hopes that a gold medal was possible. With Roger returning for the final in place of Du'aine, we had a strong team. True, the Jamaicans with McDonald and Martin were looking good. Also true, the US had Johnson. Still, we fancied we could take them on: Butch Reynolds had pulled out of the US team having injured his hamstring in his semi-final of the 400 metres individual race, which gave us more hope. Then Michael Johnson dropped out after winning the 200 metres final, the day before the relays began. We really started to believe.

The four of us – Jamie, Mark, Roger and I – were a tight-knit group. We got along well and realised we could be on the brink of doing something special. GB had won the Worlds in 1991, but no British team had ever won the Olympics and we genuinely believed we could give the US a run for their money.

We had a team meeting in Roger's room.

'This is the first time the top four guys are fit at the same time,' he told us. 'I've never experienced that before. This is a unique moment, a unique opportunity.' He gave us a short history lesson and told us about his experience with the 1991 team alongside Derek Redmond, John Regis and Kriss Akabusi. It was inspirational stuff.

He told us how they chose the tactics and the order of running themselves and suggested we do the same. The team management left us to it. Roger said, 'Listen, Iwan. I want you to run first leg and give Jamie a fighting chance.' That is exactly what they had done in 1991: against accepted wisdom, they picked one of the strongest of the team, Roger, for the first leg. 'We're going to shake the Americans up.' He wanted Jamie and I to blast it and keep us in contention to set up Mark and him for a chance to win.

I was in Lane 6 with the USA's LaMont Smith next to me in 5. I was more nervous for this than I was for the individual final; the whole team's hopes were on the line as well as my own. I took Roger's words literally, flying off the blocks, blasting the first 300 metres and leaving Smith languishing behind. Initially, at least. Maybe I was still recovering from the week's exertions, but he had almost closed the gap by the time I reached Jamie. Nevertheless, I'd run 44.7, my fastest leg ever, and we were in gold medal position.

The most painful thing about the relay is the impotence. You pass on the baton – and that's it. There's nothing more you can do to help the team win. I slowly walked off the track, watching the race develop on the big screen. Jamie was running like a man inspired. Like he had a rocket strapped to him. By the time they broke lanes at 500 metres midway down the back straight, he had a metre lead on Harrison. It was going perfectly to plan, but as I watched, the voice inside my head asking, *Has he gone too hard, too early?* got its answer. The lactic kicked in and not only Harrison but the Jamaican Martin had passed him before he handed on to Mark Richardson.

As Mark set off, we had some good fortune. Amid the crowded changeover, the Jamaican athlete had taken a tumble and lost valuable seconds. Now it really was us against the Americans as Mark battled with Derek Mills. Ricco ran 43.62, the fastest ever 400 metres relay lap by a Briton, but still left Roger half a second behind the US anchor, Anthuan Maybank.

By the time Roger was in full flow down the back straight, the three of us were together, eyes glued on the screen. As they came to the final bend, Roger made it to Maybank's shoulder. We jumped up and down and grabbed each other, 'He's gonna do it! He is!' But then Maybank kicked in the final straight and it was just too much; the three of us knew and Roger did too. He just didn't have the strength to keep with him.

There was no disappointment from any of us. We had a silver medal. Our time of 2:56.60 was faster than the 1991 gold-winning team and a European record, which no one has come anywhere near breaking since. In the post-race interview with the BBC, we were still overjoyed. 'We really wanted to win,' I began the interview. 'We gave it everything, but we can't control what the other team does.' Roger, who knew this was his last Olympics and had more reason than any of us to rue not getting gold, summed things up generously. 'This is a great team, with great strength. Not just a team for the present but a team for the future.'

We were a dream team. The togetherness was brilliant. That night on the podium as we were presented with our medals, we truly felt like brothers. What a feeling to stand there having achieved that together! As we took off on our lap of honour, the only people I could have wished to share the moment with as much as them was my parents. As we laughed and jogged our way around, I kept an eye out for them, but my hopes weren't high. Then suddenly, somehow among the 85,000 people, there they were! They clambered down to the fence and at last I was able to hug them. It capped the most fantastic day of my life so far.

We were so close to a gold, but to have a silver hanging around your neck is just amazing. I was still wearing it as I went with Roger to do a live BBC interview for *Grandstand* and then they asked if we'd do one for BBC Southampton. I thanked Mike, saying sorry that I wasn't bringing home an individual medal and that I recognised all he had done to get me here; I thanked the people of Southampton and finished off saying, 'By the way, Next, I'm not coming back to work!'

It shows how close we were feeling as a team that the four of us headed off together to downtown Atlanta. We wanted to get away from the whole hullabaloo. We found a quiet shabby bar in the side streets and celebrated as only brothers can. We chatted, laughed and drank the night away; the cigars came out (although I abstained; for all my vices, I'm not a smoker) and we savoured being Olympic medal winners.

When we got back to the Village, we went for a late-night burger in McDonald's. I decided it was time for a little mischief. Now, the security guards all used these golf buggies to get around the Village and parked them up around the place. Darren Campbell, whose youth may have been slightly misspent, had showed me how to hot-wire one using a ring pull from a Coke can. It involved pulling back a seat and inserting the ring pull in the battery which started the buggy.

Now, a few drinks had been taken, so I managed to cajole Karen Pickering, the swimmer, to come for a spin. We got in a buggy and I gave Darren's hot-wiring method a go. Amazingly it worked and we set off for a joy ride around the Village. Within a few minutes, security were on to us and were in pursuit in their buggies. A low-speed car chase around the compound ensued before we bailed out. The buggy crashed against a wall, we ran away and were never caught. I was going out on a high on my last night at the Atlanta Olympics.

In the media back home, the Games were painted as a complete disaster for the Team of Shame – as Jonathan Edwards half-jokingly called us. Matthew Pinsent and Steve Redgrave won Britain's only gold medal in a measly haul of 16 medals (10 fewer than the BOA had expected) and we finished 36th in the Olympic medal table, below Kazakhstan, Algeria and Ireland. It was the worst result since Helsinki in 1952. To make sure this never happened again, money raised by the National Lottery began to fund UK Sport from the following year.

Of course, the media exaggerated the situation. It looked worse without any golds, which was partly down to bad luck with Linford's and Tony Jarrett's disqualification and Kelly Holmes, Sally Gunnell and Colin Jackson all suffering injuries. A few more medals from them and the athletics team would not have looked so disappointing.

For the 16 who did get medals, the Games were anything but a disaster and I proudly stood among them. Being one of the few success stories – Steve Backley (silver, javelin), Steve Smith (bronze, high jump) and Denise Lewis (bronze, heptathlon) were the only other athletics medallists – brought extra focus.

'From nobody to an Olympic Silver medallist . . . It's been quite a few months for Iwan Thomas who is outstanding proof that not everything is bleak in the future of British Athletics,' wrote the *Observer*. I was riding high in the public's estimation.

(The same article also described me as the second – thanks! – sexiest man in athletics and *Company* magazine's Olympic body beautiful competition saw me beaten by Du'aine.)

When the present lets you down, you look to the future. In the sports pages review of the Games, I was seen as having huge potential. My ranking had soared as a result of Atlanta and the same *Observer* article continued that I was 'set to be one of sport's shining lights in the next millenium'. What was more, I was young and wore my heart on my sleeve – I was on the verge of tears when I didn't win and full of jokes and smiles when I did – the press and TV reporters were always pleased to see me.

And there was something else that helped me stand out. For 10 years the 400, 200 and 100 metre distances had been dominated by Black athletes. The influx of inner-city kids had taken British athletics especially to new levels. That was great – and Roger was an exception – but it also had a spin-off. I was one of the few white competitors and, what's more, I was pasty-faced with reddish hair. It was so easy to pick me out on TV in the middle of a fast, crowded race.

I wasn't quite prepared for the reception back home. Before Atlanta, I was known by those in athletics circles, and that was it. I could walk around Southampton and I was just another bloke. Now I walked down the same streets to find people recognised me and wanted to shake my hand. It was surreal. Roger ran for Team Solent and Mike organised a welcome home for both of us at the Southampton athletics stadium on a Thursday night. Roger ran the 100 metres and I did 300 metres. The place was heaving with people stretching right back over the playing fields.

I noticed the change in training too. Now people stopped to watch and dog walkers pointed me out. If I was out having a meal, they came over and talked to me. People came down to the track to watch sessions. I have to say, they were only ever warm and friendly towards me and I enjoyed chatting to them.

The father of Peter Brend, one of my training partners, had begun sponsoring me before the Olympics. He was a successful businessman who owned 16 hotels and Ford garages in Devon. He had given me a white Ford Escort Cabriolet, which was cool. When I got back from Atlanta, he upgraded me to a black Ford Probe. I wish he hadn't. It wasn't my favourite car anyway, and not only was the name of his company splashed over it but also mine. There was no way the folk of Southampton could miss me and I always imagined the words *What a big-headed prat!* going through their minds when I drove past.

My real sponsorship break came soon after I came home from Atlanta when Adidas and Asics started a bidding war for my signature. I was sorely tempted to sign with Adidas, but I took the Asics deal. I was used to being paid £4 an hour to sell clothes at Next, and here was a four-year deal, starting at £50,000 a year (plus the same again as a bonus if I won a gold medal at the 1997 World Championships) and then incrementally increasing to six figures over four years. Just for wearing their brand? That was unimaginable to a 22-year-old back from his first Olympics.

With hindsight, though, I might have been better in the long term taking the Adidas deal. Asics gave me amazing running spikes, handmade for me in Japan, and slightly more money initially, but they didn't push me anywhere. Adidas were high profile: they had David Beckham, who was endorsing their Predator boot, and really promoted their stars well, on billboards and in commercials.

In the meantime, I could now rest properly before training, earn extra money through promotions and even move out of rented accommodation. I could afford to put down a big deposit and buy a three-bedroom townhouse off Oxford Street in the heart of the city! A fashionable address in the best part of town, it was trendily decorated (including the relay baton from the final now framed on the wall) and had a cool under-house garage with a remote-control door (like the Batcave!). It was five miles from my cramped bedsit, but a different world.

And, I soon went back to Tattoo Magic. I showed the guy my silver medal and said: 'Hi. I'm ready to get those Olympic rings now.'

# Nine

# SECOND IS NOWHERE

I was into the groove now. I had my own house, I knew my way around Southampton, I had friends, I didn't have to juggle training with a job and I knew what every training session entailed, from Lyndhurst dunes to fartlek sprints to track work. I could pay my own way now and I no longer had to rely on my parents to support me. What a difference a year makes!

The end of the season after the Olympics was mad. At Crystal Palace, Zurich, Monte Carlo and other meetings, I often ran against Roger, Jamie and Mark. We were stars now and in demand. I won an *Observer* New British Athlete award, Roger was telling everyone I was the one to watch, and Kriss Akabusi was even tipping me as the next European number one.

The athletics calendar means there is always something on the horizon – the Worlds, the Europeans, the Commonwealths, the Olympics . . . I went into the winter of 1996 with such a fire in my belly! No longer did I have Jamie, Mark and Roger in my head; now I had my eyes firmly set on the next challenge, the World

Championships in Athens. Now in training I also pictured Reynolds, Young, Washington, Kamoga and, above them all, Johnson. All I could do was keep working. Was Johnson beatable? Maybe, maybe not – but I was getting closer.

I trained like a possessed animal every single session: medicine ball throwing, plyometrics in the Boys' Club on a Tuesday night, running through the forest on a Wednesday; to me every single rep of every session was a race. I'd come fifth in the Olympics and I knew, I was absolutely sure, I could do better than that. I knew the training had taken my running up a level before and felt my body could take it – so I went up another gear.

I was now being asked to do public appearances. I used to work for a company called Superschools, going to a school, showing them my medal and leading a short assembly that included some PE. The kids would line up class by class to have their picture taken with me. Every single kid in the school – and only a handful even knew who I was! After 800 photos, my face ached through the constant smiling.

I did quite a lot of that because there was reasonable money to be earned, but Mike was strict about how many I should do. He rightly insisted that training came first and I definitely wasn't allowed to do it on a hard track day.

I realised I now had some commercial value, but Mike knew I needed holding back and nurturing. I was like an excitable puppy. If he let me off the leash, I would take anything going. 'Trust me, boy,' he kept saying. 'If you win the Europeans next year, there'll be bigger and better prizes awaiting you.'

If I told him that I knew Jamie was doing a lot more commercial work than me, he laughed. 'Who cares? He ain't beating you on the track.'

In the long run he was right. My training was always my focus. I never ran for fame. I never ran for money. Yes, it's nice to be paid for something you love doing, but my hunger was for medals. I didn't care when I heard so-and-so had signed a commercial deal to advertise shampoo or whatever. I just thought to myself, *I'm going to kill them on the track this year. My feet will do the talking.*

Going back to South Africa in midwinter was a way of getting away from any of those distractions to focus on the running. I was also excited after having had such a great time the previous year, but I had a shock coming. Just like the last time, we flew to Joburg, but this time we came out of the airport and didn't take the road to North Pretoria.

'Where we going, Andy? Bentley's Country Lodge is that way.'

'You're not going there this year, boy.'

Instead of the luxury of Bentley's, Andy had arranged for us to stay in the Pretoria Police Academy. For the six weeks I was there, all I had in my room was a metal sprung bed and a thin mattress. I even had to buy a pillow and some toilet roll. There was no TV. The showers were communal. There were no locks on the bedrooms or the toilets, and there were bars across every window. At night a vicious dog roamed the corridors, so we were afraid to leave our rooms.

The only real interaction with the police came after training one Friday. The senior police guy approached us and said, 'Awright, boys? You coming for a drink?' They took Tim and I to a club in the grungiest part of town. It was weird; just full of police slouching around with their guns in their holsters watching strippers. We ended up getting drunk with them.

'You're going to get your head down and work hard this year.'

I recognised those words: Andy may have been the one to speak them, but I knew he had been planning this with Mike. They'd decided we'd had too much of a good time at Bentley's and needed to be out of temptation's way. The training college had a basic gym, a crappy four-lane athletics track and not much else. In the afternoons after training, Tim and I crawled through a hole in the fence to the swimming pool so that we could swim and sunbathe.

I got into the best shape possible because there was nothing to do, no distractions. We trained, ate and slept. On repeat. To his credit, Andy didn't escape to a five-star hotel, but stayed there with us – maybe just to be sure we weren't having any fun. In some ways it was like being in prison or living like a monk, but in hindsight I can see it was the best winter of my career and the perfect preparation for the 1997 season.

I was entered in the Engen Grand Prix series with Tim again. This included a rare 600 metres run in Roodepoort, where I was up against Hezekiél Sepeng, the 800 metres silver medallist at Atlanta. The 600 metres was new to me and this was at altitude; I could easy misjudge it and leave myself gasping and sick. So I asked Tim for his advice. He said, 'I wouldn't go out too hard, you might blow up,' So, I thought I'd run within myself, jogging round for the first 400 metres in 48 and then speeding up in the final 200.

I should have gone off hard and done 400 in 46 seconds and tried to hang on. But what I vividly remember is that just before we got to the 400-metre mark, a loud whistle was blown in the crowd and Hezekiél Sepeng shot away. He was 20 metres up the track by the time I responded. It turned out, of course, that it was his coach who blew the whistle. Still, it was interesting doing a distance that wasn't familiar, and 600 metres at altitude was toughening me up. I came in third and the time I did was pretty decent, which showed me I was strong even at that time in the season.

Mike's Easter warm weather trip to Portugal came around soon enough and this time I had a camera crew following me. Filmmaker Mark Craig was making a fly-on-the-wall documentary. I'd got to know him in South Africa early in 1996 where he was filming a similar documentary on Tony Jarret called *Olympic Dreams*.

Tony was a 110 metres hurdler (and part of GB's 4 × 100 metres relay team), and had won medals in World Championships since 1993 and narrowly missed out on a bronze in the 1992 Olympics. He took silver at the 1995 World Championships and was one of the GB team's big hopes for a medal in Atlanta.

That year in South Africa, Mark was filming Tony. I knew I was still a nobody in athletics, but I kept teasing him. 'You should be filming me, mate. Look, I love Tony Jarrett, he's awesome, but come on! I'm the future. I'm rock and roll.'

'Yeah, but he's Tony Jarret. He's an amazing hurdler. It'll be a great programme.'

'I'm not disputing that, but I'd be much more interesting to watch.'

And so it went on.

On Mark's final day in South Africa, a few of us went to look round a flea market. While we were there our van was broken into – and all his equipment and all the film was stolen. Mark was devastated. We did what we could to help, but soon the others got tired of hanging around with him and went back to the hotel. I thought someone should help him out, so I stayed and went round the Joburg police stations with him. We had no luck. (In the end, Andy Norman got word out to the criminal underworld and got everything back – no questions asked!)

Fast forward a few months to Atlanta. I'm doing the lap of honour after the 4 × 400 metres, desperately scanning the crowd to try to catch sight of my parents when I see a familiar face with a distinctive mullet haircut: Mark. Tony Jarrett had been disqualified for obstruction in the quarter-finals of the hurdles, but here I was celebrating a silver medal. 'Oi! You long-haired twat,' I shouted over to Mark with a huge smile on my face. 'I told you that you should have followed me!'

When I got back to Southampton he wrote to me and said, 'I'll never forget how kind you were to me in South Africa. You're obviously going to come through. I should have done a documentary on you – how about it?' So, self-subsidised, he followed me with a camera for two years.

*Second is Nowhere* was broadcast on the BBC in 1999 (just my luck it was up against the Spice Girls documentary!). My first words in the documentary are a breathless exclamation of 'Fuck me!' after an exhausting sprint on the dunes. Mum had sat down to watch it with Dad, and on hearing that, she jumped up: 'Ooh, ooh, I'll make a cup of tea!' They were disgusted. The 40-minute film was, however, a great portrayal of who I was at 23, showing the pressures, frustrations and, above all, the burning ambition I had to reach the top of the sport.

Mark was there in Portugal at Easter 1997 to film us training with Mike. The training was tough but, apart from me, none of my crew were professional athletes. In the documentary Mike refers to me as wanting to be 'the eternal student' and notes how I was often the one leading the lads astray. At one point he is seen laying down the law. Complaining about the attitude of the group, especially the late nights before training, he says: 'As far as I am concerned, you come here for athletics first and holiday second.' However, the intensity of the sessions meant we could train for only an hour or two a day, so we had plenty of time on our hands. We were in our twenties, so naturally we had some fun – not much of it conducive to peak fitness; plenty of beers, sitting around the pool and playing football.

Mike wasn't keen on us playing football – and I had been warned. It was too easy to injure your feet or joints. So I couldn't tell him that I was taking a penalty kick when I felt a sharp pain in my knee. I just kicked the football at a weird angle and felt my knee pop. I'd had a couple of small injuries over the winter, but this was more worrying, especially with the World Championships not far away.

Thankfully, by the time the season started, the knee wasn't giving me too much trouble. Once again, Mike's winter regime had delivered me at my peak early in the season. At the European Cup meeting in Munich in late June, I showed

I was in good form by running 44.47 in my relay leg. (Relays are often faster than individual times because the changeover means you sometimes cover a shorter distance or are already in motion as you start.) A week later in Sheffield, I raced in the individual 400 metres and recorded 44.49. Quite a few watching said I could have broken the 44.37 British record that Roger had set the previous year at the AAAs, if I hadn't started celebrating 15 metres from the line. I knew I could go even faster, though. And a few days after that, I did, taking my PB to 44.46 in the pouring rain in Lausanne. I was creeping nearer that record but was still a tenth of a second away.

I was so far in the groove it seemed I was running fast without even trying. I felt I had much more in the tank – and so did the commentators and spectators. Going into the British Championships (which also served as the World Championship trials) in Birmingham, I was the favourite to win. I was feeling so confident that I knew if I ran my race no one could touch me. Roger was absent, still recovering from illness, so effectively it was a battle between Mark, Jamie and me for the two confirmed places. Mark was running well too, but I'd just beaten him in Sheffield, while Jamie had finished a disappointing fifth in that race.

Alexander Stadium, Birmingham, 13 July 1997: 44.36 seconds. Those were details I'll remember for the rest of my life. I had just run faster over 400 metres than any other Briton, ever. My primary thoughts that day, though, were really just to beat Mark and Jamie and qualify for the Worlds in Athens. In a way it's thanks to those guys pushing me that I ran so fast that day. It was a perfect race for me: I ran in Lane 4 with Mark to the left of me and Jamie to the right. I went out hard and closed down Jamie pretty quickly, but still had Mark in my shadow. In the final 100 metres, I felt so strong. There was no way he was catching me.

When I crossed the line, I didn't realise I'd broken the record. I looked up at the scoreboard and saw it said 44.36. I looked away in disappointment for a second. I'd only managed to equal Roger's record. Then I looked again. *Hang on,* I thought. *That is the record!* Just a year earlier, open-mouthed and in awe, I'd watched Roger Black in this race. Now I had broken his British record. It was pretty hard to take in.

The first guys I spoke to when I finished were the race floor managers, Wilbert Greaves and Tony Barden. They handed me a bottle of water and directed me over to the press and TV for interviews. Over 25 years later, I see those same faces working alongside me whenever and wherever in the world I'm doing infield presenting, and it always takes me back to that special day.

I was so dehydrated that the dope testing after the race took three hours and I had still had a three-hour drive back to Southampton that night. I was giving Tim a lift, but was tired and lost in my own world. I still hadn't given much thought to beating the record. Suddenly, Tim broke my reveries with a tap on the leg.

'The British record. You got the record!'

I looked across and shook my head. He shook his too.

'I can't believe it. Eric Liddell, David Jenkins, Derek Redmond, David Grindley, Roger Black, Iwan Thomas. It's you. You're on that list.'

It was a record that would stand just short of 25 years.

The reaction was explosive. 'This man just gets better and better with every single race,' said Brendan Foster on TV. 'He has the authority now to take the race by the scruff of the neck.' The back pages of every paper carried my photo and there were articles every day.

Roger was magnanimous, especially as he wasn't able to defend his title. 'Iwan doesn't have to think now, it comes naturally. He can't run slowly, just as I couldn't last year. It was physically impossible. Iwan will run very fast.'

Even Mike was prompted to speak: 'Iwan is the best I've had. Watching him run is majestic, like the *Queen Elizabeth* sailing out with a couple of tugs behind.'

I didn't have a lot of time to take it all in. The World Championships in Athens were due to start in two weeks. I was the second ranked 400 metres runner on the planet that year and, although the first – a certain M. Johnson – hadn't competed in the US trials, the committee had bent over backwards to give him a wild card entry. Still, rumours continued to circulate saying that he would not be fit enough to run.

The World Championships entailed running four races in four days – enough to test anyone, no matter how godlike, and stamina was one of my trump cards. I felt the weight of expectation on my shoulders, but in the form I was in, I was supremely confident. Why shouldn't I be the World Champion?

Well, I got to Athens and immediately discovered two reasons why not. Firstly, almost immediately after the AAAs, my knee flared up again. I was in pain every time I ran and went back to cortisone. I hadn't been able to train at all, but there was no way I wasn't going to race. I could bear the physical agony much more than the despair of not running.

The second was a little more difficult to overcome: Michael Johnson was here. But even so there was hope. He had been struggling with a hamstring injury since the final in Atlanta and we'd recorded similar times since the beginning of the season. Only a few weeks previously he had pulled up running against Donovan Bailey in a showpiece race, The World's Fastest Man. Could he be struggling to find form?

The World Championships in Athens was an altogether different beast to the Olympics. It was just about the competition; no distractions, no free MacDonald's or outdoor cinema screens. The British team was based in a hotel in gridlocked central Athens in August – it was hot. So hot that the racing was scheduled for either early morning or late night.

The first heat was at eight in the morning. I was usually fast asleep at that time, but I had to be up at five. It went well, though; I ran without painkillers for the first time in ages, my knee stood up to the rigours of racing and I won my heat comfortably. The quarter-final went just as smoothly. I won in the second fastest time of all those through to the semis. Johnson caused a bit of a stir, taking it so easy that he only made the semi-final as a fastest qualifier. No one was under any illusions, though; he was still the one to beat.

I was landed with a tough semi-final. I was up against seriously good athletes in Johnson, Davis Kamoga, Jerome Young and Roxbert Martin. I ran 44.61 and came in fourth, coasting in at the end because I was safely ahead of Martin. That was fast; Tyree Washington had won the other semi in exactly the same time. I'd made the final and I felt good. I had more in me and still felt a silver medal was definitely within my grasp. Could it be a gold? Johnson had run 44.37 in that semi. I need a PB to beat him or hope that the race schedule had taken its toll.

The year before, I'd raced behind Roger Black when he'd taken silver at Atlanta. It looked as if he never had any intention of going for the gold. He let

Johnson do his thing and raced the rest of us, knowing he was almost certain to finish second. In the end he finished second behind Johnson and bagged that silver easily. Job done.

Should I do the same? I fancied my chances against the rest of the field. Four Americans: Johnson, Washington, Pettigrew and Young. A Ugandan in Davis Kamoga. Three Brits: Mark, Jamie and myself. I was in a similar position to Roger. Except . . . Roger was 30 years old in Atlanta. It was silver or nothing for him; he'd never get another chance. I was just 23 and in great form. What did I have to lose?

There were still doubts over Johnson's form. He'd had little competition all season. What if someone challenged him? How would he react? Maybe he would buckle under the pressure.

As an approach to take, this was a massive gamble. It would take someone in the form of their life – maybe an idiot with too much confidence in their own abilities – to take it up. I knew just the person.

I idolised Michael Johnson. We all did. It was an honour to race against him. He was an absolute legend. He had gone 8 years and 59 races without losing, but that run had just come to an end. Recovering from injury and not up to full fitness, he had finally been beaten by Antonio Pettigrew in June at the IAAF Grand Prix held in Paris. Here, racing for medals, someone had to try to beat him into silver and take the gold. No one ever had. But was this the time? Maybe I should wait for a one-off race. Only, for me, it felt like now or never. I decided to do it in the World Championship final in front of 100,000 people in Athens. Brave or foolish?

Have you ever wanted something so much you feel you can will it to happen? I ran that World Championship final over in my head a hundred times before it happened. I knew what was going to happen on every step of that race. I had it all worked out. In the British Championships I had gone out hard, put Jamie and Mark under real pressure and relied on my strength to finish off the race. It had worked to a T. No one had done that to Michael Johnson – not in my memory anyway.

Mike had come out to Athens to watch me and I outlined my plan to him. 'Do you think it could work?'

He nodded thoughtfully and said, 'You go for it, boy.'

I visualised the race. *I match Johnson step by step in the first 200. Coming around the final bend, I look across and he's still there, but his usual cool, concentrating face has started to crack. He's beginning to feel the pressure. We're neck and neck all through the final straight – it's just me and him, there's no one else around in this version – until the final few metres. He's flagging. He tries to keep up, but I dip and take the victory. I'm bathed in golden light. Euphoric.*

I played that through in my head so many times I really believed it would happen. He hadn't been put under pressure in a race for ages. He wasn't at his peak. He was injured. This was the time. I knew it wouldn't be easy. I was in the difficult Lane 2, while he had the prime spot in Lane 4 and it would be difficult to pace myself on the stagger, but I was convinced I was going to beat him.

I was so hyped. As I headed for the starting blocks, I mumbled away to myself: 'You've got this. You've fucking got it. Come on, you can do it, this is it, you're going for it, we're going now . . . '

I took a few jumps, a deep breath, nervously adjusted my vest and positioned myself in the blocks. My heart was pounding. The gun went, and I was off. I'd taken just one step before I heard it go again. I was so pumped that I had false-started for the first – and only – time in my career. I was deep in the zone, though, so the risk of disqualification by false-starting a second time wasn't going to change anything. On the next start, I was on a hair trigger once more: my reaction was the second fastest after Johnson.

I put everything out there from the starting gun. I ran like a sprinter – around 10.6 – for the first 100 and had already closed down Tyree Washington in Lane 3. I wanted, I needed a fast first half of the race. Going down the back straight, it was fast, but I didn't feel it was too quick, I felt so good.

I can see Johnson ahead. I'm getting closer and closer. I've caught him. It's all going to plan. I can almost hear him thinking, *What's this idiot up to?* Johnson's PB for the 200 metres was 19.3 whereas mine, at the time, was 21.1. I go past the 200-metre mark in 20.7; faster than I'd ever run that distance, even when running the 200 metres race.

This is the moment of truth.

But not like it was meant to be.

I come off the final bend with 110 to go and suddenly I know I am in a world of trouble. All I can think is: *I've blown it. I've gone too fast, far too fast.* But it's too late to ease back, the damage has been done.

David Coleman said in his commentary: 'Thomas is relying on pure strength now', and he was right.

I have nothing left. I'm running through sand and go from first to sixth in the space of 10 metres. The reality sinks in: I've failed. I didn't care now if I came sixth, seventh or eighth. Mark Richardson beat me, and it just didn't register.

I was so gutted. I was in despair. I'd really thought I could do it. I wandered over to the side of the track to be by myself, slumped to the ground and tried to pull myself together. Phil Green, one of the GB team managers, came over to commiserate. 'Bad luck, mate,' he offered. 'At least you had the balls to try.' Now, Phil had short shorts on with nothing underneath. I looked up as he said those words and got an eyeful. Maybe it was a deliberate attempt to cheer me up. I tried to summon a smile, but I wasn't in the mood. I went off to the warm-up track to find Mike and cried my eyes out. I'd blown it. Big time.

The *Sunday Mirror* ran an article describing me as 'Champ of the Week', the guy who 'went for broke – victory or nothing – and for 300 glorious metres even looked as though he could do the impossible and beat Michael Johnson.' Or was I 'Chump of the Week'? 'Yeah he made a bid for glory and all that, but let's be honest – he allowed himself to get taken in by the hype . . . He ran the 200m instead of the 400 – and saw silver turn to sixth.'

Most of the pundits agreed that I had been too audacious, but I had no regrets. I had confidence in my own ability and still believe now that Johnson was beatable that day. His winning time of 44.12 was the only time in his career he won a World Championship or Olympic gold in over 44 seconds. I refused to concede that I got the race wrong, but that didn't mean it didn't rankle.

Would I do the same thing again? Maybe I would if I was in the same form and with the same mindset as then. Then again, with hindsight, I could have run for a medal. A silver or a bronze were there for the taking. I had little time to sulk over it. The following day saw the start of the 4 × 400 metres competition. I had to pick myself up and go again.

The GB relay teams always had a good spirit. As low or high as we felt after our individual performances, we left our feelings in the hotel room when we joined together as a team. On the track, my rivalry was intense, but Jamie, Mark, Roger (who, despite missing out on the individual 400 metres, was part of the team) and Mark Hylton (who ran the first heat for Mark Richardson) were all friends and we had no problems bonding as a team. The final was a chance to exact revenge for the Olympics. The US team were once again without Johnson, and again we sensed it could be our moment.

I went out first, running 44.8. Roger, just recovered from illness, ran second leg, tiring at the end to let the American Pettigrew stretch out a five-metre lead in the final straight. It was all so familiar. Jamie once again went off so fast. He closed the gap, went past the US runner Chris Jones, but by the time he set Mark off we were a metre back with the Jamaicans on our shoulder. For Roger in '96, read Mark in '97; he did everything right. He closed down USA's Tyree Washington, attacked him off the final bend and when that failed, tried again. Same old . . . We got closer than before, but still finished in silver position with less than two-tenths of a second separating the two teams.

We stood on the podium that day as silver medallists, while the United States team smiled their way through 'The Star-Spangled Banner'. We were proud, but how much better would it have been to be hearing our own anthem with gold medals round our necks, soaking up the feeling of being World Champions in front of 100,000? We never found out.

In 2008, 11 years later, Antonio Pettigrew stood up in a court room in San Francisco to testify that he had been injecting human growth hormone and EPO, both banned substances, at the time. We'd lost out on gold to a drug cheat.

My first reaction was surprise. I had never suspected Pettigrew of doping even though he ran a phenomenal time of 43.2 seconds in his leg of the final. Jamie was wiser. 'Have a look at the race, it's a joke. He comes up the home straight like Speedy Gonzales.'

Pettigrew didn't look like I assumed drug users looked like: bulked up, muscular and with bad skin. He was skinny, there's was nothing on him. He was like a whippet. I liked him, and I never like a cheat.

Maybe I was naïve, but I never saw evidence of drug use in athletics. It's an individual sport, you train with only a small group and don't get to see what's going on elsewhere, but I was never approached by anyone or saw any sign of performance-enhancing drugs being taken. It never even crossed my mind. I was super-cautious with anything. I was drugs tested so many times, I was even paranoid about taking ibuprofen or aspirin. I sometimes wonder if I was tested so much because they knew I was clean; I was an easily ticked box.

I never wanted to have that attitude where I found myself lining up for a race and looking at seven competitors and thinking *You know what, I bet he's a cheat* or *He looks dodgy* or *He's improved a lot this year*. It wasn't somewhere I ever wanted to go. I assumed all athletes were clean unless it was proven otherwise.

The IAAF eventually stripped them of their title and awarded the gold to us, but then claimed that too much time had elapsed to award new medals. It took a Facebook campaign and letters (many from Jamie's dad!) to force them to change their mind – and even then UK Athletics sat on the medals for eight months wondering what to do.

Finally, in 2010, I received a call from UK Athletics saying that they had my gold medal and would I like to come pick it up? I was given my medal by Cherry Alexander, a great long-serving official, one I have always had time for and still see regularly at meetings. She came out of a pub in the outskirts of Birmingham and handed me my medal in a shoe bag. I was alone, waiting in the drizzle in a pub car park ridden with potholes in the West Midlands. It looked like some dodgy deal playing out. The most unglamorous medal ceremony ever. A million miles away from standing with your team on the podium in front of thousands in a balmy evening in Greece. Apparently, they had been having a board meeting in the pub and said, 'Oh yeah, he can swing by and pick it up.' I suppose it was something; Roger Black got his in the post.

Opening the shoe bag was immediately dispiriting. With the exception of Pettigrew, the US athletes had refused to return their medals, so the IAAF produced new medals. Mine was nothing like the real thing. It had no weight and, instead of the classy Athens logo, it had an IAAF stamp 2000 copyright (four years after the actual race) and no mention of Athens whatsoever. As Jamie said, it resembled a chocolate coin you get at Christmas. A hollow gesture.

To their credit Welsh Athletics arranged a special ceremony for Jamie and myself at the Senedd, but we have never had our moment – unlike the Beijing 2008 Olympics women's 4 × 400m relay team whose place was upgraded and who received their bronze medals in front of a big crowd at the London Stadium. To be fair, British Athletics still try to get the four of us together at one of the big meetings . . . maybe one day.

I was – and the others were – I think, understandably bitter. We were robbed of experiencing a once-in-a-lifetime moment; of taking a lap of honour and celebrating with the crowd and family; of enjoying the financial benefits of being World Champions (in my case a considerable bonus from Asics); and of coming home as heroes. I think, at the time, the IAAF brushed it under the carpet. They wanted to play down the problem of drugs in the sport and move on as quickly as possible.

As disgusted as I was that he had cheated us and the ambitions that I wrecked my body trying to fulfil, I felt for Pettigrew. It's easy to see how the pressure to succeed and the financial rewards for those who managed to cheat the system can seem to justify the risk of getting caught. And at least he came clean. He didn't have to admit he was doping back in 1997. Tragically, Pettigrew committed suicide just months after we received the medals; it was a terrible fate for a once great athlete who had won gold fairly and squarely in the 1991 World Championships in Tokyo.

Back in 1997, I was still just a silver medal winner, but I had made progress. In the autumn, I received the British Athletics Writers' Association Athlete of the Year award. It was a prestigious award, one that put my name alongside the nation's great athletes over the decades, from David Hemery, Brendan Foster, Daley Thompson, Steve Ovett and Seb Coe right through to Kriss, Linford and Roger.

Now I was on the VIP list in the top clubs in Southampton, sometimes hanging out with England internationals Matt Le Tissier, James Beattie and other Premier League players. And, I was now recognisable enough to feature in a BBC ident. It referenced how I said I felt like I was running on sand in the last 100 metres of the final and then cut to me running in the dunes, with a voiceover saying: 'He now trains on sand.'

Despite the award, regardless of my British record, never mind being one of the stars of the sport and for all the pundits saying how good I was going to be, I still had so much to prove to myself. It was going to be another tough winter . . .

# 3.00am. 16 June 2021

*I'm in a dark place. My body is screaming to stop, while my mind is saying,* Keep going, you're going to be OK. *I am just counting down the checkpoints. I constantly do deals with myself.*

Get past the checkpoint and you can walk for a minute.
Get over the hill and you get another painkiller.
Another 10 miles and you can have a can of Coke.

*I embrace the pain. It's like a superpower for me. The more I suffer, the closer I am getting to the finish line. I welcome the hurt. I keep telling myself that pain is weakness leaving the body. I picture how I'll feel on the finish line, just how great I'm going to feel.*

*It's going to be worth it.*

# Ten

# THE SWITCH

Tuesday, 5 August 1997, Athens: the day of the World Championship final.

Have you ever wanted to hurt somebody?

I was arguably the second best athlete in the world that season. Within touching distance of gold. Except. The best was Michael Johnson. The greatest 400 metre athlete ever. The man in the golden shoes, with a packed stadium roaring him on, stood between me and a gold medal. Nevertheless, I had my plan and just maybe it would work.

We had already been to the first call room at the warm-up track and there were now just us finalists, no phones, no music, no coach, just us and our thoughts as we prepared to do battle. It was quite a long walk – through a strange system of tunnels – that led us from the warm-up track to the main stadium. The route took us underneath the main road into the final call room.

It was a lonely walk. No longer any friendly faces around, but also time for me to engage my inner animal, a time to get inside my rivals' heads. Even just a small stare would do for many, but not the great Michael Johnson: he was unshakable, a tough-minded man out in front, literally so on this long walk.

In my head it felt like it was just Michael and myself walking to the stadium. Gladiators. Me or him. As we walked on, I looked around and it was just that: the other athletes had fallen behind. We turned a corner and all of a sudden we were at the top of a cold concrete staircase. In a split second my plan was forgotten, my mind whirred and from somewhere I sensed a different, wilder opportunity. I clenched my fists in a rage.

I'm not a violent man but I felt the urge to push him. His word against mine . . .

———

He looked a bit of a bastard. A single-minded, arrogant, uber-confident kind of guy. His eyes were steely and his expression blank. He walked to the start like he owned the track, treating the other athletes with contempt. You didn't want to go near him. I knew him well and always welcomed his arrival. Because that was me. An alter-ego, a monster that I became when I raced. When there was something on the line, my whole mindset changed. I wasn't angry or emotional, I was really calm. But I wasn't me. I was a cold-blooded killer . . .

In most elite 400 metres races, it is hard to pick a winner. The eight runners on the blocks will have reasonably close PBs and the top six will finish within a second of each other. Those places will be decided by tenths or even hundredths of a second. That split second is in the mind. And goes to the athlete who wants it most, the one who can push themselves that much faster. The body can only take you so far; the mind has to do the rest.

People underestimate the power of the mind, but top athletes know how to use it. Galvanising your body and energising your performance. Focusing on that one notion: winning is everything. You're there for only that. It's all about confidence, determination, controlled aggression and channelling physical power.

Then there is the external perception; how you look to your rivals and how you make them feel. When I'm racing, it is me against the others. In the Olympics I wasn't running for PBs or records; they happened as a consequence. I was racing to beat the others – that's all that counted. If I could unnerve them, make them have doubts about their own ability or think I was on it before the race had even started, I already had an advantage.

Spectators and TV viewers see the athletes appear on the track and make themselves ready for the race. They usually look focused and composed, but like those swans paddling furiously underwater they are hyped and nervous. They've been psyching themselves up all day and have been in or around the stadium for hours building up to this moment. More than enough time to warm up thoroughly, check out your rivals, talk with your coach and get yourself in the zone. Far too much time.

I didn't have any special preparations. I liked to keep myself to myself. Do my pre-race warm-ups, chat to Mike, slap my thighs a bit to wake up my legs and focus on the race. But inside, something was changing. I'm a friendly guy. I like people and want them to like me, so I enjoy being helpful, kind and making folk laugh. I respected my rivals and fellow professionals and genuinely wished them the best. I could be like that on the bus on the way to the warm-up track, but already inside I was changing. I called it the Switch.

I tried not to look at rivals during the warm-up. Mark Richardson was a beautiful runner. He flowed, moving across the track effortlessly. I knew that watching him running could be unnerving. I always tried to look good during the warm-up. If I had to walk past rivals, I stood tall, almost on tiptoes. Given that I'm 1.88 (6' 2") as it is, I'd be taller than most, towering over Mark and Jamie. I liked to stick my chest out and strut like a peacock as I did my strides around the bends. I cut an intimidating figure – strong, confident and imposing – and I let them project their insecurities on to me.

Things may seem tense out in the warm-up area, but you have your routines to concentrate on and your coach and friends to chat to. Sooner or later, though – anything from 10 minutes to an hour before the race – it's time to report to the call room. This is where the race begins. Like check-in at the airport, you sign in and then you can't leave. Officials check your numbers, logos and spikes and you wait – and wait.

Call rooms vary. There can even be a series of two or three call rooms for different processes. Sometimes you are transferred from one to another and often it is one of many sectioned-off areas with just two rows of chairs like a doctor's waiting room. At that point you're on your own. Just athletes and race officials are allowed in – and no electronics are allowed.

The call room is an area unique to athletics. For me, this is the place where many races are won or lost. The eight of you are pretty much of a similar ability, and the mentally strongest, the one able to hold his nerve and stick to his race plan is often the one who emerges victorious.

The call room is like a cage. Often it is in the bowels of the stadium, with no natural light and bare walls and floors. The overriding silence is peppered with a series of echoing sounds: the muffled hum or cheers of the crowd somewhere above you, the rustling of papers, the sounds of spikes scraping concrete and the occasional orders or name checks barked out by the race officials.

It's seriously intimidating. Imagine a boxing match where the two fighters spend 30 minutes to an hour staring at each other before walking out to the ring. In the call room you are sharing a space with seven people who can ruin your chances of glory – or possibly even your career. Athletes react in different ways. They might quietly wish others luck, do stretches that don't require space, slap their thighs and legs, but mostly it's just their thoughts and emotions running wild. The air is buzzing with nerves, impatience and expectations. My mind was set in stone. I might give a nod or a few words to athletes I knew, but however long I had to wait, nothing could shake my resolve.

All athletes try to get in the zone. At some point, whether it is on the way to the stadium, in the warm-up area or on the track, they get into race mode. Some hype themselves on the track. In the last race of the 1997 season, the Berlin Grand Prix, I was at the starting blocks, when I suddenly heard this shouting and bawling like a street fight kicking off. In the next lane to me, the American sprinter Butch Reynolds was calling himself every name under the sun – motherfucker this, asshole that, pussy the other. He was a brute of a man; muscular, standing around 1.93 (6' 4") and a good 10 years older than me. He may have been shouting and swearing at himself – but it put the fear of God into me.

Roger Black, on the other hand, was the opposite. His style was super-relaxed, almost zen-like; while other runners were stretching and pacing around mumbling to themselves, I imagined he was listening to folk music and dreaming he was in a flowery meadow. I was ready to go to war. I'd get myself hyped up by listing to something fierce like Prodigy's 'Firestarter' and though I might have sometimes looked fidgety at the start, it hid an inner calm and controlled aggression.

No one taught me the Switch. I don't even remember when I first became aware of it. It just happened. I don't think it was there at the BMX racing. Sure, on the gate, I was focused, I concentrated on what I needed to do to grab the holeshot, but that was as far as it went. I think it's more likely that something clicked at the School Sports Day. When I heard the Pig doubting me, willing to bet against me, an angry surge of determination swept through me. And I never forgot that feeling. It happened again in that first race of 1995 when I beat Du'aine Ladejo. His T-shirt riled me and took me to another competitive level.

To get into the Switch, I did nothing. I just went through the motions and let it happen. Something clicked and I would be a different person. All I thought about was winning. It was total. I shut everything else out: my recent times, arguments with girlfriends, nagging injuries or my rivals' form – they all got packed in a box and stored away in the far recess of my mind. I was focused, fired up, and ready to go to battle. To me, it was a matter of life and death. I was a gladiator in the Colosseum. Kill or be killed.

It was an energising feeling that supercharged my body. Something like an out-of-body experience. Losing wasn't something I thought about; the idea of not winning was inconceivable. It wasn't contempt for my rivals, more like disdain. I wanted them to feel under threat, even those I counted as good friends. There are stories about athletes mocking other runners' form or telling them what they were going to do to them on the track. I never bad-mouthed anyone, but I had a mood, an aura and a look that said all I needed to say.

The European Championships in 1998 was an exception when I pushed it further than usual. There was still an hour and a half to go before the race and I was coming to the end of my drills and strides at the warm-up track. I could see Mark Richardson walking towards me, doing leg pick-up drills. He was in Lane 3 – and so was I. As he approached, I stood firm, thinking, *Come on then, I'm going nowhere. You can move around me if you want.* He looked at me and I looked him straight in the eye. Then he looked down at the floor and moved to another lane. I went over to Mike.

'I've won it. I'll beat Mark.'

'No, he's in great shape.'

'His head's gone. I know.'

In that race, the athletes had to be driven from the warm-up track to the call room in the main stadium. I made sure I got on first and sat on the front seat. One by one, all seven of my rivals had to walk past me – and I eyeballed every single one of them.

I knew I'd beaten Mark before I got in the blocks. He ran the worst race he'd run all year. I always felt that showing Mark my confidence chipped away at his, revealing his insecurities. When he saw me, he would think: *Fuck, he's so up for it* and shrink a bit. I really like Mark and I feel guilty about that now. I can only say I did it because he was such a naturally talented athlete and I feared his ability on the track. I never did it to Jamie. Rightly or wrongly, I just didn't feel as threatened by him. And I wasn't bothered by Roger. Sure, he might beat me, but if he did I thought he'd never do it again. Our trajectories were crossing: he was on the way down and I was getting faster every race. I knew it was just a matter of time – and every race was, I believed, my time.

I was far from the only one who had that power. James Cracknell, double Olympic gold rower, could switch like no one else I knew – even for events I just saw as fun. Years later, after I retired, I was sitting next to him on the VIP bus to the London Marathon. He had his headphones on, so I tapped him on the shoulder.

'What are you listening to?'

'I can hear you, mate,' he replied, and he showed me the unattached headphone plug.

'I just don't want anyone to talk to me – I'm in the zone.'

He then showed me the split times written on his arm for points during the run. 'If I'm not on schedule at halfway, I'm giving up. If I don't run under three hours, I'm not bothered doing it.'

That was another mindset altogether. Switch plus some!

The desire to win ran so deep within me. It was as true running in the woods when I was training in Southampton as it was in front of 80,000 people and a gold medal at stake. I hated losing. I didn't hate myself for losing. I never beat myself up for not winning a race, but I hated the feeling of losing. And when I did, I'd swear this is never ever going to happen again.

No matter what kind of injury I was carrying, I didn't feel pain once the race started – or if I did, I just ignored it. My body was like a finely tuned supercar driven by my mind. As long as my body didn't physically break, I'd push it as much as I could. And no matter how much I liked my rivals as people or friends, I had absolutely no feelings for them in those 44 seconds on the track.

Psychiatrists have identified an ability in psychopaths to switch any feelings of empathy on and off. Some can switch at will whereas others are driven by a subconscious impulse. An otherwise normal person becomes a ruthless operator. They're just one bad mood away from murder. It's a trait that's also been recognised in businessmen making cut-throat deals and Olympians at the top of their game.

That story I told at the start of the chapter about wanting to hurt Michael Johnson? Every word was true. Would I ever really have done it? I suppose I have to think not, but the thought swirled around my head. There was no sense of morality. It was: *How can I win? How do I make sure I win?* I was single-minded and desperate. My mind could be so strong. That was the X factor that took me to the top. When I was in the right mindset, no one among my rivals could touch me.

Eventually there came a point when the Switch didn't work. When the injuries kept coming after 2002, I lost faith in my body to run as fast as I wanted. Underpinning all that certainty and positivity I once had was a feeling that I really could beat anyone – anyone on the planet. But there came a point when that was all just bravado. I knew I was kidding myself. Without the confidence, I just couldn't summon the power that had so often given me the edge. I tried. I pushed myself as hard as I could, but the inner belief was gone. That's when I knew it really was over.

Years later, when the relay boys met up for a reunion drink, the conversation turned to the mindsets of athletes. How some athletes could seem so motivated on one occasion and uninterested on another. How some went to another place in their heads when they raced, a few even turning into different people altogether. We even began to wonder if it might be a kind of mild disorder.

Roger turned to me and said, 'Well, you had something going on, Iwan – you were special.' I think I knew exactly what he meant.

# Eleven

# MAGIC POST-IT NOTES

'Your focus has to be completely on athletics now. That's where it's got to be. If you do not win either the Europeans or Commonwealth Games, your commercial value will plummet . . . When it comes to it, it doesn't matter what anyone else says – what Andy Norman says, what I say, what your mates say. When you walk out on to the track there's only one person there, and it's you. Everyone else can walk away. You can't.'

Mike was reading the Riot Act in March 1998. He knew this was my make-or-break year.

I carried the pain of that evening in Athens in my heart all winter. The fact that I'd let a chance get away, in the World Championships of all races, rankled with me every single day. But I refused to hide or sulk. I confronted it head-on. I knew the knee injury hadn't helped, but I wasn't looking for excuses. It just came down to the fact that I hadn't been fast enough or strong enough. But I would be.

In interview after interview, I told anyone who would listen that I would be back. 'I'm going to keep on training like I do and I'll have my day,' I told the BBC. 'I will be World Champion one day.'

I meant it.

I never wanted to feel the hurt again, I never wanted to miscalculate a race like that ever again. I had a new attitude. I was already training full-on and I'd massively cut down on nights out; I was so focused now, so serious about what I wanted. I wanted to be European Champion.

Without really thinking about it, I developed new superstitions. I wouldn't touch Lane 2 on the track in Southampton. It became a thing. I knew there was a chance that I could get beaten by Mark in the Europeans or the Commonwealths in 1998 and for me the number two meant silver. I wouldn't have that; I only wanted gold. I didn't mind Lane 3 – I knew I'd never get a bronze – but never Lane 2; I'd even rather run in Lane 1.

Other things were more psychological. I never parked next to the athletics stadium in Southampton but would drive up to the car park for the adjacent ski slope even though it took me longer to walk down. There were 76 steps down to the track but, more importantly, there were 76 back up. When the others asked me why, I said: 'I just like it, it's a bit more private', but the truth was, I knew none of my rivals were doing that. My quads would be stronger than their quads. When I was exhausted after training, I forced myself back up those stairs and was invariably sick somewhere up those steps. If I didn't stop somewhere to throw up, I felt disappointed. I wanted to get back to my bed that night with my legs on fire, having done not just six 300s but also those steps. Those 76 steps could be the difference between silver and gold.

I had also been reunited with my lucky charm. I lost it the previous year when my house was burgled. One morning about 10 a.m., I was still in bed on the top floor of my three-storey town house. The phone by my bed rang twice, then it stopped. Seemed odd, so I picked it up. It was Tim.

'What are you doing?' he asked.

'I'm in bed. What d'you mean?'

'I just rang and you picked it up and hung up straight away.'

'Nah, not me.'

'I could hear breathing.'

'There's only me here.'

'Then someone answered your phone.'

I cautiously started going downstairs and nearly tripped over a vase that had been placed on the steps. I screamed 'Oiiiii!' as loud as I could and charged down the stairs. I could hear scampering as whoever was there legged it out the front door.

They stole a DVD player and a load of DVDs and chucked it in an Asics bag full of kit, some of it unwashed, including my spikes. None of it mattered to me except for one memento: the medal my grandfather had won for running for Wales in 1929. It was attached to my running spikes with a cable tie and I touched it for good luck as I went in the blocks every time I raced. It was personal and irreplaceable. I went on BBC South Today on TV and asked for its return. I said I didn't want anything else back and wouldn't go to the police if only they would return the medal engraved with A.C. Thomas.

There was no response. The whole robbery freaked me out. I put the house on the market and sold it in a day. I'd had it with the city centre and bought a converted officers' mess, dating back to the Crimean War, in a village just outside Southampton.

Three months later, though, Mike came to training with a smile on his face. 'Guess what I've got,' he said and unclenched his fist to reveal the missing medal. The police had raided a crack den in the city and a policeman saw the spikes and kit and remembered seeing my plea on TV. I was so delighted and grateful. I thought, *What are the odds? It really must be lucky.*

It didn't bring me much good fortune, though. Early 1998 was so frustrating. I tore my hamstring. I was sitting around for weeks, just itching to get back to training, and once I did, it was jogging and stretches. My carefully planned preseason training was wrecked.

Only on Andy Norman's now seemingly annual trip to South Africa did things start coming together. This time, though, Andy had taken things to another level. Not quite as bad as the police college, but tough in another way. Potchefstroom was a university town an hour north of Joburg – the Loughborough of South Africa. With the students all on holiday, it was like a ghost town. For two months all I had was a track, gym, restaurant and a cinema that endlessly showed *Titanic* and *Tomorrow Never Dies*, but having missed so much of the winter training because of the hamstring tear, I needed some warm weather and focus.

There was so much resting on the coming season with the European Championships and the Commonwealth Games both in the schedule. Before that, however, there was the small matter of the British pecking order to decide. Roger had announced it was going to be his last season, Mark had changed his coach and joined Roger's group under Mike Whittingham, and although Jamie had suffered from an injury in the winter and a bad early season virus, he was now back training with former World Champion Frankie Fredericks. Meanwhile, I couldn't get my season going. I had a series of inconsistent and frustrating results in my early races. I was getting faster, but the rate of progress was slow. And I was running out of time.

The Bislett Games in Oslo in July – a legendary competition that has hosted the best athletes in the world through the years – was the biggest race so far this season. No exhibition race but a top-class line-up featuring Young, Pettigrew, Washington, Richardson and Johnson and now a part of the newly established Golden League. Across a series of seven meetings, the League put up a jackpot of $1 million in gold bars for anyone who won them all. He had the gold chain, and the gold shoes – now Johnson was after the bullion to match.

Mark Richardson was in Lane 1 and Johnson, who had been given his choice of lanes, had a favourable run in the middle. I was furthest out in Lane 6. Oslo was just a six-lane track, so I was going to be running blind on the outside. What's more, the spectators are hanging over and banging the advertising boards once the race begins, creating a gladiatorial atmosphere. They're right next to me, able to reach out and grab me.

I ran a completely different race to the Worlds, running within myself in the opening 100 metres. So much so that Tyree Washington was on my shoulder as we came out of the first bend. I kept just ahead of him down the back straight and into the final bend. As we hit the final 100 metres, there was a line of five and me a pace behind, but one by one they dropped off. I kept looking across expecting to see Johnson forging ahead as usual, but it never happened. Coming to the line, it was Mark, Johnson and myself. Although he knew he wasn't on his A-game, I think Johnson thought he could stroll it and still win easily. He was gobsmacked to see two men finish ahead of him.

Only Pettigrew had beaten him in the 400 in recent years – and that was when he was coming back from injury. He had a face like thunder after we crossed the line and was so pissed off that he ignored my customary outstretched hand after the race and stormed off to the changing rooms. To be fair, he did come and find me in the bar later to apologise – and, to be even fairer, who wouldn't be cheesed off after blowing the chance of winning a million dollars? He never did pick up the big prize, the US athlete Jeremy Wariner becoming the only 400 metres athlete to claim the now defunct jackpot in 2006.

I came second in that race. Mark ran a PB of 44.37 and finished ahead. It was a hundredth of a second off my British record and the fastest ever 400 metres from the inside lane. People were raving about his performance and I had to listen to him jokingly gloating in his after race interview with Steve Cram. 'If I can run 44.37 from Lane 1,' he said, looking over at me, 'you look out, Iwan. I'm gonna be fast this year!'

I was disappointed not to win, and I have to admit that I was worried. Mark looked in great shape; he could well take my record off me. But I was absolutely buzzing too. In my previous races that season I had been struggling to run under 45 seconds. I'd been beaten by Mark in every race. Now I'd run 44.5 in the outside lane – improving my season's best by a whopping half a second and finishing ahead of Michael Johnson. The season was finally coming together, and I was excited for what was to come.

Mark was becoming a problem, though. He was flying. By the time we had got to the European Championship trials, he had beaten me five times out of five races that season. He was the man of the moment and I was portrayed as the number one who'd been knocked off his perch. I just couldn't beat him and I can't deny that it grated.

He credited Roger Black's sprint coach Tony Lester for giving him confidence to increase his speed, but I too was about to get some help and it came from an unexpected place. I had a call come up on my mobile – a Southampton number, but I had no idea who it was. I answered and this magic voice boomed out the other end: 'Iwwan! It's Busi – Kriss.' He said, 'I got your number off Mike – I still live local and I wanted a word with you.'

I was amazed. Kriss Akabusi was my inspiration in athletics. I had watched him run that last leg in the 4 × 400 that took gold in the 1991 World Championships in Tokyo over and over. He had timed his run to perfection, going past Pettigrew at exactly the right second in the last few metres, giving the American no chance to respond. Kriss had been a hero for me ever since, but he had retired before I started running and our paths had never crossed. Now here he was inviting me to his house.

He lived in a big house in a classy neighbourhood on the outskirts of Southampton. I was in awe as the gates opened and I went down the long drive. There in the doorway was the man himself, greeting me with his massive trademark smile. Inside, the house was amazing. Soft deep carpets, huge drape curtains, shiny mahogany. It oozed luxury. Kriss was a great runner and had invested his money wisely. I knew athletics could be a lucrative sport, but I was still shocked how well he had done.

As I sank into the velvet sofa in Kriss's front room, he said: 'You like my house, don't you?'

What could I say? 'Wow, yeah. It's stunning.'

'You can have all of this,' he said. 'Houses, cars, the world is at your feet.'

I smiled and nodded. And I thought to myself, *Where on earth is this conversation going?* I looked back at him and waited.

'So?' he said. And then a pause, that smile and finally, 'What's going on with you?'

It took me back. He hardly knew me, but he'd got straight to the point. *What did he mean?* I thought for a second. *What was going on?* I could kid myself that it was all going pretty well, but when someone you admire asks you that bluntly, you can only give a straight answer.

'I just can't beat Mark,' I told him. 'I had some injuries. I'm fit now, but I still just can't get the better of him.'

He looked at me and with a more serious face said, 'Yes, you can. You can beat him.'

So here I am, submerged in the sofa of one of Britain's great athletes, waiting for him to share the secret of winning. I look into his big sparkling eyes. Was he going to offer to coach me? Was there a tactic no one else had told me?

I'll never forget it. Very calmly, he said, 'All you have to do is find the man inside.'

Was that it? Psycho babble, hippy stuff? I'd never heard any athlete or coach talk like this before.

'What d'you mean?' was all the response I had.

'I've seen you run,' he said. 'I've seen the fire in your belly. I've seen how good you are. Listen,' he continued. 'What do you want to achieve this year?'

'I really want to become European Champion.'

'Right. Great. Do you believe you can do that?'

'Yes,' I replied. 'I know I can.'

'Really?'

I didn't have a chance to answer that one.

'First, you've got to really believe you can be European Champion. You've got to see it shouting at you everywhere you go. You are European Champion.'

I didn't get it. Then he gave me a pad of Post-it notes.

'I want you to write "Iwan Thomas European Champion" on all these. Stick them on every mirror, in the fridge, on the oven door. Everywhere you look, you'll be visualising yourself as European Champion.'

I thanked Kriss, it was really good of him to spare me his time, but I'll be honest: as I drove home, I didn't know what to think. If all there was to it was a few Post-its, why wasn't everyone doing the same? What did that have to do with running fast?

I went home and told my girlfriend what he'd said. 'It's a bit weird, isn't it? But,' I admitted, 'I'm doing it.' I'd already decided. I would do anything if it gave me an extra 0.001 per cent chance of success. So, armed with a marker pen and Kriss's Post-it notes, I wrote out 'Iwan Thomas European Champion' and began sticking them throughout the house – on the bathroom mirror, on the kitchen cupboard, on the inside of the front door, on the bed headboard, on the kettle, on the arm of the sofa, on the dinner table, on my sock drawer, on the inside of my shoe bag, even on the bottle of tomato ketchup.

Who knew the power of budget stationery?

It changed everything.

My mindset became totally different. I could feel myself getting stronger and stronger every day. I had an extra zip in training. I was so confident, knowing I was getting quicker. 'Where are you, Mark? I'd shout in the car as I drove home from a session. 'I'm coming for you!' I was so utterly convinced I could beat him.

Kriss Akabusi! He's one of the most inspiring men I've ever met – and I'm so proud to know him.

---

The British Championships at the end of July was crunch time. They served as the trials for the forthcoming European Championships in Hungary: the first two qualified automatically and the third place was at the discretion of the team managers. Jamie and Mark Hylton were capable of causing an upset, as was Solomon Wariso, who had switched from 200 metres at the age of 32, but Mark, Roger and I were a fair way ahead of the field.

In a way the pressure was off me. Mark was on a roll and unbeaten so far this season, and while I had run fast, I was yet to produce a string of good times. He was given the tag of 'favourite' and was predicted to break my British record and then follow up with a gold in Budapest. Meanwhile a lot of the press was focused on Roger, who was desperate to earn a chance to win an unprecedented third European 400 metres gold.

Roger raised expectations when he ran the fastest time of all the semi-finalists, but Mark and I (in that order again!) strolled through in our semi. I ran the final just as I had the previous year when I took the record, going hard in the first 100 metres, steady on the back straight, then pushing on the top bend. With 100 metres to go I was still a few metres behind Roger and Mark and I needed to place in the top two. I didn't panic. I just relied on my strength to take to the line, coming in ahead of everyone and running 44.5 again. I celebrated with a raised arm as I crossed the line as much in relief as joy. I had beaten Mark for the first time that season (and on his birthday too; he wasn't happy).

Effectively that ended Roger's career. He knew he would never beat me (or Mark) again. He was fourth at the trials, beaten by Solomon Wariso who, to add salt to Roger's wounds, immediately said he would rather run the 200 metres in Budapest if selected (he wasn't and was entered for the 400 metres).

Roger dropped out of the relay team in Hungary and would soon announce his retirement. It was really sad to see him have to finish, but few have such glittering careers. Over a 10-year period, he won medals at the Europeans, Worlds and Olympics. He suffered injuries that would have finished many athletes and refused to let a congenital heart condition stop him from following his dream. I was honoured to take part in his farewell race at the Don Valley Stadium in August 1998.

Even more, it felt like this was my time now. The expectation to win at the Europeans was coming from all directions – from the press with headlines like 'Battling Thomas opens up gold trail' and 'Thomas looks right on time' to Dad saying, 'You can do it. You are the British Champion and no one is going to come close to you this season.' And I was happy to heap pressure on myself too. I'd run bigger races – Olympic finals and World Championships – but none ever seemed as important as the 400 metres in Budapest.

I looked at those Post-it notes again. Iwan Thomas European Champion. It was working. I was hitting form at the right time. It would happen, I was sure. With four weeks to go until Budapest, my knee was hurting again, but I just had to carry on.

Out in Budapest I was still running well and clocked a decent 44.82 in the semi-final. Even so I'm not sure I've ever felt as nervous before a race.

'You've got all the advantages. Don't worry, you'll win,' said Mike, building me up on the eve of the final. Adding, not so reassuringly: 'The only problem is if Mark runs a blinder . . . ' Thanks, mate.

That night, I barely slept. I was so scared of losing because this was mine to win. *Just don't run like a headless chicken in the first 300 and you'll be fine*, I told myself over and over.

On the starting line in the final, I was up against a couple of really good Polish athletes in Robert Maćkowiak and Tomasz Czubak, but to be honest it was only going to be Mark Richardson standing in the way. Beat Mark again and I'd win.

Mark went off really fast and it was tempting to go with him. But, as I had told myself enough times already, I wasn't going to make that mistake again. It meant I was still trailing him going into the last bend, but I kept to my own pace and when we emerged on to the home straight, I felt so strong. 'Thomas coming away,' croaked Coleman on commentary as I went clear. 'He's the powerhouse in this race.' The others all just fell behind and I powered on to the line. There was clear daylight – a half-second – between me and Maćkowiak in second when I finished and my time of 44.54 was enough to take Roger Black's European Championship record.

'Iwan Thomas European Champion' was no longer just words. It meant so much. It felt such a relief to have my first individual gold medal around my neck, finally. Until then, I had been feeling I was on the verge of something really good, but now I felt secure. I was walking 10 foot tall, feeling I could do anything, win anything.

The 4 × 400m just reinforced that feeling. It was an event that GB had won in every competition since 1982 and we were in no mood to be the first to lose – even if there was no Roger to run anchor. Mark Richardson and I were rested for the heat on the day after my individual gold (replaced by Sean Baldock and Solomon Wariso), but we were back for the final alongside Jamie and Mark Hylton on the following day.

The Polish team were the only ones to fear. Mark Hylton ran a really good first leg and by the time Jamie hit the end of the stagger on the second, we were in the lead. It was a really good run from Jamie considering he had just recovered from a virus, and he had a metre or so on the Poles once he passed the baton to me.

I was up against Piotr Haczek, who had finished fifth in the final. I was still flying and immediately extended the lead. I eased up at the end of the back straight and Haczek closed the gap a little. Then I pushed again through the last bend and was gone. 'He gave him hope,' said Coleman on the TV commentary. 'And now he's trying to destroy him.' I had four metres on him by the time I handed the baton over. Mark ran anchor. Chasing him was Robert Maćkowiak, the Polish athlete who had beaten him to silver in the individual final. Mark had been brooding over that ever since, so there was no way he was going to let this go. He came in a couple of metres ahead of the Pole and I'd won another gold.

The competitions were coming fast now. By winning the European Championship, I had won myself a place in the IAAF World Cup – an invitational competition in Johannesburg for the champions of Europe, Africa, America and Australia.

The race pitched me against the best of the best and a chance to earn my biggest prize money yet: a £50,000 prize for first and £30,000 for second. That was the upside. The downside was the racing was at altitude with no time no acclimatise – and was going to take place just two days before the Commonwealth Games. Many athletes going to the Games were skipping it and others told me I was mad. I had no qualms, I was on a roll. No one was stopping me getting on that plane.

It turned out to be the toughest race I ever had. At altitude, with a fierce headwind and a top-class field. My main threat was the US champion Jerome Young, who was also in tremendous form having run 44.09 earlier in the season. But when I reached the home straight, I found myself neck and neck – not only with him but also Troy McIntosh of the Bahamas and the Nigerian Clement Chukwu.

It was still a four-man race with 20 metres to go, and at that point I confess I did think about money. There was £50,000 on the line and I wanted it. I just about got in ahead of Young in the dip at the line: 45.33, a pretty good time in those conditions. I certainly paid for my efforts, throwing my guts up as soon as I left the track.

Twenty-four hours later I was back at the track for the 4 × 400 metres with Jamie, Mark Hylton and Sean Baldock (Mark Richardson had gone off to the Commonwealth Games). I was down to run the last leg, but I was knackered and pleaded with the boys: 'Don't leave me too much to do. I'm knackered and I've got the Commonwealth Games tomorrow.' On the handover I was in fourth place and two metres adrift. I was thinking, *For fuck's sake. I really don't need another hard race*, but I gave everything. I went past everyone but couldn't catch Jerome Young. Second to the Americans yet again. We shared about £30,000 as a team and the lads were jumping around having earned a nice little payday and all I could think was *You bastards – you left me too much to do.*

Back in the spring when we were training in Potchefstroom, I'd got friendly with Steve Backley. Because it was so hot, we had to train in the morning, which left the whole day to fill. Steve and I drove to a nearby lake, to sit with a couple of beers and do some fishing. I didn't like fishing much but always enjoyed Steve's company.

After the World Cup in Joburg, I was chatting to Steve at the celebration dinner. He asked me about the Commonwealth Games. 'When you get to Kuala Lumpur, when are you racing?'

'I fly in, have some kip and race the next morning.'

He looked at me like I was crazy. 'Pay for an upgrade. You'll be grateful for the extra leg room.'

As usual with Steve, it made sense. I did try to do as he said and book business class to Malaysia, but my credit card wouldn't work. Steve, being the bloke he is, used his card.

He was dead right and I thanked him in my head as I stretched out through the long journey. I needed the rest. I hadn't been exaggerating about my schedule. I landed in Kuala Lumpur late in the evening and was on the track the following morning. Everyone was asking me about jet lag and my lack of preparation. My attitude was if I couldn't spend a month there getting acclimatised, it was better to just turn up and run. No time to feel the jet lag or change in altitude, just go with it. If my body doesn't know what time it is, how can I suffer? As for preparation, I was running as fast as I ever had. I was on autopilot. I'd get on those starting blocks and it just happened. I went fast without really thinking about it.

The whole Commonwealth Games experience was so different to Canada four years previously. There I'd been the open-mouthed student marvelling at the facilities, the athletes and the free steaks. Now I was the captain of the Welsh team, chatting to the likes of Jonah Lomu and having to make speeches. Around the Village people were shaking my hand or I heard them saying 'Look, there's Iwan Thomas.' It felt surreal.

I got through the heat next day, a quarter-final the day after, and was looking at a semi-final on the third day. However, as I had warmed down, I felt my joints in my lower back seize up. It was agony. A disc in my back was giving me such pain that I was unable to walk properly. I rang my parents in tears, telling them I was injured and I was going to have to drop out. They were sympathetic and supportive. 'Don't worry, you've won the Europeans, that was the one that mattered. You've had a great season.' But I was devastated.

I had one tiny sliver of a chance. An old friend of mine was at the games: Torben Hersborg. Back in 1995, he was the guy who had sorted my hamstring. That had been pretty amazing, but it was going to take a real miracle worker to get me fit overnight. I had no choice: it was let him try or cry myself to sleep.

So at 11 in the evening, here I was, sneaking him past the Commonwealth Games security and smuggling him into my apartment in the Village.

'I will work on you all night. Give me until tomorrow before you drop out.'

'Torben, it's pointless. I'm in such pain, I can't even walk.'

He wasn't deterred. He set an alarm to go off every hour through the night. I'd get back to sleep and in no time he'd wake me again and get to work. It was the most painful treatment ever. I was black and blue from the rubbing and prodding. Around four or five in the morning, something clicked. Was there hope? I got a few hours' kip and, come the morning, I could move OK. It was some kind of miracle.

If that wasn't ridiculous enough, it was matched by what happened next. The semi-final was to be the funniest, most memorable and quite astonishing race I ever ran. I was in Lane 4 and Jamie Baulch was in Lane 2. I was in the shape of my life, but Jamie, also running in a Welsh vest, had been struggling that season. So, as we took to the blocks, I said, 'Jamie, if you're up there with 100 to go give me a yell. Stay on my shoulder and I'll drag you through to the final.' I go off as normal. Down the back straight and I can't see him anywhere. Then I come off the top bend and I suddenly hear his voice.

'Iwan. You c—!'

Now, it's not big or clever, but around the Village Jamie and I used to play this game. We'd sit among the Americans who were always loud and one of us would say a swear word – sometimes the worst of swear words – and the other had to say it louder. We'd end up shouting it as loud as we could across the table.

'Iwan. You c—!', he shouts really loudly.

I look over my left shoulder and I couldn't believe it. Jamie is waving.

We're on the home straight of the semi-final of the Commonwealth Games with the Jamaicans hunting us down and he's starting the game! What could I do but shout back?

'You what? You want some? Come on then!' And I beckon him on.

'Come on. If you think you can beat me, catch me up.'

We spend the last 80 metres talking. It was unheard of – and the race wasn't a slow one, either. There were good runners like Troy McIntosh taking part. The two of us came home one and two. It was so easy. I felt like I was jogging, and when I crossed the line I thought I'd run around 45.8. I always had a pretty accurate awareness of my time, but I'd actually ran 44.61, just missing the Games record, and Jamie did a season best in 44.83. We were just so relaxed, it hadn't seemed a real effort.

In the BBC television studio, Roger on commentary duty was open-mouthed, asking, 'If he does that in the semi-final, what is he going to do in the final?' My only fear was that we had gone too fast and would suffer the next day.

We had a laugh after but had forgotten about it by the time we got back to the Village for dinner. As we walked into the canteen, the New Zealand rugby sevens team stood up and gave us a standing ovation. They had been watching endless replays of our high-speed chat on the big screen. Better still, the Australian broadcasters had overdubbed the footage.

'Hey, Iwan, fancy going to the cinema tonight, mate?'

'Nah mate. Let's go for fish and chips. You want some?'

I made the start of the final. I was completely knackered from being up all night with Torben, from jet lag after the flight from South Africa, from competing in the AAAs, then the Europeans and the World Cup in individual and relay competitions, and now three races in two days. I'd gone from running fast naturally to dragging my exhausted body to the start line and hoping it would do the rest.

*Come on. One last race*, I told myself. *Let's just see what I can do.*

There were some decent athletes in that final. Sugath Thilakaratne from Sri Lanka, Arnaud Malherbe from South Africa, Davian Clarke from Jamaica and, of course, Jamie. There was only one man I felt was a threat, though. My mate Mark again. Was he getting faster? Or had I seen him off for the season?

I can only think I ran on pure adrenaline. I really wasn't sure how much I had left in the tank. I was careful not to go off fast, but found myself just ahead of Mark as the stagger unwound. Into the last 30 metres when I was usually so strong, I found myself struggling. I looked across with 10 metres to go and Mark was closing in. I was just longing for the finish line to get closer.

It was close. The closest finish I'd had all season and impossible to tell who had won. I was shattered and immediately turned to my friend Doug Turner, a 200 metres runner who had stayed to watch me. 'Have I won?' I kept asking. 'Have I won?'

Mark had run me so close with his best race of the season at 44.6, but I had beaten him again with a Games record of 44.52!

I was so exhausted I had to hitch a lift on the BBC camera buggy to do my lap of honour. For an instant, as I rested my broken body, I felt an incredible feeling sweep over me. Relief, delight, disbelief and excitement – all tinged with an overwhelming desire to sleep for days. I had done it, won two gold medals, then travelled halfway across the world and won another. Then it struck me: *Oh shit. I've still got the 4 × 400 to do.*

The heats for the relay began early the next day, but the team management had told me I could skip them – they had enough in reserve to get through. So Mum and Dad took me out to dinner to celebrate. It was great to see them, to get my feet on the ground and enjoy a nice bit of Thai food and a beer.

I got back to the apartment that night so pleased to see my bed. I've never needed a good sleep as much. I fell asleep seconds after my head hit the pillow, but it seemed like only minutes later that I was being shaken awake by Deleth, the Wales team manager. It was six o'clock in the morning.

'What's the matter?' I said, still half asleep.

'I can smell beer on your breath.'

'Yeah,' I said squinting in the light. 'I had a beer with my dinner. I've got a day off.'

'No. Sorry. We've discovered we've got a really tough heat. We can't risk resting you. You're going to have to run.'

So, knackered, I dragged myself to the track for the 4 × 400 heats. The Welsh team was made up of Jamie, who maybe had gone too fast in our semi-final blast and missed on out a medal, coming fourth in the final; Paul Gray, who had also missed a bronze in the 400 metres hurdles just 20 minutes before this race; and 19-year-old Matt Elias. We got through that heat, coming in just behind England, who had given Mark Richardson a rest, which didn't go unnoticed by me.

England – with Mark back and Wariso, Hylton and Paul Slythe – were probably favourites to take gold, while Jamaica with Roxbert Martin and Michael McDonald looked strong and South Africa with my 600 metres rival Hezekiél Sepeng and Arnaud Malherbe were capable of springing a surprise. For Wales, my mate Dougie Turner replaced Matt. Dougie was one of the few who had also been in the World Cup in South Africa and had suffered for it. A European 200 metres silver medallist in the summer, he was gutted not to even make the final here.

When I took the baton for the last 400 metres, Jamaica had a reasonable lead, with England in second. The lads had done well and put Wales in third place. I had a familiar figure ahead of me: Mark, a good 20 metres in front. It flashed through my mind: *How sick would he be if I denied him again!*

I had him in my sights and I was intent on reeling him in. I got pretty close. If I'd had a day's rest like he had, I reckon I could have done it. In the end he crossed the line a second before me – just beyond what my body could muster.

I could have dropped out of that race because I was so knackered, but I was so pleased I did it and was thrilled to help get a Welsh record and a bronze medal.

This was the most incredible end to a season that had started so badly. In less than a month I had won gold at the European Championships, the World Cup and the Commonwealth Games. Back home, my profile had risen again. The bouncers at the casino in Southampton, who had previously turned me away with a 'Sorry mate, no jeans', now welcomed me with 'Good evening, Mr Thomas.' And McDonald's gave me a free food gold card, which they only ever gave out to footballers.

The phone was constantly ringing and I was in demand like never before. A lot of it was TV, a step up from taking school assemblies. I was a regular on *A Question of Sport*, appeared on *Blue Peter* and did my first chat show on BBC's *Onside*. On the comedy sports quiz *They Think It's All Over*, not only was I a panellist, but I was also the panel – the backdrop was a picture of me. It wasn't just TV, though. I modelled for Katherine Hamnett, one of Britain's top fashion designers, and perhaps best of all for a cocky young man, I did a naked centrefold (wrapped in a Union Jack flag to cover my modesty) for *Cosmopolitan*. Wow, life was changing!

I was really proud to receive both the SJA Sportsman of the Year and BAWA Athlete of the Year awards in December. Both were acknowledgements that I was one of those who had put British athletics back on its feet after Atlanta and were making the sport popular again at home. I'd laughed when some people had tipped me to win the BBC Sports Personality of the Year for 1998, but the overwhelming response to that summer and winning those awards set me dreaming. I bought a sharp new suit and had my hair cut especially. Well, what if I won live on TV in front of 12 million people?

It was unlikely. Not only was I up against the likes of Arsenal captain Tony Adams, tennis stars Tim Henman and Greg Rusedski and fellow European gold medal winner Denise Lewis, but Michael Owen, who had starred for England in the World Cup, was the runaway favourite – you could only get 1–5 on him at William Hill.

Owen had been England's star at the World Cup in France and was an absolute shoo-in – and a worthy winner. Nevertheless, I was a runner-up and was as thrilled as anything, if a bit nervous, to pick up my award from athletics legend David Hemery.

A couple of weeks later I was named the BBC Welsh Sports Personality of the Year, the first time for five years that an athlete had won the award. After the ceremony, I was chatting and some bloke came up to me: 'You should have won the BBC award, Iwan. You got stitched up, you did.'

'Too right, mate,' I replied joining in the fun. 'What's that Michael Owen done apart from score a good goal against Argentina? I've won every single major championship this year – it's an absolute joke!'

I was just mucking about and I hadn't been tabloid newsworthy for long enough to know when to keep my mouth shut, so I thought no more of it. It turned out the guy was a reporter from the *Daily Mirror*. Sure enough a full page feature appeared with a picture Michael Owen and a headline that read: 'What has this man done to deserve the BBC's Sports Personality of the Year? says Iwan Thomas.' The next day they followed up with The Great SPOTY Debate, in which some members of the public backed me while others trashed me with comments like: 'I'm sure Iwan Thomas's mummy is proud of him, but who the hell is he?'

It caused enough of a stir for me to send an apology to Michael Owen. All very embarrassing.

By this time, it was getting difficult to keep abreast of all the calls and letters. I'd never been in this situation before. Some I just dismissed as pranks. I nearly did that with the letter from Madame Tussauds, thinking it was some kind of wind-up. Nope, it turned out to be real. In one of their public votes to see who would be next to have a waxwork, I had won.

They came round, and had me laid out on a turntable like a slab of meat – naked except for the skimpiest of pants. They were spinning me round and photographing me from every angle. They put dots all over my body and measured absolutely everything – everything! Every single measurement was exact to the tiniest detail. The weirdest thing I remember from the process was when they walked in with an enormous box just full of fake eyes – taking one out at a time as they attempted to match my eye tone. It took six months of absolutely painstaking work to make the waxwork.

I had to go to London a few times so the sculptors could do some corrective moulding. They told me that the Spice Girls were having their models made next door.

'They keep seeing your model and want to meet you.'

'What? No way.' Spicemania was in full flow and they had just played massive concerts at Wembley Stadium.

'Yeah, they kept saying what a shame it is you keep missing each other.'

The Spice Girls wanted to meet me! I can't describe how weird that felt.

Some people are disappointed by their likeness, but I was blown away. It was good to go with my parents to unveil the waxwork, but better still that I was accompanied by Charles Lipton. I was so proud to share the moment with the man who had given me such encouragement and I know that he felt equally proud of my achievements. Charles would die the following year, and to this day I'm grateful we were able to spend that special moment together.

These were good times. Cool Britannia had thrown the likes of Tony Blair, Liam Gallagher, the Spice Girls, Gordon Ramsey, Baddiel and Skinner and David Beckham together and I'd arrived with my bleached blond hair bringing athletics to the party. I was cheeky, confident and enjoying the spotlight. I loved being recognised, I loved training with my mates, I loved racing, I loved being the second fastest quarter-miler in the world. I was loved up.

And it was only going to get better . . .

# Twelve

# FALLING APART

I was still on cloud nine when training for the 1999 season began. I might be the hottest thing in British athletics, but I knew I'd only just got started. No way was I ever going to be distracted by the appearances, party invites or plaudits that now came my way. I knew what I was – an elite athlete – and I'd remain that only if I carried on training as hard as I had done over the last few years. So winter came and once again, I threw myself into the dune hill runs, the muddy forest sprints, the fartleks and the circuits.

As winter training progressed, I felt pain. That was nothing new; I'd lived with various injuries for the past four years. I ran through it because that's what we did with Mike. 'An athlete's body is like a finely tuned Ferrari,' he liked to say. 'What might seem a tiny injury to an ordinary person is exaggerated a hundred times.' His advice was always to pretend it's nothing and carry on. The pain in my left foot continued to get worse through the winter. On those forest and other runs I'd get excruciating shooting pains in my ankle every time I put my foot down. I was living on painkillers, sometimes crying because it hurt so much, but I didn't stop. 1999 was going to be something special.

After my 1998 treble golds, I was the one of the biggest stars in British athletics. The general public aren't interested in athletics in the winter months. But the real enthusiasts were happy to see me talking things up on the radio and in the press. 'Yeah, I'll be raring to go when the season starts,' I told them. Sure, I would need to make up time later – because of the foot injury, Mark and the Americans would already have an advantage over me – but having to put in the effort never phased me.

As I forced myself through those torturous, tough winter runs, I dreamed of the forthcoming South Africa training break in the spring. Sunshine, BBQs, swimming in the pool, running on the track . . . Getting away from the miserable English winter would do me the power of good. It had set me up so well for the early season in the previous couple of years. With a change of scenery, sunshine on my back, training at altitude and a renewed focus, I'd be back on course. And, if I needed an added incentive, we were going back to the luxury of Bentley's Country Lodge. Andy Norman was taking his family out with him this time, so it was no expense spared.

In South Africa, the warm days, facilities and good company meant the training stepped up a gear. And the vibe was so positive. After a couple of days of training on the quality tracks in South Africa, though, the ankle was hurting more than ever. 'Andy,' I said. 'This isn't right. I'm in so much pain.'

He sent me for an X-ray. It showed nothing; no break. 'Everything is fine.'

I thought, *It's me, I'm making too much of this.* So I went back to training. I gritted my teeth and soldiered on, every day feeling my ankle getting worse and worse. There was a meeting in Roodepoort coming up and, just a couple of days beforehand, I had to admit there was no way I was in a position to race there.

The race series was a big deal to the organisers and spectators and I was one of the star attractions. I needed a good excuse to drop out of this one at the last minute, but Andy Norman didn't want to spook them into thinking I wouldn't be fit for the other races. So he got creative. A few days earlier he had seen me playing with his son on the trampoline and this inspired him to tell the press: 'Iwan won't be running this week, as he got injured bouncing on the trampoline.'

Well no one, including me, knew what was actually up, so that was as good as anything. Some stories are just too much fun not to believe and Andy had come up with an absolute cracker. The South African press had a right good laugh. To this day many people still believe that jumping about on a trampoline was what triggered my ankle injury.

The quicker I got it sorted, the sooner I'd be back on the track. I pulled out of my remaining commitments in South Africa and flew back to the UK for MRI scans and to see ankle specialists. There, the doctor's diagnosis was bad. I had a stress fracture in my ankle. Not only that, but I'd had it for months. And ignoring it meant that I'd built up fluid, a cyst, in my ankle.

The problem was where my fibula joined my ankle – and getting to it proved a real problem for surgeons. The only realistic solution was to go to America for pioneering surgery which involved detaching my foot and drilling vertically upwards through the fibula to drain it. They warned this was potentially a career-ending operation, but as far as I could see, I had no choice. Doing nothing wasn't an option. It would mean sitting out the season, the rest of the year and maybe more – but if that was what was needed for me to get going again, then that was what it had to be. Would I be up to speed for the Sydney Olympics, September 2000? It was touch and go.

Then a miracle happened. A doctor from John Radcliffe Hospital in Oxford contacted me with an alternative plan. He said he could operate on the ankle using keyhole surgery and drill down through the bone rather than upwards. He was really confident and talked me through every stage. Wow! My prayers had been answered. I would be back training by the autumn. Plenty of time for Olympic preparation.

My foot might have been in plaster and I was hobbling around on crutches, but I was on the road to fitness. I was young, there was plenty of time. Roger Black had faced similar long absences when he was older than me and he came back to break the British record and take silver at the World Championships. I'd be back, faster and stronger than ever.

I went to the World Championships in Seville, but only as I was narrating *Pot of Gold*, a TV documentary describing how the National Lottery was funding athletics. I was filming pieces to camera in the stadium and just being there hurt. I so wished I was running not filming. I stayed strong, reminding myself that I wasn't the first athlete to take months out – it's an occupational hazard. By the time the final came around I was back home. Sitting on the sofa with my foot, still in plaster, sticking out in front of me. I tied myself in knots watching Jamie and Mark – really wanting them to do well, but maybe not too well at the same time.

Michael Johnson set a new world record of 43.18 in that race. Despite him delivering a time that was over one second faster than I had ever run, this provided some consolation. He had been injured all year, missed the US trials and was in the finals only due to a new rule allowing defending champions to enter. And he was 31. I was 25, so there was plenty of time for me yet. My dream of being World Champion would have had to wait anyway. Even fit, I'd never have beaten him then: it was a really fast race. Mark ran 44.65 and only finished sixth.

I'd also been lifted by some brilliant news. Months before, I'd received a letter – on proper, expensive, headed paper – saying I was to receive an MBE in the Queen's Birthday Honours list. It said: 'Top Secret' and I wasn't allowed to tell anyone I'd been nominated. I thought, *Bullshit*. Convinced it was a joke from one of my old university mates, I ripped up the letter. When another letter arrived saying that I hadn't responded and requesting I now respond immediately, I thought, *Shit, this might be for real.*

I was pleased as punch to be the only still-competing athlete on the list and so proud to be able to receive the medal from the Queen at Buckingham Palace accompanied by Mum, Dad and Gran. (What really made me laugh was that Gran, who lived in an ex-council house, refused to go to the toilets in the Palace, worried that they wouldn't be clean enough.)

I made sure I was there in plenty of time. When I'd gone to receive my Athlete of the Year award from the Duke of Edinburgh, I got stuck in traffic and he'd left by the time I arrived. The press kindly reminded me of that for my appointment at Buckingham Palace, saying MBE stood for 'Must Be Early'.

I put my best suit on and, to mark the occasion, put my crutches aside, wore a sock over my plaster cast and hobbled along instead. The Queen had obviously been thinking along the same lines as me when she said, 'Will one be ready for the Olympics.'

'Yes, Ma'am, that's the plan,' I replied.

But I was finding the route back to fitness more frustrating than I anticipated. The doctor's 'couple of months' proved a bit of an understatement. As one minor injury followed another, I struggled to get back to full training. It was only by the start of the 2000 season that I was finally getting quicker. I was beating my training group, but that meant little on the track when I'd be up against Mark and Jamie or even the newcomer Jared Deacon.

Missing a whole winter meant I was always playing catch-up. It hadn't helped that to compensate for not being able to train every day, I had spent more time in the gym and had bulked up. A change of shape was going to slow me down a little, but regular training would sort that. I was confident I could still run fast enough to get an individual place in the Olympic team.

Sydney was the only focus that year. After missing a year, I was so ready to be back among the big hitters. Not training for 12 months was a major obstacle. Usually when athletes miss a season it is literally that, a season, and they are back training in the winter. I didn't get started until well into the New Year. Even so, I was positive I would make the final. That would be enough to say I was back – a statement of intent. When I was asked to go out to the Gold Coast early in the year, with high jumper Dalton Grant and triple jumper Ashia Hansen, to look at the facilities as part of British Athletics' Olympic recce team, I really felt part of the set-up. They were clearly counting on me to be there just as much as I was.

And then I tore my hamstring. Just as things were finally coming together, I faced another five or six weeks out. Crap timing. I'd only just be back running in time for the AAAs, which were serving as the Olympic trials, and running three races in two days was unfeasible. The stress on my hamstring was just too much to risk. If it went again, that could be the end of my season.

The selectors were understanding. They knew I had a race lined up soon after and I remember Graham Knight, the main selector for the 400 metres, rang me to say, 'Don't worry, we'll give you a couple of weeks to prove your fitness.' Mark would almost certainly win in Birmingham, Jamie would come second, and they would be able to give me the discretionary third place. This was reassuring to hear, although both Graham and UK Athletics firmly dispute this happened. Their position was: 'there was a possibility a place would be left open' but that I was 'never told that if he didn't run in the trials a place would be kept open. We can't do that'. Clearly our recollections differed because by the end of August, I thought I would obviously be their best option to win a medal.

Sean Baldock, an up-and-coming athlete, only went and put a huge spanner in the works. From nowhere he ran a massive PB of 45.20 at the AAAs, coming second to Mark Richardson and ahead of Jamie. He had bagged the second guaranteed place on the plane and given the selectors a real dilemma: Jamie or me?

Jamie's season best was 45.38, while I had run 45.85 in Budapest in my first race for over a year. I had shown I had got over the ankle operation now and the hamstring was just a temporary injury that could happen to anyone. I would only be getting faster from now until Sydney. As good a mate as Jamie was, it was a no-brainer.

A week later, I was back running and flew out for a race in Sweden. I was excited to be back racing and had something to prove: my fitness. It's a nice summer's evening and I'm down on the track warming up, thinking to myself, *This feels so good. I'm ready. Things are looking up.* I was in the best mood. 'I'm going to absolutely smash this,' I said aloud to no one in particular.

My phone rang and it was a friend at home. I had time for a quick chat and a laugh. 'Hi, mate. What's happening?'

'They've only gone and selected Jamie Baulch.'

Words failed me. I couldn't believe what I heard. I sat on the track and tried to process it. *Why now? What about their promise?* They had nearly a week before the selection deadline. None of it made sense. I ran the race in a fog of confusion and anger. I remember coming into the final hundred metres thinking, *What's the point? What am I doing this for?* I won the race. I didn't run that quickly, 45.6, but I proved I was getting faster and wasn't injured.

I couldn't contain my anger, frustration, disappointment. And I unloaded it all to a journalist straight after the race. I told him, in choice language, that I couldn't believe the selectors had gone back on their word and not given me time to show my fitness.

As I was boarding the plane home from Sweden, I had a call from my agent. 'Listen,' he said. 'I'm going to meet you at the airport.'

'OK,' I replied, a bit surprised. 'Why? What's happening?'

'I think there's going to be a bit of attention surrounding you after what you said.'

I spent the whole flight mulling it over. I was still feeling betrayed and angry, but also wondering what the reaction would be back home. Had I gone over the top? It was just an athletics story, surely it wasn't so big that the press would be all over it?

British Airways staff met me off the flight and escorted me out through back corridors. When I finally emerged through the customs gate, I was gobsmacked. I felt like a pop star caught in a scandal. There was press everywhere, lightbulbs flashed and a barrage of shouted questions came in my direction.

'Who lied to you, Iwan?

'Which member of the committee was it?'

I was giving them all the 'No comment' line, wondering what the bloody hell I had got myself into.

A 'clear the air' meeting was arranged for me to talk to Graham Knight and the UK Athletics Performance Director, Max Jones, at the home of UKA Chairman David Hemery in Marlborough. Hemery was kind and remained neutral as we thrashed it out. I insisted that they had told me they would give me time. They denied it – and have continued to do so. This was stalemate and doing me no good. I'd still been selected for the relay team. I vowed to put the whole sorry business behind me and concentrate on preparing for that. Roger might be gone, but we were going to get that gold this time.

Ironically, I nearly did get selected to run in the individual 400 metres. I had been named as first reserve for the individual selections in case of injuries and withdrawals and now a chance arose. A year previously, Mark Richardson had tested positive for the banned steroid nandrolone, but he denied any wrongdoing.

The IAAF, however, were not satisfied and referred the case to an arbitration panel, which they scheduled for the first day of the Games. Mark knew that the five days he was given to prepare was not enough and in asking them to reschedule he would forfeit his place. It was desperately sad and unfair – and less than a year later the IAAF reinstated him, having found that he had taken nandrolone accidentally in a supplement.

With the opportunity to replace Mark being discussed, I was forced to admit to myself and to the committee that since the race in Sweden I hadn't made the progress I needed. Although I still believe – and results in Sydney made my point – I should have been selected, I wasn't interested in entering the individual 400 metres just to make up the numbers. Maybe the whole incident had left too sour a taste. It was a big decision and one I thought through a lot in the days when it became an option. I was the European Champion; if I couldn't do myself justice, I would rather not run at all.

So I went to Sydney as a member of the 4 × 400 team. I felt like a spare part; one of those athletes with no chance and there only for the fun of it – the kind who go to the opening ceremony, as Linford had described back in Atlanta. It was a great Olympics and I got to enjoy myself. There was a Speedo party on Bondi beach, the kind of event I would never have even thought about attending four years earlier.

Even though I wasn't competing, I offered my full support to the other 400 metres runners and winced when Jamie and Sean Baldock both crashed out in the heats, running around 46.5. Only Daniel Caines, the late replacement for Mark, made the semi-final with a PB of 45.37. I watched the final with tears in my eyes, knowing that if I was fully fit I'd have been among the medals.

Finally my turn came with the 4 × 400 metres, such a strong event for Britain for years. We had a decent team, if weaker than the recent past, with Jared Deacon, Daniel, Jamie and myself on third leg. I ran no better than the others. I wasn't great, running 45.26 in the final and we trailed in sixth (although credited with fifth once the US were disqualified after Pettigrew's confession).

Whatever the disappointment, the Olympics had proved one thing: the 400 metres was an event that had not moved on. Johnson had retired, but no one had taken up the mantle. In fact, the 44.7 seconds I'd run to finish fifth in the final in Atlanta would have won me a bronze in Sydney. No one in the world was running sub-44.6. With an injury-free run-up, I could be in with a chance, and 2001 also meant the World Championships in Edmonton, Canada.

As the 2001 season got underway, things were definitely looking up – despite a stop-start winter. I ran 46.53 in Helsinki, 46.16 in Moscow and 45.95 in Dublin. It wasn't fast, but it was a start and I wasn't carrying an injury. In the AAAs I finished second to Mark. A guaranteed place in the World Championship team? Nope. Not with the way my luck was going. I ran 46 flat – just outside the 45.72 qualifying time for Edmonton.

I had to get to Canada. Once I was there, anything could happen. I had one last chance, running at a meeting at Crystal Palace. I messed up badly. I set off too slowly, not wanting to blow up before the finish, and I finished a tenth of a second outside the required time. I was kicking myself. I was faster than that – I had no doubts. I'd let myself down. I'd do anything to rewind the clock 24 hours and try again.

A few days later there was a British Milers' Club meeting at Watford. I enquired if they would host a 400 metres race at the meeting. It was past the deadline, but it was as much about self-esteem as anything. I just wanted to prove to myself that I could run faster than I had at Crystal Palace. They agreed on the basis that I find seven others to race. Having enlisted Mike's help, I recruited a line-up of friends like Robert Lewis, Danny Jackson and Simon Ciaravella and set off for Watford.

On a balmy summer evening in Woodside Stadium, in front of a few hundred spectators, I ran like it was an Olympic final. I gave it everything and came in at 45.70 – two hundredths within the qualifying time. Was it too late? I'd missed the deadline by less than 24 hours, but surely they could overlook that? I rang Max Jones at British Athletics straightaway. He said he'd call the IAAF and check. It was now out of my hands.

'Don't worry,' Mike said in his most reassuring tone. 'It'll be fine. You'll get the nod. Just wait and see.' I wasn't so sure. I'd had so much bad luck over the past couple of years, it just didn't seem likely to me that they would bend the rules. It was an agonising wait and I'd practically given up when I was out in Southampton having a Friday night curry with my mates and received a call from Max. As I tucked into my usual prawn madras, I learned I was in.

My grin said it all. My luck had changed. I had a bounce in my step and I had such faith in myself to get somewhere near my old form. Johnson wasn't going to be there – and I was. I told everyone that if there was a possibility of winning the thing, I was going for it. 'Well, Goran Ivanisevic won Wimbledon as a wild card, didn't he?' I asked the *London Evening Standard* reporter.

'The chances of you winning are longer than long,' Brendan Foster told me when I got to Canada.

'What do you mean? 20–1? 50–1?'

His expression suggested they were even longer.

'Whoa! I'm having some of that!'

In Edmonton, I ran a reasonable heat in 45.9, but two races in two days proved too much for a body that was still refusing to get back to its best. Rather than get faster, I came in last in the semi-final in 46.72 and that killed me. Edmonton had a weird set-up with steps going up to the mixed zone, where you have to pass through the massed press and TV groups. I barely made it up the steps, pausing to throw up halfway up – I could have been back at the Southampton track.

The relay was a similar story: I disappointed myself and the team and we never bothered the medal positions. For all my efforts, I really shouldn't have bothered. On one hand I was telling everyone I was so sure I could get back, and I absolutely meant it. I wasn't bullshitting people. In my head, I was the same person who had run 44.36 – I'd done it before and I could do it again. Then, on the other hand, somewhere a small nagging doubt had taken hold. *That was three years ago. What if my body just couldn't do it now? What if it never could again?* My willpower and self-belief were overcoming those doubts – but had now swapped from being a strength to a weakness.

And yet, there was always a tantalising glimpse of sunshine behind the clouds to egg me on. I'm a born optimist. I don't need a lot to give me hope. I finished the season with 45.82 in the pouring rain at Gateshead and I was healthy. That was as good as it had been for some time. By the time 2002 came around, I'd missed only four days' training since October, which was the most I'd managed since '98. Were things finally looking up?

2002 was the year of the Commonwealth Games and the European Championships. I was the reigning champion in both and desperately wanted to defend my titles. 1998 seemed like another life now. I knew I couldn't go on doing the same things and getting nowhere. I couldn't face another winter in Southampton. So, for the first time ever, I decided to leave Mike's group (with his blessing) to do some warm weather training.

In February, I joined Linford's group in Brisbane, Australia. It was just the tonic I needed. Jamie, Darren Campbell, Matt Elias and Katharine Merry were all there; great friends who also happened to be top-class athletes. It was a fantastic camp in terms of being around the best in the business. I loved training with those guys. If I was ever going to turn the corner, this was going to swing it. I threw myself into it with a new zest.

It was a new environment and a different kind of training, much more speed-orientated with lots of 250s on the track. I was used to the dune and forest runs and other strength training that Mike put us through. I gave everything, they were such an inspirational group, but it really didn't suit me. Turned out, in fact, to be another poor decision. I just wasn't fit enough. I eventually pulled a calf muscle and was out for another two months. Another big setback – and I was devastated.

I recovered in time for Mike's Easter camp in Portugal and, for once, my body was holding up and my times were looking good. I ran my fastest 300 metres for years. If I could get back to even 80 per cent of what I had been, I would be ranked in the top three in the world. I'd waited so long and now the future had opened up once again.

Slam! The very next day, the final day of training, my hamstring went. It was a frustrating, soul-destroying, endless cycle: new start, promise, injury, recovery, new start . . . *Jesus*, I thought, *how much bad luck can one person have?* This was bang on time to ruin the start of the season.

The hamstring kept niggling away. I flew to Bratislava for a race, only to pull out after the warm-up when it didn't feel right. Then I skipped the Welsh Championships. Thankfully, the Welsh Athletics Association were really supportive. They showed a lot of faith in giving me an unconditional place in the team for the Commonwealth Games in Manchester, without me having to prove myself. They needn't have bothered. Three weeks before the Games, I ran in the Welsh Games in Cardiff and was terrible. Although it was a wet and windy night, I knew a 47.17 time was just not good enough.

It was the beginning of one of the worst weeks ever. At the British Championships a few days later, I was no better. I finished fifth in the semi-final, still failing to break 47 seconds and in doing so missing out on the chance of defending my European title.

I drove home in floods of tears, running through the gamut of self-pity, self-doubt and anger – and desperate to get back to being the athlete I had been. A week later in Dublin, I ran 47 flat and came in last. The writing was on the wall in screaming capital letters.

Once, I had been the darling of the press. Now they had given up. The *Daily Telegraph* said I had expressed 'an unhealthy self-loathing' in my post-race comments while the *Guardian* wrote, 'He looked a poor imitation of the man who four years ago had steamrollered all in his way.' With days to go before the Commonwealth Games, I withdrew from the individual competition. There was just no point.

I was desperately in need of cheering up and the relay competition came up trumps. Wales had a good squad: Jamie; the new AAA champion, Tim Benjamin; and Matt Elias, who had just won the silver in the 400 metres hurdles. We fancied our chances even up against tough opposition in England, South Africa, Jamaica, Australia and the Bahamas. I ran a good second leg in the semi-final, but again, two races in two days was too much. In the final, Tim had given us a solid start, but all I could do was keep us in it. Fortunately Jamie on third and Matt Elias on anchor did a fantastic job and Danny Caines, running for England, only just held him off at the finish. We had a new Welsh record and silver medals. If I had been fully fit, I think we could have taken gold.

That, I realised, was the last medal I would win. It was time to be brutally honest with myself. The dream was over. I was fighting against myself. Putting myself through so much effort and anguish for what? A chance to let myself down on the world stage.

My optimism had finally been drained dry. That ankle surgery had never really worked. From 1999 onwards I never completed a whole month of training. I'd manage a couple of weeks, then something would go. I was broken beyond repair. My knees flared up, then I'd pull a hamstring, then my ankle pain returned – I even got bitten by a bloody dog while running in the woods.

And yet, for some reason, I told myself quitting was not an option. I needed to please those people who stood by me, I had to honour my commitments to my sponsors and I wanted to prove everyone wrong. I was still the British record holder and I was bloody-minded.

In the full face of the obvious facts, with blind faith in my ability and, perhaps most significantly, not knowing what else I could do – I soldiered on. No one ever tried to convince me otherwise. No one took me aside and said, 'Listen Iwan. Your body is broken, mate. You're not coming back. Don't fizzle out – walk away now.'

God, how I wish they had.

# Thirteen

# DVDS, NEEDLES AND VOLTAROL

*Don't think about it. Just run. It might not even happen.* I was miles from home in Eastern Europe, about to start a race in which, for once, I wasn't concerned about winning. *Just run.* How many times had I been in the blocks and worried about injuries? This was new. This time I was running in order to tear a muscle. I knew that I had to get injured. More injured than I already was. My lower leg was already hurting before the race even started. Warming up was agony. *Ignore it. It doesn't matter.* That was why I had to carry on. I waited for the gun. Things had to get worse to get better. *It's not madness. It's the right thing to do. Run.*

---

The quarter-mile is a mean bastard. A torture rack of an event. One that demands ultimate commitment. If you don't put your body on the line, it spits you out

– and if you do, it grinds you down slowly. As Mike Smith said, 'You have to work bloody hard to go nowhere at all.' That requires punishing strength and speed training in order just to get on the starting line. And plenty more if you want to win. That same effort is what ultimately breaks you and stops you enjoying the sport into which you put so much. That's the curse of the 400 metres. It's going to end you, the key is how much you have achieved when it does.

And that's a *when*, not an *if*. Unless you're lucky or a physical freak, it's going to get you. Look at the successive British 400 metres record holders from 1985 to 2023: Derek Redmond, David Grindley, Roger Black and me. All talented runners and utterly dedicated trainers and all with careers racked and ruined by injury when they, and I, should have had so many more years in the sport.

To most quarter-milers and many other athletes, injuries are an occupational hazard. There's usually little warning. Maybe you feel something, an ache or minor sensation, but it's easy to ignore or explain. There were moments when I thought: *Is that a twinge to my calf?*, then I dismissed the idea, put it down to cramp or exhaustion or paranoia, and then the adrenaline of a race masked it completely. The sensible athletes are careful. They know that injuries are more likely after overtraining and over-racing. But the sensible are never the fastest; that's reserved for the reckless gamblers – and all I ever wanted to be was the best, so I had to be all-in.

What fuelled me when I was a younger runner was this positive feeling that I could do anything. It might have been the speed with which I went from schoolboy to Olympian, but nothing fazed me about the sport. I savoured the rigours of training and I loved pitting myself against others on the track. If I lost, I doubled up on the training in the certainty of winning next time. Injuries were minor inconveniences to be ignored or endured. So a strain or a pulled muscle? I was unstoppable. Yeah, the invincibility of youth.

I was no different to most of my rivals in getting injuries and maybe missing a race. But I felt none of them trained as hard as I did. It was a matter of pride for me. Hard yards, pain, exhaustion, vomiting and near destruction – in my head all this was required to knock thousandths off my time.

I got my reward on the track. I got fast quick. I ran 47.94 in my first AAA British Championships in 1993 and in only four years took the British record at the same event in 44.36. I was having such fun, making such an impact in the sport. I fed off the praise and the pride of those I cared about, the cheers of the crowd and the media spotlight. I was the centre of attention and revelling in it. I never stopped to think that it would all catch up with me – and even if I had, I'm pretty sure I wouldn't have cared. I was living, training and running in the moment.

I can't talk about my injuries without talking about something that is complicated and difficult for me to write. Mike Smith was a brilliant coach. He knew the 400 metres inside out and had a magic knack of preparing me perfectly for each new season. He got the best out of me and I loved him like he was my father. But Mike had one blind spot (I'm tempted to call it an Achilles heel): he had never been an elite athlete and he never understood injuries.

There was always some needle between Mike and Roger Black. Mike had taken him to the peak of his career, only for Roger to leave for another coach. It hurt Mike a lot and so when I beat Roger, that brought him more pleasure than me beating anyone else.

When I first got to know Roger, I asked him why he'd left. 'Mike just doesn't understand injuries,' he said. At the time, that seemed ridiculous to me. He was a superb coach. I hadn't been with Mike that long and he had already improved my times so much. I defended him, saying: 'He's a great bloke, of course he understands.'

By the time I realised what Roger meant, it was too late. Mike was a great coach – when we were in our early twenties and superfit – but the stress and wear we were putting on our bodies was never a concern. He had a one-size-fits-all approach to training. 'This is what we do, now get on with it.' He had no truck with niggles, resting up – it was always 'Just two more reps, come on now!' We'd go to Portugal every year for warm weather training and went straight from doing one track session a week to one a day. A lot of the group returned with injuries, but Mike never seemed to put two and two together.

All the injuries I suffered were internal. They weren't cuts or gashes. On some, bruising might appear after several days, but mostly it was just the pain that indicated something was wrong. And pain is such a subjective thing. I could say it hurt a lot, but what did that mean? That I was soft and couldn't take a little discomfort? Or that, knowing I was a tough trainer, it must be bad if I was complaining? Mike didn't recognise levels of pain. You ran through it until you couldn't. There was no middle way.

In those first few years we were made for each other. His old-school methods and my insatiable appetite for tough, painful training went hand in hand. I willingly lapped up every gruelling session and – honest to God – couldn't wait for the next one. I didn't need any encouragement. In fact, I was like Mike's deputy, egging on the rest of the lads to work harder.

Just as I had been desperate to please Dad when I was racing BMX, I just wanted to make Mike proud of me. I savoured the rare words of praise I got from him like a vintage wine. When I was competing, I looked to Mike for pre-race advice, and he was the first person I'd go to or call when I finished. Speaking to him after my biggest successes was worth as much as the medals themselves. 'Well done, boy,' he said when I won the European Championship. 'You looked really strong there. That was really something, you know?' He could have done a 10-minute speech and I wouldn't have felt prouder.

I constantly ask myself, *Why didn't I say more to him?* I could have stopped and said 'Sorry, but something doesn't feel quite right' or 'My hamstring's feeling a bit tight – I'll just do the three reps.' Midway through a session I could have said, 'Listen, Mike, I'm a bit tired today, I'm going to take it easy.'

If I had done, I would have had a longer career – no doubt. I've so many regrets. Maybe if I'd listened to my body, taken a couple of days rest, I wouldn't have torn a hamstring or got an injury which put me out for two months. I could have, should have argued back. It wasn't in my nature, though. I was the *let's have it*, gung-ho guy. I never let the training group beat me at anything and I really did love the pain. I felt it was giving me super-strength, and never stopped to think what it was doing to my body. I was also the puppy-dog schoolboy who cared too much about Mike's reaction. I didn't want him to be annoyed or disappointed. He could be really pushy and I had no answer to that. And he sulked – knowing it would get to me. Sometimes, he didn't talk to me for days. He was a funny bugger was Mike.

It's easy to criticise. Being an elite coach isn't easy. You're dealing with different personalities – slackers and grifters, those who'll talk and those who just get on with it – and varying abilities – those who learn and keep improving quickly, those who have run as fast as they ever will, and those dealing with injuries and personal issues. All the time the coach is trying to do the best for all of them. It's a thankless task.

Mike was the person who saw more in me than a good athlete; he saw a great athlete. He kept faith with me in the student days when I found excuses not to make it down to Southampton to train; he tolerated my high spirits when he really wanted seriousness; and he carried on believing in me when many had given up. For many coaches it was just about the sport; Mike cared about me.

My lifestyle didn't help, either. I never stopped. In that 1998 documentary, Mark Richardson calls me the Gazza of the team, and he had a point. I always liked having fun and being the entertainer. Even back in 1994, as a wide-eyed 20-year-old at my first Commonwealth Games, I was pushing it. I split my lip trying to do a double backflip off a diving board just before the 400 metres heats. In Portugal in 1998, I injured my knee playing football – something Mike always discouraged – and that injury could easily have jeopardised my season.

I was too afraid to let go of being liked. If I agreed to calm down and never go out again, that would change who I was. Sally Gunnell, Linford and the others, they all said: 'Iwan, what a character!' and that was what I wanted to be. Midweek, I didn't pass up when the guys said, 'Coming down McCluskey's? It's half-price beers until 10', even if I knew I was racing again on the following weekend. In 1998, just before the British Championships, I was at a house party in Cardiff. Dressed as Rocky Balboa and dancing like a madman. There was no way Mark would have done that, or Jamie (and he lived in Cardiff!). Six days later I broke the British record.

I had the same restless attitude to racing. I took everything offered to me, even if I didn't feel 100 per cent fit. I could be limping, but I'd warm up and still race. As long as I could run, I just switched off the pain at the sound of that gun.

In 1998 and '99, many coaches might have had a word. Might have taken me aside and said, 'Don't take on too much this year. You're doing the European, Commonwealth and World Cup, so how about limiting yourself to three or four grand prix races?' Not Mike. He'd say, 'You're in great shape, lad. You've got Zurich next week, you're in Lane 4. You'll be back on Thursday, and on Saturday you're in Lausanne.' I was travelling twice a week and living out of a suitcase. What kind of serious athlete lives that kind of life?

I wished there had been someone to offer me advice. On the other hand, I might not have listened. Try telling a 23-year-old earning good money at those grand prix races to slow down.

All athletes get injuries. The body just isn't made for the kind of strain we put on it. I had countless groin strains, twisted ankles, knee flare-ups, pulled hamstrings, quad/calf/thigh muscle pains and shin splints. The occupational hazard for a professional. You rest and take some painkillers or run through it and soon come back.

1996 to 1999 were the Cortisone Years. When you are young you just want to race – sod the consequences. The first cortisone injection I had was 45 minutes before the Olympic final in 1996. It was within the rules – and the only way I was going to make the race. The pain and stiffness in my hip had reached the point where I was having difficulty walking, let alone running.

The cortisone jab is unpleasant and, for the first time at least, a bit scary. The medic comes over with this bloody big needle, sometimes about 10cm (4 inches) long and it has to go right into the cavity of the joint. This isn't like a blood test or a flu jab that you can watch; you have to turn away. And it really hurts. But it really works. It is a localised anti-inflammatory that goes straight to the muscle – in this example, my hip flexor. Within half an hour I was running normally and it would be a week before I felt it again. They're not magic, though. They don't heal an injury, they just mask it and you can only ever have a maximum of three cortisones in the same area.

A lot of my injuries weren't that bad. They just came at the worst moment. They never happened in the depths of winter when I could take time out of training in the knowledge I could catch up. They came, those muscle tears and sprains, as soon as I went into that sheer speed phase of training. And the nearer this was to May, the further behind I would be as the season started. If it happened mid-season, I was in the lap of the gods. Maybe I'd miss a race in Estonia or Cardiff; a pity, but it couldn't be helped. But maybe they came at the worst possible time: before the AAA's Olympic trials, before the Commonwealth Games, before the World Championships. Then the frustration and exasperation were 10 times as painful as the injury.

Patience and rest, the two necessities of dealing with an injury. Then there's me, hyperactive and with a low boredom threshold; I really wasn't suited to being laid up. I could rest after training or if I had a big race coming up, but I was always the guy who said yes whenever anyone suggested a pint or a club. I liked people, I was a bit of a hedonist, I didn't like sitting still. And yet for seven years I spent more of my time sitting than actually on the track. And it wasn't as if I couldn't run.

OK, I'd spent most of the season out with a torn hamstring in 1995 – but I was 21 years old then, and that's different, knowing I would come back with my best years ahead. Now I was 26 and approaching the peak of my career and wondering if I would ever be fit again. In a matter of months I went from being the great hope of British athletics to hobbling around on crutches with no idea when I'd be back on the track.

I was one of the top athletes in Britain, in the world. Michael Johnson had tipped me as the one to take the crown when he retired. And I knew, really knew, that I could do it. When I was fit, it came so easy. I'd float round that track. Fast and strong and always feeling I could go faster. Except for Johnson there was no one better than me in 1998.

I was a professional athlete. It was what I was paid for and what I did. How long can you be an athlete and not run? Back in 1995, it hadn't been a massive deal. Young athletes, especially 400 metre runners, get injuries. Even in 1999, it was OK. I had shown I was among the world's best; I was still in the papers. 'Iwan's on the road to recovery', 'Iwan's eyeing gold in Sydney', 'Iwan receives the MBE with his foot in plaster'. Even in 2000, people still had faith (just maybe not as much as me).

When I went out to Seville to watch the 1999 World Championships, I met up with my sponsor, Asics. My contract with them was coming to an end and they were keen to re-sign me. They offered me a three-year deal at around £60,000 a year before bonuses, pretty much the same as they had given me four years earlier. Since then I'd become the European and Commonwealth Champion and held the British record which no one looked like breaking any time soon. It didn't seem overgenerous, so I turned it down. I was so confident I was worth more than that and soon to be valued a lot higher. I said, 'Give me £70,000 for two years and we'll negotiate again then.' It was a gamble, but I truly thought we'd be talking at least £100,000 by then . . .

Now every time I got an injury, it felt like a countdown clock had started. Every second that passed away was my status, my currency, my commercial value ticking away. How soon would I be back? I'd scan the meetings scheduled for the season. Nope, nope, nope – maybe that one?

I missed racing so much, it dogged my waking hours and my nights. I regularly had dreams of being on the blocks, of steaming down the back straight, feeling the surge of energy in the final hundred metres and making the desperate dip at the line. I dreamed of being as fast as I was, of seeing the surprised reactions of rivals and coaches amazed I'd recovered so quickly. And I'd wake still on a high for a fraction of a second.

One of the most frustrating things was that I knew that there were people out there cheating. Drug cheats who never seemed to get injured and had 10 good years in their careers. There I was, watching athletics through tears on TV thinking: *Why me, why me* and all I ever did was push my body a little too much to be the best athlete I could be, to make people proud of me.

There were probably drugs out there that I could have taken to get me back racing sooner. I don't know where I'd have got them and I was never willing to find out, let alone take anything. Maybe I could have taken a year out, doped and come back better than ever. I think others did that, but it wasn't me, and it never even occurred to me as an option.

I sat at home watching the team in major championships. I watched Mark, Jerome Young, Antonio Pettigrew battling it out, thinking: *I'd have been up there, I could have won that.* British athletes were coming in behind them with times I used to do in my sleep. I don't want to be disparaging, they were really good athletes and were there on merit, but it was bitterly frustrating. *If I can just get fit, they'll never beat me.*

It was a brutal watch. My dream seemed to be slipping away. There were so many tears. Through drenched eyes, I would watch athletes winning medals and think, *That should be me.* I had so much self-hatred. I couldn't understand why my body kept letting me down. This had been happening since 1996; I should have realised that it couldn't take the workload.

With the benefit of hindsight, I should never have put myself through all that. Over and again, I thought it would work out and all be fine. Everyone else could see the signs but me. They were all thinking *he's put on weight, he's done too much gym work this year and bulked up; he hasn't got the speed any more; he's lost that strength in the final 100 – it's not going to work.* I wasn't going to take that. Proving the doubters wrong had been a motivating force since the School Sports Day, but willpower could – can – only take me so far.

Being injured was like a prison sentence. I had no idea when it would end or what to do. I was given recovery dates that kept getting moved back, or I got over one injury and just as I thought I was on the road back to full fitness, something else went.

I was still reasonably high profile in the media and featured on the radio, TV and in magazines, but that just made me feel a fraud. Every time I heard people refer to the often-injured England footballer Darren Anderton as 'sicknote', I thought, *Yeah, that's me.* I got tired of being asked, 'How's the recovery going?'; 'Are we going to see you back soon?'; 'Will you make the Olympics?' I just wanted to lock the door and hide away.

Maybe I should have taken up a hobby; done jigsaw puzzles, made model aircraft or taken up knitting. I was going out of my head with boredom and frustration. Stuck in the house with no structure to the day, sometimes just staring at the walls. I watched crap daytime TV and endless action movies on DVD. Every Monday I was down at Blockbusters, buying at least two DVDS and building my own collection; I must have bought over a thousand films. There's a limit, though. There are only so many *Rocky* and *Rambo* films or so much bickering on Jeremy Kyle that one man can watch. And yet, the sport continued without me. I read *Athletics Weekly*, watched competitions on TV, saw Johnson getting better as I got worse, and Jamie Baulch running in races where I should have been. It was tough.

I learned to live with pain. From an intense throbbing right down my thigh to a searing bolt of agony that flashed through my ankle. At times my arms ached from walking on crutches, my knees were swollen and burning, I could have a stabbing pain in my calves or some mysterious unplaceable discomfort that came and went.

No matter what the pain, I had to be so careful about what I took. I believed I was the most drug-tested athlete on the planet (at times I wondered if it was because they knew I was clean, so it was an easy win for them).

You are responsible for anything found in your system, regardless of how it got there or whether you were trying to cheat or not. And the list of what you are prohibited from eating or drinking is extensive too because these can mask drugs or themselves be performance-enhancing. I was allowed only a very limited amount of caffeine and no Lemsip, Nurofen or cough remedies, but I was allowed strong painkillers prescribed by doctors. I needed them just to perform everyday tasks and popped painkillers like they were Smarties. I lived on Voltarol and other anti-inflammatories – anything that was OK by the IAAF. God knows what I was doing to my insides.

Injury was such a lonely place. I desperately missed the training, the meetings, the socialising, but even when I was able to get about, I didn't want to go out any more. My mood swings were vicious. I was hell to live with – grumpy, snappy, moody and irritable. I provoked rows with my girlfriend over nothing. I didn't even realise I was doing it. I was just being a total arsehole.

I didn't want to see people – or for them to see me. As much as people cared, they didn't know what I was going through. They were all so well-meaning and said things like, 'Don't worry, you'll get back running soon. You'll be fine.' I didn't want to hear that. I was brimming with resentment. The sport had kicked me in the teeth and left me to rot. I was so bitter and angry over everything; my bad luck, the futility of all my efforts to get fit, and the platitudes and the advice (however well-intentioned) that I was being given over and over again. I just wanted to reply, *What the fucking hell do you know?*

A comment I got a lot was, 'C'mon Iwan. Try to stay positive, you'll heal quicker.' When I was desperately struggling to keep things together, this didn't seem helpful. *What a load of bollocks*, I replied in my head. *It's a torn hamstring – and me thinking: 'It's nothing, I'm almost ready to run again' isn't going to make the slightest difference. It's fucking science for God's sake.*

In the end, though, I thought, *Why not. I've tried everything else.* When I tore my hamstring yet again, I was determined to be optimistic. I refused to dwell on the injury, I told people how well it was going. I was the old positive

Iwan. And, you know what? It worked! In about 10 days, I was up and sprinting again.

Ultimately, two injuries put paid to my career. The first started out in the winter of 1998, when I was running through a lot of pain in my left leg. I went to South Africa in the new year, hoping in vain that the warm weather would help it heal. I ended up coming home and, as I've already explained (see page 153), discovering the problem was a cyst in my ankle meant I now had the difficult choice of deciding which surgery to choose. I was a reasonably high-profile sporting name at the time, so there was quite a lot of kudos for the surgeons and doctors who got to treat me. Their promises ('although there are always risks') of speedy recoveries were music to my ears, but they didn't deliver. Agreeing to the keyhole surgery at the John Radcliffe Hospital in Oxford was a mistake. He cleared the fluid, but the injury never fully cleared up; it would flare up regularly and pain was never far away.

It was a year after that surgery before I ran again. From then on, I was playing catch-up. Adding to the problem is that an injury simply means the body compensates. With my left leg not quite right, I put too much pressure on the right leg and tore my right calf. I tore my hamstrings at least 10 times. I was plugging away despite running only 46.5 or 46.3, crap times. I just couldn't go any faster. I was able to train only two or three times a week at the most – and was kidding myself that was enough to compete with the best.

The second big injury was the plantaris tendon; the most pointless and annoying tendon in the body. It runs down the back of your lower leg from the calf to the Achilles, and can damage either, but – and wait for this – it performs no useful function in the movement of the leg. Its only use is for a graft and many people (it may even be as high as 1 in 5) don't even have one – and never suffer or even notice.

However.

The thing can be a source of pain. I partially damaged mine in 2002 and it affected my Achilles. I had a number of cortisone injections to try to help it heal, but it didn't get any better.

The physio sat me down and said I could have an operation to snip it. Apparently it then curls up, withdraws into the calf and stays out of harm's way. I'd be out for a while, but it would never bother me again.

There was another option: I could rupture it on purpose. I'd have to run flat out, knowing, even hoping, that suddenly it would snap. Something like subjecting myself to self-circumcision! A nightmare.

It didn't go in training, so I flew off for the race in Bratislava just to rupture the tendon and get on with my career. It was my most bizarre race, running in the hope of suffering a serious injury. The starting gun went and I went out fast. Nothing. I was running well, I was winning. Into the back straight I was still leading, then . . . *phut!* It was like I had been shot in the leg by a sniper in the stands.

For all I was anticipating and willing it to happen, it came out of the blue. The tendon had snapped apart. Relief but excruciating pain at the same time. *What do I do now?*

I couldn't stop. That just seemed wrong. I'd come all this way, I was going to finish that race.

Somehow I ran on through the pain and came home in seventh place. Self-mutilation in Bratislava. Just one more desperate attempt to get fit again . . .

---

You read of those people who get trapped and cut their own arms off and think: *How desperate must someone be to inflict that kind of torture on yourself?* That was the situation I'd been in; trapped by the injury and desperate enough to take drastic measures. Back in the hotel that night, I was in such pain that I couldn't sleep. I lay on the bed. *You've done the right thing – everything's going to be cool. Don't worry.*

I was wrong. Back in the UK, a scan showed me I'd been unlucky. And only partly ruptured it – neither one thing nor another. Now I was going to have the surgery anyway.

The world of injury can be a desperate and strange place. I was willing to take any advice or tips. 'You should go out to Germany and see this guy, Healing Hans,' Linford Christie said to me. 'He'll have you up and running in no time.' Linford had torn his hamstring at the World Championships in Gothenburg in 1995 and this doctor had got him back running 10 days later.

He was talking about Doctor Müller-Wohlfahrt, who had been the Bayern Munich and German football team doctor for years. He had become a go-to medic for sporting superstars and celebrities, with clients ranging from Michael Jordan, Usain Bolt and Diego Maradona to Bono and Pavarotti. When I flew out to Munich to meet him for the first time, I walked into the waiting room in this unassuming building on a Monday morning and found, already seated, Colin Jackson, Paula Radcliffe and Boris Becker. Müller-Wohlfahrt really was the doctor to the stars.

Müller-Wohlfahrt mixed conventional methods with homeopathic treatment, a whole lot of massage and some weird stuff. It was controversial and a lot of medical experts dismissed his methods as hocus-pocus, insisting that his success basically relied on a placebo effect that was due to his mythical status. But he had a track record as long as your arm and, having spent years on treatment tables, I was ready to try just about anything. I spent a lot of time and money going back and forwards to Munich.

Back then in Britain, dealing with muscle injuries basically was all focused on RICE – Rest, Ice, Compress, Elevate. The Germans, way ahead of the game, preferred a lot of heavy massage. Müller-Wohlfahrt was on to that and a whole lot more. His rule of thumb was: 'If you can get to me within 24 hours of tearing your hamstring, I will bleed you out.'

First of all, I lay there in my pants as he pummelled me to within an inch of my life. It felt more like he was trying to end my career than save it. He hit so hard and dug so deep, I felt like his fist was going to come out the other side. I'd never had treatment like it.

Then came the injections, or 'infiltrations' as he called them. With a huge syringe he pumped Actovegin, basically calves' blood, into the area around the hamstring. At one point I had 36 needles sticking into me. Then, he fixed me up to an IV drip containing a mix of homeopathic preparations and vitamins like magnesium and zinc. Bizarre.

Many people had warned me about him, and among their many reasons was that he made you see a physio who liked you to go naked. I was relieved that hadn't been part of the treatment and guessed they'd been having me on. But when Müller-Wohlfahrt had finished with me, he sent me across Munich on a train to see this mad physio.

This guy put me on the bed and said: 'Calvin Kleins off!'

I said, 'Sorry?'

'Knickers off!'

I lay there naked and this geezer put on a rubber glove. I was open-mouthed.

'Whoah, what's happening?'

'Me no English.'

With that, he plugged his glove into a machine and started massaging my belly. What I discovered he was doing was draining the lymphatic system.

Müller-Wohlfahrt was like no other doctor I'd encountered. When I first met him, he looked like Keanu Reeves. 'He's 65, you know,' someone said to me. I was like, 'No way. He looks about 30.' I sometimes see him on TV now. He's in his eighties but has a full jet-black head of hair and looks so young. Maybe he's found some potion for eternal youth.

The treatment was controversial back in the early 2000s. Actovegin had even been banned by the International Olympic Committee around the Sydney Olympics in 2000, but the ban was lifted within months when it was discovered to have no performance-enhancing potential. It all seemed so weird at the time, but now, of course, it is commonplace in Britain.

Back at home, I saw Bryan English, at Chelsea FC's training ground in Cobham. Bryan had been the Team GB doctor, and had latched onto Müller-Wohlfahrt's methods quite quickly. He'd adopted the tough physio and herbal injections too. Jesus, they were painful and I had to go four or five times. You can't knock it, though. I went from not being able to walk after tearing a hamstring to being back on the track two weeks later. It was some kind of miracle cure.

Could I have avoided the injuries? Maybe. If I had been less bullish about training. If Mike had been a more sensitive coach. If I'd been based somewhere like Loughborough with fantastic medical resources. If I had been less impatient to get back to the track. But even then I might just have been average. After all the injuries, the best I ran was 45.5. Most 400 metres runners have never run that quick, but it was a second slower than those at the very top, and that just wasn't good enough for me. Would I swap all I won in 1998 for a 10-year athletics career with nothing to show for it? Absolutely no chance.

At the tail end of my career, when I was injured at Loughborough, my main training partner was Chris Rawlinson, a 400 metres hurdler. He had Commonwealth golds (including beating the Wales team with me in it in the 4 × 400m) to his name. Together we went to see a British Athletics physio named Dean Kenneally, a tall, clean-cut guy and a typical Aussie, always full of jokes and piss-taking. As we entered his office, he was busy on the phone. He looked up at the two of us, smiled and announced down the phone in his broad Aussie accent: 'I've got to go, mate. Just walked in are a has-been and a never-will-be.'

Brutal, but at least I had been something.

# 5.00am. 16 June 2021

*I'd been OK 10 minutes ago. I'd got through the 70-mile checkpoint. I've got this, I thought. I convinced myself that it was going to get easier after that. All downhill from here.*

*Then I turned a corner to face the biggest bastard of a hill I'd encountered on the run. Gene Thibeault, ultrarunner and author, once said: 'If you start to feel good during an ultra, don't worry, you will get over it.'*

*In disbelief, desperation and ridiculous optimism I scanned the way ahead for a signpost directing me down some other route. Nope. That was where I was going: up. Up the path that wound its way to the very top. What was that? Half a mile? A mile?*

*My body was like a sulking child, dragging its feet as I hauled it up the hill. I was halfway up a stretch with a 60 or 70 per cent gradient and bent over double with my back, shins, calves and ankles screaming at me. I hadn't just given up running, I'd now given up walking: I was on all fours. Crawling up a monster of a hill that was out to kill me. My knees were getting scratched and cut by the chalk and flinty path, and with no shade at all I could feel the sun burning through to my back.*

*'Get up,' I shouted to myself. 'Get up and walk. Just another few hundred metres. Please!'*

# Fourteen

# DOG DAYS

Alexander Stadium, Birmingham, 2007: I'm just taking it all in. Smiling from ear to ear, waving furiously, stopping to chat and have a laugh. I'm on my last lap of honour, having run my final race before my retirement. The crowd are on their feet applauding and shouting. Friends, fellow athletes, family, celebrities, they have all come to give me a send-off and salute the finest quarter-miler this country has ever seen. Iwan Thomas, Olympic Champion, World Champion, the man who had broken his own British record three times . . .

In my dreams . . .

I had plenty of time to daydream after 1999 as my sporting dreams slowly fell apart. How might my life have gone if I had been able to race to my full potential? I am in absolutely no doubt I could have beaten my British record. OK, beating Michael Johnson, who ran 43.84 to take gold in the Sydney 2000 Olympics, might be stretching the imagination a little, but 44.39 would have won me a silver. After 2001, there was no Johnson and so . . .

. . . and so it went on with the what ifs and the maybes.

Things came to a head by 2002. It had finally dawned on me that I was never going to reach those 1998 highs again. No one else in Britain was doing that or anything like it either. Daniel Caines had a PB of 44.98 but no one else was near the 44.5 mark. I was still ranked in the top five 400 metres athletes in the country and, if I stayed clear of a major injury, I believed I could still compete.

However, if I was to get back to something like my best possible form, I had to make some changes. Southampton wasn't equipped for an athlete in my physical condition. My body needed more attention, I needed to be able to step off the track and get a massage or take an ice bath. I couldn't face another winter training alone or sitting at home waiting for an injury to heal. Even when I was fit enough to join the sessions, I found that the love of training which had once driven me had now dissipated.

It was a massive decision for me to split with Mike after all he had done for me. He had taken me to levels beyond my dreams. His training schedule had been perfect for me and when I was injury-free he had brought me to peak fitness at exactly the right time. We had an odd but close relationship. He played the father figure down to a T and was encouraging, disappointed, angry, proud, reassuring and no-nonsense in equal measures. Meanwhile, and just as often, I moved from being Jack the Lad to eager-to-please, vulnerable and sulky to totally driven. We were made for each other.

I hated thinking he might be disappointed in me. I wasn't moving on or rejecting him, I never would. I was just desperate to find some way to full fitness, a need for change. As they say, it wasn't him, it was me.

Mike understood. He'd seen what I was going through and was totally on board. I think I'd been the bonus for him, the icing on the cake of a great career, and he knew as well as I did that we had come to an end. Whether it was his age or my troubles, he had lost his enthusiasm too. Hardly surprising; he'd spent 50 years giving his heart and soul.

I had considered switching coaches and locations before. Especially after hearing that Michael Johnson trained differently to the 400 metres runners in Britain. He'd do lots of short quick stuff like 25 × 60 metres. That always intrigued me. In 2000, I was on an Olympic recce for British Athletics out on the Gold Coast in Australia when I bumped into Johnson filming a Nike promo on the beach. He was there with Clyde Hart, his long-time coach. I approached Hart about becoming my coach, thinking it was a way to re-energise my training. He seemed pretty receptive to the idea, but pretty soon it became apparent that Johnson – who was always guarded about his training – wasn't keen and that was the end of that plan! I also considered joining Mark Richardson and the others at Windsor, but didn't feel I could do that to Mike and the idea never got off the ground.

So, I went to Loughborough to train with Nick Dakin. He was a top 400 metres coach, a big, softly spoken guy with plenty of experience and a great reputation. His training group included top athletes like the 400 metres hurdler Chris Rawlinson, the Jamaican hurdler Kemel Thompson and the talented 800 metres runner Mark Sesay. Just like in Southampton, I used their strengths to help me; Mark was strong on the longer runs, while Chris was an animal in training who gave it everything and pushed me so hard. Sean Baldock, although not part of the group, regularly came to train with us.

I called Nick 'The Shadow'. He was always there. If you didn't see him, you might think, *What's he got us doing 3 × 300m reps for?* Then you looked round and he was right behind you. In fact, he was everywhere, it was freaky! Out of nowhere, he'd appear, holding his stopwatch. Nick wasn't like Mike – he really didn't know how to handle my ADHD, my moods, jokes and energetic personality – but he managed to get me into the best condition I'd been in for some time.

To go from training at Southampton with its half-built stadium and no toilets to the Loughborough high-performance centre was a real eye-opener. The facilities were something else: two different gyms, state-of-the art indoor and outdoor tracks and fantastic medical rooms. I was able to get treatment twice a week from a specialist medical team and a massage after training, and sports scientists tested my lactic levels and gave biomechanical advice.

*What might have happened if I'd been accepted to study there when I was 18?* That thought crossed my mind more than once. And it wasn't just me wondering, either.

George Gandy, the legendary British endurance running coach and director of athletics at Loughborough, was one of many who brought it up. 'How come you never came to university here?'

'Because you dickheads rejected me!'

'What!'

I settled into the winter training, which resembled Mike's programme with perhaps a little more gym work. I wasn't expecting an overnight resurrection of my career. I wasn't going to be running 44.5 – the gold medal/world record level – any time soon, but the Olympic Games in Athens in 2004 seemed a reasonable ambition. However, I was running surprisingly well as the 2003 season got underway and, well, just maybe the World Championships in Paris were a possibility?

In Norway, at the end of June 2003, I ran under 46 seconds and in Florence, just a month before the trials, I clocked 45.58 – the fastest I had run since the Kuala Lumpur final in 1998. And it was the quickest British 400 metres so far that year. A week before the trials, I ran well again with 45.78 in Madrid – just outside the World Championship qualifying time of 45.55. Like they say, it's the hope that kills you . . .

In Birmingham, I made the final and fancied my chances, if not of finishing in the top two, then of coming in under the qualifying time. It was possible, I just had to repeat that Florence run. Then the gun went and almost immediately I felt the searing pain in my Achilles. I was despondent but struggled on, searching for that inner force that once seemed so powerful. It was futile. I came home last. Yet another false dawn.

'If I don't run 44.8 next year, I'm going to retire,' I told the *Daily Telegraph* at the end of 2003. I ran 46.52 in California in April, but that was about as good as it got. I didn't get out of the heats in the British Championships. The Athens Olympics – my hoped-for last hurrah, the one competition I had been hanging on for – came and went. And the year got worse. I damaged my plantaris tendon soon after, and that was that. I ended up entering that race in Bratislava in order to tear the muscle. And, as you know, that didn't work.

Despite my declarations to the press, my own ever-lower expectations and an increasing sense of futility, I soldiered on. It's easy with hindsight to wonder just what I was expecting to happen. Brendan Gallagher nailed it in an article for the *Daily Telegraph* in 2002: 'Thomas goes from glory to a horror story,' said the headline. Gallagher himself wrote, 'If Thomas was a boxer you would throw the towel in. It's too painful to watch any more. But Thomas is the proudest of men . . . Hyperactive by nature, workaholic by inclination and fretful by temperament, nobody could have tried harder. Perhaps that has been the mistake.'

---

'Do you want to be an athlete or be a celebrity?'

It was late 2005, the off-season. Nick Dakin crossed his arms and looked me in the eye.

It was a fair question. I'd just told him that I'd agreed to be in a TV show. It had been such a shit year, I'd just had an operation on my Achilles, I was limping and feeling I was fighting an uphill battle to even compete on the track, so the slog of winter training had lost its appeal. Instead I could be pampered in a TV studio and put up in a swanky hotel. Earning good money. The decision wasn't difficult.

There was something else: I was 32. Not some fresh-faced kid who'd had his head turned by a soft option. Ultimatums from Nick just wouldn't cut it any more. However much I had dragged it out, my athletics career wasn't going to last much longer; it was time to explore my options. I'd been kicked in the nuts one time too many by athletics, and wasn't prepared to take it any more.

I offered my hand out and said, 'Thanks, Nick, it's been great.'

After over three years there, that was Loughborough and myself finished. I'd done everything right there. I'd done the tests, rested when told and followed the coaches' instructions. And still it had got me nowhere. Time to go home.

After finishing the TV show, I was back in Southampton. I went round to see Mike. I'd always stayed in touch with him. He was my anchor. 'I know it's over,' I told him as we sat in his front room. 'But I just want to give it one last go.' Mike had his doubts. He worried about my commitment and my focus, not to mention my fitness, but my enthusiasm and optimism went into overdrive. How could he resist? Soon we were planning it all out, like two old cons planning one last heist.

The previous August, Jamie Baulch had announced his retirement. I still wasn't ready to quit and had been given a place in the Welsh team in the 2006 Commonwealth Games. I'd made the 4 × 400 metres squad and still had a chance of running in the individual. It was my last chance and I was prepared to do anything to remind people just who I was.

'OK,' he said. 'You come back to Southampton. There will be no media, no personal appearances or nights on the town, your arse is mine, right?' And it was. I quietly got on with my training and – amazing! – I was running injury-free. It really felt like I had finally turned a corner. *This is it*, I told myself. *This is for real. Win and walk away.* In my head, it was that simple.

The Commonwealth Games were taking place in Melbourne that year and were scheduled preseason in March. I hadn't raced at all yet but had done some trial runs, and I was quick. Like I had gone back six, seven years. I was in great shape. For once everything seemed to have fallen into place at the right time as I went out for my last training session with Mike, 10 days before I was due to fly out to acclimatise in Australia.

Towards the end of the session we were doing 80m reps and I felt a slight twinge. Nothing much, but why risk it?

'Ah, Mike? My hamstrings feel pretty tight.'

'You'll be alright. You've only got two runs left.'

There was no argument. There never was. I went back to the start line. Midway through the very next rep, it tore. There were no words. My mind went blank and my heart sank. Disbelief, anger, self-pity, utter resignation, all welled up inside. I sat in the car and the tears fell.

I've still got that Commonwealth Games kit in the loft somewhere. I never took it out of the bag.

I didn't retire. I just couldn't bring myself to utter those words. I hadn't been able to walk away with my head held high. I never had that final hurrah or an emotional send-off. I never had the chance to say goodbye – to the people, the fans, the sport. I just fizzled out. The pain of that didn't, though. It became the hardest thing to live with.

---

*You're lying. You're scared and can't face the truth.* Those thoughts would taunt me. Every time I posted a time I couldn't bear to look at, every time I came away from the physio, every time I fronted up to the press, every time I lay on my bed and thought about the future. *This is so much worse than everyone thinks*, barked the voice in my head. *You're not coming back. Not now, not ever.* I shut it out. I couldn't face that. I had reached such heights in 1998 and been so sure that this was just the beginning. It was obvious that I would be going to a level that no British runner had ever reached, and I had a few good years to get better and better. I was in my mid-twenties, and time was on my side. In 1986, Roger Black had broken the British record and won the Europeans, and then he missed three years due to injury. He came back and won again four years later. If he could do it, then why shouldn't I?

At first, it was about focus. I just had to get fit. That was all that counted. If I was on crutches, sitting watching endless TV or jogging slowly around the track, unable to train properly, that was just part of the process. But as time went on, the reality began to eat away at my soul. Maybe I had too much time to think. I wasn't a great one for self-reflection, but when you've got no training, no competition, no appearances and bugger all else to concentrate on, your mind does start to wander.

To the outside world I was still happy-go-lucky Iwan. Laughing and joking, going out and still trying to be the life and soul. It was what I did, and it was hollow. I was exhausted keeping up a pretence that everything was fine. It wasn't. I was living a lie, and hurting. It burrowed away at my self-esteem. Who was the real me? The guy who trained like a beast, ran 44.36 and scared the great Michael Johnson? Or the one who could train only three days a week and struggled to run a sub-46 and make the top three in the British Championships? I pretended I was the first of those for so long, that soon I was going to be that fast again. To do otherwise was to rip my soul apart.

As much as I could endure untold physical pain, I was simply unable to cope with the emotional pressure in the ensuing years. I certainly wasn't going to admit to anyone that I was feeling down.

For a start, I was to all appearances an alpha male: a big, tough guy who took this kind of thing on the chin. In the tunnel at races, I had been the one staring people out – no one wanted to catch my eye. Even people I got along with, like Mark Richardson. I gave them all a look that said, 'You don't want this as much as me, do you?' I never showed weakness – ever. And I wasn't about to start.

Then there were my mates. I didn't train with professional athletes; my training partners were down-to earth guys. They were never successful enough to make a living from running and they worked hard for a living. I couldn't go to them and say I was getting depressed about my situation. I was still a celebrity and I was earning a decent living as an athlete. They were struggling with mortgages and had every right to look at my car and my luxury four-bedroom townhouse in the nice part of town and say, 'Yeah, tell us some more about your problems, Iwan.'

Of course, I know now that they wouldn't have reacted like that. I should have talked to them. They would have listened, and it would have helped.

I still saw Mike regularly. With a cup of tea we put the world to rights. We never discussed injuries or my career. It was an unwritten rule that we didn't talk about athletics, and that was the same with most of my friends – it was just somewhere we didn't go.

I didn't talk to my parents or my girlfriend either. I didn't know how to begin. I didn't want to admit to them that what had been was as good as it was ever going to be. Everything had gone wrong. How might they understand what I was feeling? And what were they meant to say?

Instead I shut myself away. I internalised my fears, bitterness and hurt and it did me no good. At times I struggled to get out of bed and life was a zombie existence. Many of those days are a blur. Moping around the house. Going through the motions. Doing household chores with no thought or purpose. Watching a film and not really taking in what was going on or reading a newspaper or a magazine with absolutely no interest.

I didn't like myself any more. I didn't like the person I had become – bitter, frustrated and negative – but couldn't see any way out. I was so angry. I was angry with the sport that had done this to me and angry with my body that had let me down at the worst possible time. Pyschologists call it embitterment, a feeling of being betrayed and not being able to do anything about it. Generally this is true of those who have lost loved ones or whose relationships have come to an end, but I had lost my identity, my career and my drive and saw no way of getting it back. I was no longer *Iwan Thomas – athlete*, I was just *Iwan Thomas* – whoever the fuck he was.

There were some really dark times when I couldn't stop sobbing, numb for hours on end and/or unable to get out of bed. Many of those moments are just a blur now, but one incident in particular stays in my mind. I had been home alone, watching athletics on TV, probably the European or World Championships. I wasn't a drinker at home, but this time I got the whisky out. And I started crying. I went out into the night, taking the bottle with me and walking down to the Solent. I sat on this platform about 20 metres high, staring down into the dark waters. When I finally finished it, I threw the empty bottle in and watched it splash, then sink. I sat there for ages, fixated on where it had disappeared and thought, *That's what I want to do, disappear.* It took all my strength to stop myself from jumping in.

For quite a few years after I finished, I 100 per cent hated athletics. I'd keep up with the 400 metres, but found it difficult to stomach watching championships on TV or going to race meetings. I thought it was a cruel and vindictive sport. I had put so much effort into being the best athlete I could possibly be, and it had spat me out. And, as ludicrous as it now sounds to me, I even hated the athletes. They had escaped my torment and they still had a career. I was scornful and resented seeing people I still regarded as lesser athletes than me running in GB vests.

Those feelings were still evident in 2012 when London hosted the Olympics. I was working trackside and interviewing athletes and all the time thinking, *You lucky fuckers. You do not know how lucky you are to be at a home Olympics, at the prime of your career.* I'd have given anything for 1998 to have been the London Olympics. How great would that have been? Maybe I could have given up more easily if I'd had that kind of high? It wasn't anything personal against those athletes. They deserved to be there. It was pure jealousy and self-pity, but it was eating me up.

Being loved and liked was life blood to me. I thrived on being appreciated, whether it was for being helpful and decent, for making people laugh or for being good at what I did. I had always sought approval and in sport had found a means to earn it. Originally it came from my dad, then from my friends, from Mike, from people in athletics, from spectators and, eventually, from the general public. Coming through customs on the way home from a competition and having one of the officers tap me on the shoulder and say: 'Loved watching you beat those Americans last night' made me feel 10 feet tall.

Success gave me a shield. It gave me the confidence to express my personality publicly. I could be effervescent, jokey, opinionated and even slightly risqué or controversial. That's who I am, but it was so much easier to show that side of me when I was a winner. I could chirp up with silly comments and people were more likely to say: 'He's a right character, that Iwan Thomas' rather than 'Who does that bloke think he is?' I was successful and people wanted to like me.

*Was.* Was successful.

Without athletics, what?

I missed the buzz, the spurt of adrenaline of racing and I missed the pain of training. I desperately wanted to drive my body so hard that I had to puke. What I was feeling did hurt so much, but this was different. A suffocating, anti-energy that could never replace the agony of the burn and extreme fatigue of lactic acid.

---

Athletics was so central to my identity. To most people outside of my family and close friends, it was who I was and was my way of communicating. All through those years after 1998, I carried in my head a stopped timer. Stopped with my fastest time illuminated in big numbers. That defined me. And now 45.9, 46.6, 47.4 – every extra fraction of a second chipped away at my self-worth.

I had no idea what else I could do. When I called my parents and spoke with bravado, they tiptoed around the conversation, anxious not to upset me. They knew the future was a no-go zone.

Pretty much everyone else did too. No one said, 'Don't worry, you'll be OK. There will be plenty of work for someone like you.' I just couldn't imagine any kind of future.

I had a degree in Sports Science, and I knew I wasn't an obvious candidate for an office.

I was finding it all so hard to deal with, and it took until 2011 for me to do something. My agent, Sue, prompted me to see a counsellor. She was one of the only people I felt I could tell what I was going through. I rejected her suggestion at first. I'm not the first sportsman – or, come to that, the first man – to be reluctant to reveal any weakness and embarrassed about having mental health issues. It was a secret I held for years.

Eventually, though, I made an appointment with a therapist recommended by Sue. They were based in Harley Street, London, and I drove up feeling nervous, slightly worried about being spotted by the press or someone I knew and with no idea what was going to happen.

It wasn't easy at first. I found it difficult to talk about issues that seemed totally unrelated to how I felt. When she asked about sporting achievements and disappointments, I was fine. When we got onto my family, my schooldays, my relationships, my emotions, I clammed up. It took a while for me to open up, but eventually I was able to sit and talk about my life and my thoughts for an hour. I felt comfortable talking to a stranger. We went through everything, right back from being left at boarding school to not having any closure on my career.

It was all fine, but in my head nothing changed. I still felt lost, empty and full of self-pity. I was stuck in neutral. After a year of paying a fortune in petrol, counselling fees, parking, the congestion charge, I decided that I'd had enough. 'I'm sorry. I'm wasting your time and definitely wasting my money. It's not working.'

'It will work. It will suddenly click.'

'Well, it hasn't clicked yet and I don't think it's about to.'

With that I left. I'd tried it and it wasn't for me. *It is what it is*, I thought. *I'm a crocked has-been who needs to be a bit tougher.* Six months or so later, it dawned on me that things we had talked about were still floating round in my head. I thought about my desperate need to achieve and to be valued, my restlessness and physicality, and I understood now that these had all been satisfied by the training, competition and the prestige of athletics. The therapist had been right; it clicked. I came to understand more about how I had come to be this person and began to work out how I could still be me, but not an athlete.

By 2013, a good 18 months after my first counselling session, I'd met and was seeing Anna. I was ready to like myself again. Taking on media work and being recognised for something other than athletics played a part too, but learning to live with myself, my achievements and my disappointments still took time.

Having not gone back for years, I returned to the BBC Sports Personality of the Year ceremony, over 10 years after I had been a runner-up. This was the year that Ryan Giggs won and I was seated in the front row next to Phil 'The Power' Taylor, the darts player who dominated his sport for two decades. The boxer David Haye made a beeline for me to shake my hand, but what astonished me was to be recognised and greeted by so many of the stars there: David Beckham, who was late, came past and stopped to say: 'Alright, Iwan!' like I was an old friend. This was recognition from some great sportsmen and women; I was remembered! I'd had a short time at the top, but like a firework I'd shone brightly while I was there.

I was 23 when I broke the British record and 24 when my career began unravelling. I was so young, some might say vulnerable, and the up, then the down all happened so fast. I was in no position to cope. I lacked the emotional resolve, as well as the confidence to reach out for help, wallowing instead in anger and bitterness. It took time and help for me to come to realise that I had achieved something and made an impression.

Now it was time to move on.

In the summer of 2016, I was invited to an event hosted by Heads Together, an initiative spearheaded by the Royal Foundation of the Prince and Princess of Wales, to tackle stigma and change the conversation on mental health. Somehow, I found myself flipping burgers with Prince Harry (not a sentence I ever thought I'd write!). I dropped a burger on the ground, put it back on the barbecue and joked that I was going to say he'd done it. We were soon having a bit of a laugh.

Maybe it was the right time, the reason we were there, but suddenly I opened up to him. For the first time ever, I was talking about the dark clouds that had shrouded my life for nearly 10 years and I was opening my heart to a prince – a guy I had never met before. I certainly hadn't planned it, but it felt good to get it out there and support a campaign that expressed so much about what I had been through.

# Fifteen

# CELEBRITY ANYTHING

'You've done alright, you have.'

'What d'you mean?'

'You're 1 per cent of the 1 per cent.'

I couldn't just walk on after that. 'Yeah?'

'Yeah. Think about it. Probably 1 per cent of the population make it to the level you did in sport. And, only 1 per cent of those are still relevant 20 years later.'

It was just a bloke I happened to be passing while walking my dog, but it made me think. Things like that helped give me a lift when I needed it. Maybe 'relevant' was pushing it a bit, but I took it. Among my contemporaries on the track, I'm one of few still keeping busy on TV. I'm still out there.

A man's got to make a living. That's how it all began. I hadn't had a proper job since Next. The athletics had seen me alright. It was simple: get fit, run fast, earn money. I never earned footballer-level sums, but I was doing pretty well. I ran into Kriss Akabusi once when things were really going well and had just had my first ever tax bill: over £50,000 and I was stunned. How could I owe that much? I stopped Busi as he passed and told him. He didn't even stop. He laughed and said just how many more times that his own tax bill was! I thought, *Hey, it wasn't meant to be a boast.* But it did get me thinking how much I might earn . . .

When the phone stops ringing, your sponsorships begin to run down and there's precious little sign of winning race money, you begin to wonder where the next cheque will come from. That's where I had got to by the beginning of the 2000s. I was still doing OK – I'd always been super-savvy about money – but the future was approaching fast. Maybe it had all come too easily, and now I could see it coming to an end just as quickly.

I'd already turned down some interesting offers. I was offered a mouth-watering sum to run the London Marathon in 1998 and was sorely tempted. I loved a challenge and, well, the fee, whoah!

When I told Mike about it, he just laughed. 'It'll ruin your career,' he warned.

'But I wanna do it,' I whined.

He was right of course. And I knew he was. It would have totally screwed my best ever year.

A few years later, there was talk of me playing for the Cardiff Blues rugby team. Again, it was an interesting challenge, but at that point I still believed I could make it back to the top in athletics. Besides, I'd been through enough pain already. Being hit full on – and from all sides – by 100 kg (16 stone) of muscle seemed to be pushing things a little too much.

Around 2003, I was driving down the M3 when my phone rang. It was a call from a number I didn't recognise.

'Hi! Is that Iwan?'

The line wasn't great.

'Yes. Speaking.'

'How you doing?'

'Yeah great, how are you?'

The guy was chatty and seemed to know me and, not wanting to be rude, I played along with the small talk.

'I'll get to the point,' he said eventually. 'I've got a fantastic script. It's going to be a blockbuster – just perfect for you.'

I was a bit confused, but eager not to throw away an opportunity. I said, 'A blockbuster? That's great.'

'I'll send it to your agent then,' he concluded and we swapped our cheery goodbyes.

Excited and a little confused, I rang Sue straightaway.

'What is this about? Is this my chance,' I gabbled. 'You've got to call him back now.'

She did. And then came back to me, laughing as she spoke. The movie was indeed a big deal (it was *Big Fish*, which would win BAFTAs and Golden Globes), but the guy thought he was calling Ewan McGregor not Iwan Thomas. Damn, just my luck.

In the end, the offer I did take up was pretty physical too. In 2005, just after I had Achilles surgery, ITV approached me to do a show called *Celebrity Wrestling*. It was scheduled for prime-time Saturday night viewing for 10 weeks. It was similar to the *Gladiators* series, which I had enjoyed watching, and it sounded like fun, but I was still recovering from the operation and didn't think I was up to any physical activity. When I told them as much, they said that there was still a couple of weeks before the trials with their trainer Stuart Taylor. He was going to be testing various celebrities to see if they had what it takes to be a wrestler. What did I have to lose?

I went along to the studios. I told them I'd had surgery less than a month ago and that I would have to go easy on my foot. I would be able to give it only 40, maybe 50 per cent.

I should have known I wouldn't find it possible to do that. I tried to take it easy, but that wasn't in my nature. As the film and the casting crew looked on, I hobbled around on one leg and practically ripped Stuart's head off.

I was still training in Loughborough at the time, and they weren't impressed when I told them I was taking time off for a TV show. That was when Nick Dakin asked me if I was serious about being an athlete. It was a fair question. I was disillusioned. I'd been worn down by the injuries and disappointed that

Loughborough had been unable to end that cycle. I wasn't able to train much anyway for months, so why not take an eight-week break?

I wrestled as 'The Dragon' and had a fantastic costume: black trousers with flames down the side and a cape with dragons on each shoulder breathing out dry ice. The show was tacky and cheesy and fun, with 'Rowdy' Roddy Piper hyping it up as the in-your-face MC. We did get good ratings in the first week, but on the second we were up against the return of *Doctor Who* on the BBC. By episode five we were relegated to a Sunday morning graveyard slot.

The actual wresting was surprisingly aggressive, several celebs having to stand down after getting injured. I had some tough head-to-heads. Particularly gruelling was the head-to-head with the military-trained James Hewitt, aka 'Gentleman Jim', in the semi-final.

The show was roundly panned, but I really enjoyed it. I'd had a taste of TV and I liked it.

Without ever knowing how it might happen, I had always felt that television was a possible route for me after athletics. I felt comfortable in front of the cameras and the public generally seemed to take to me. It made me feel wanted again and I was well suited for many of those celebrity shows: ultra-competitive, never shying away from a challenge and having an energy and a sense of fun.

If anything helped me get over the darkness that permeated my life after athletics, it was the TV work. It wasn't as intense as running for your country, but it spoke to many aspects of my personality – the adrenaline-seeking, the sociability, the competitive spirit, the search for identity – which I had been so badly missing.

I was up for *Celebrity* anything. Having endured one nightmare of a sudden collapse of a career, I was going to make hay while the sun shone. I was fortunate enough to find a great agent in Sue Barrett. She not only spotted and created opportunities for me, but through the years she has really looked after me.

I took on whatever was on offer and gave it my all. I did *Ready Steady Cook, A Question of Sport, Through the Keyhole, Superstars, Brainiac: Science Abuse, Tool Academy, So You Think You Can Be A Single Parent* and a load more that I've managed to put to the back of my mind. OK, some were less enjoyable than others, but I had a great laugh. Especially *Car Duels* where Steve Redgrave and I raced each other in Reliant Robins and *Celebrity Stars in Their Eyes*, when I went on as Chris Martin and sung Coldplay's 'The Scientist'. Who'd have thought the boy who was too nervous to stand up and read to the class would sing on TV? It was pretty nerve-wracking, but I loved putting myself through that.

It's easy to say now that I should have been more discerning. People were probably saying: 'Oh no, it's that athlete bloke again', and I do now regret doing some of the, well, lower-budget programmes. But I was throwing myself into a new life, learning as I went along and searching for an identity that wasn't just a clapped-out athlete. And in the meantime, it was paying the bills.

*Celebrity MasterChef* was excellent. I was as nervous as I had ever been on the track when I signed up for the show. The kitchen was a foreign country to me. I was hardly able to boil an egg. So I was pretty pleased with my second place. I went one better in *Deadline*. That was a celebrity journalist competition where we competed to put a magazine together. I spent six weeks as a paparazzi photographer and writer, covering gossip and celebrities. I managed to survive to the final and was genuinely chuffed to hear Chief Editor Janet Street-Porter utter the words 'Iwan, you can hack it!' Especially as I was given a cheque for £50,000, some of which immediately went on a Ducati 1098 motorcycle that I'd promised myself.

In 2012, I got a great break. I received a call from *The One Show*, which was looking to do a feature about heart defects among sportsmen and women. A study had come out saying that something like 40 per cent of extreme athletes had caused irreversible damage to their hearts. The BBC sent me up to Liverpool John Moores University, where I interviewed some doctors and then had my own heart tested. They seemed pleased with how I came across and the feature went down well, so I was asked to come back and do more.

'We've got a job in Scotland. Can you leave now and we'll be filming tomorrow?'

'Yeah, yeah. I'm on it. I'm on my way.'

These commissions were not money-spinners, at least not sums I was used to: a long day, maybe stretching to two, three minutes of final film and I'd be paid £500. Not superstar rewards, but nice work, and I was getting it. I'd joke to my mates that I was off on another 'Scotland 500'. *But*, I'd be thinking whenever they called, *it's* The One Show, *and if I don't do it someone else will and they might never call back.* So I'd jump at the chance.

It was prime-time BBC and gave me real credibility as a presenter. I ended up doing a 10-year stint on the show. For a large part, I was a roving reporter. It wasn't just sports issues. I reported on amazingly random subjects. Travelling around the country, chatting to people, I felt I'd really fallen on my feet. One week it was a story on epilepsy, and the next I was baking bread in an old people's home or abseiling in a cave. I did so many cool things on that show. My biggest interview was with David Cameron in 2014. I think Dad was more proud of that than any of my athletics success. 'Ooh, I saw your son interviewing the Prime Minister on *The One Show*!'

TV work gave me a respect and self-worth that I thought I'd never find again. I was good at it, and I enjoyed it. I always loved being busy and now the phone was ringing again. In 2012, I was in such demand that I had only four days off all year. And earned more that year than I had at my peak as an athlete.

This gave me a route back into athletics too. In 2011 Channel 4 invited me onto their commentary team for the World Championships and a year later I was a pundit for them on the Paralympics in London 2012 – including the live closing ceremony. Around the same time, I started as the infield host at Indoor Diamond League Athletics meetings. It was so good to be back as a meaningful contributor in the arenas where I used to compete. I'd be there hyping the crowd up, introducing the athletes and interviewing all the stars. I originally stepped in only for a weekend, but they kept asking me back to do more, so I must have been doing something right.

Trackside, I felt at home straightaway. I might not have been running myself, but down among the athletes, all that tension and focus came back. I could feel what they felt so vividly. I'd have loved to be on those blocks next to them. I still get so much from the infield work, and the buzz from the crowd is just incredible. It can feel like a rock concert out there, when the crowd's excitement is at fever pitch. I've now hosted every World Championships since 2017. That's the longest stint anyone has ever had. It can be hard work with very long days, but I must have earned the respect of the organisers to keep being asked back.

The last 10 years really had been a whirlwind. And by now I'd finally emerged from those days of despondency, when I didn't know where my life was heading, what I was going to do or even who I was any more. I'm so grateful for the opportunities I was given on TV, especially on *The One Show*. They enabled me to feel good about myself; I had discovered that I was capable of doing something other than run fast. I had reinvented myself as a presenter and reporter, and I felt wanted in that role. A new generation didn't care or even know that I was once an athlete. I was sitting on a train minding my own business, when a child near me said to her mum, 'Look. There's that man from *MasterChef*!' Her mum pointed out that I had actually been a top athlete. For the first time in years I began to like myself.

TV, though, is a tough place for someone who thrives on being liked. I was used to athletics, where the public have their favourites. Ultimately that all depends on being successful. TV is different. Especially on 'reality' or celebrity shows. People like or loathe you for what often seemed the most illogical, ridiculous reasons. Some off-the-cuff comment you make, the way you do your hair, a look – or even just the cut of your jib. It is a fickle world and you can feel so exposed. Today, social media magnifies all that too. The negative comments can be really hurtful. You can get 99 nice comments, but it takes only one critical or abusive remark and it's back to feeling paranoid and insecure.

In 2015, I was filming a BBC series that I really enjoyed. Called *Natural Born Winners*, it featured former sportsmen in sprinter Donavan Bailey, rugby player Gareth Thomas, superbike champion James Toseland and me. We took on each other and local champions in lesser-known sports around the world. We filmed the first, a Man versus Horse fell run in Wales (I managed to tweak a hamstring while training for it – nothing changes!), and then went to Turkey to shoot an episode on Turkish oil wrestling. You can never say I wasn't up for a challenge!

It was while I was out there that I received a call from my agent. She immediately warned me not to respond to what she was going to say because she didn't want the crew there to realise what was happening. She then proceeded to hum the *Strictly Come Dancing* theme – the daddy of celebrity challenge shows. I had been so pleased when they first approached me and completed an interview before we began filming for *Natural Born Winners*, but I hadn't allowed myself to think it was going to happen. Now it was actually happening. *Wow.* Just *wow*.

The only problem was the timing. I'd already signed up for this series and still had episodes in India and Japan to film. What's more, I was now ensconced as the presenter on *Chequered Flag*, part of BT Sport's MotoGP coverage – what a job for someone who loves motorbikes as much as me! – and that required my attendance at races every other weekend. Still, busy was something that had never bothered me and I wanted to do *Strictly* so badly. I couldn't and I wouldn't turn it down.

As bad decisions go, it went about as well as the 1997 World Championships. It managed to ruin both shows. From that moment on I took my foot off the pedal in the *Natural Born Winners* challenges. Now I was scared of getting injured and blowing my *Strictly* chance, so I went at them far too cautiously. That isn't me. I have to give everything and I want to win. I hated not doing myself and the programme justice because it was really good fun and had the makings of an interesting series.

I was fully up for everything about *Strictly*, though, and went full-on camp. I was there in wardrobe asking if my trousers could be even tighter and if I could have extra sequins. It might have been a world away from wrestling with Donovan Bailey, but it was so interesting meeting people from different worlds. We were all in the same boat – intensely nervous about having to dance on TV.

Did I think I already looked good on the dance floor? I always thought I was alright. I was no John Travolta but no dad dancer either. As a teenager, I had fancied myself as a bit of a b-boy and could even remember a few breakdance moves. But dancing in front of millions on TV? I'd been on *Let's Dance for Sport Relief* back in 2010 in a group with Jamie and a few other Olympians – and I swore I'd never dance on television again. Now I'd put myself up for an even bigger challenge.

The *Strictly* experience was the best and worst TV experience I've had. I was so excited to be part of it. You start off doing a group dance together and that feeling of being part of a close-knit group of celebrities was immediate: I bonded with Jeremy Vine, Peter Andre and Ainsley Harriott straight away. The producers were watching us dance to see which professional they would select to dance with which celebrity. I struck up a good connection with both Karen and Natalie from the start and was convinced I would partner one of those two. So, I was pretty surprised when it was announced that I would be dancing with someone whose path I was yet to cross: Ola Jordan.

This was Ola's tenth series. She was popular with the public and had won the series with Chris Hollins in 2009. I was pretty chuffed to be selected to partner her. In fact, I was so hyped that when it was announced on the live show, I lifted Ola up on my back and caused her to have a small, but not revealing, wardrobe malfunction. A slightly embarrassing start and maybe an omen of things to come, but when we came off stage it was Ola who was apologetic. 'I'm so sorry.'

Those were her first words. I didn't understand. She was convinced that the show's producers were determined to get rid of her. They had sacked her husband the year before and now she made a good case to me explaining why they might not be happy with her. She had publicly criticised the pay differential between the dancers and judges; defied the show's bosses by releasing a steamy calendar which clashed with *Strictly*'s wholesome family image; and taken part in the Channel 4 celebrity winter sports series *The Jump*, tearing a ligament in her knee which prevented her from appearing in the finale of the previous season of *Strictly*.

I told her I was really happy that she was my partner. And I meant it. She was a great dancer and I was totally up for it, determined to do everything I could to give a good show of myself. It was ultimately down to the public. If we danced well enough, there wasn't much anyone could do about it. What could go wrong?

After discovering who our partners were, the competitors had three weeks to work on their opening dance – in my case a tango to 'Keep On Running'.

Trouble is, I had to fly straight off to Japan to film *Natural Born Winners*. I would get back with just two days' rehearsal time. Poor Ola had such little time to get me in shape for the dance. In both BMX and athletics, a natural talent had taken me a long way. My hope was that the same innate ability was about to kick in with my dancing. It was always going to be on a wing and a prayer.

To make matters worse, it had become common knowledge that I was cutting it fine. Peter Andre let the cat out of the bag in an interview with Nick

Grimshaw on Radio 1 saying, 'Iwan's a really nice lad, but he's up against it, he's only got two days to learn the dance.'

Stepping onto that dancefloor knowing I wasn't going to look good was probably the scariest thing I'd done.

The tango didn't go down well. OK, I know it wasn't great, but I thought the judges were harsh. There was a long list of criticisms and 'plodding' was mentioned more than once. I don't think any competitors have had such a reaction to their first dance. But the judges had heard that I had not had time to put in the full rehearsal and decided that I wasn't really committed to the show. They assumed that I wasn't taking it seriously, that I was only in it for the money.

We came second to bottom on the scoreboard and although there was no elimination until the following week, the judges had put down a marker: we were poor. It was always going to be an uphill battle from there, but their comments had struck home and I was determined to show what I could do.

This time it was the cha-cha-cha to the LMFAO hit 'Sexy and I Know It'. No matter how hard I wanted to succeed, learning that dance was so difficult. I had no problem with the fitness side, but I struggled with the concentration required to learn the steps and the timing. It soon dawned on me that I was not a natural on the dancefloor. And I hate being rubbish at anything. Getting the dance wrong was frustrating and infuriating. I was willing to work as long as it took to get it right, but we didn't have that time.

The dance, which featured me ripping my shirt open at the beginning and then later digging out some of my 25-year-old breakdancing moves, did not impress the public or the judges. I'd injured my hip flexor in rehearsal which didn't help, but that's no excuse. It wasn't good. We found ourselves in a dance-off with Jamelia and her partner Tristan MacManus and were unanimously voted off by the judges. We had the ignominy of being the first couple to leave the show.

Sensitivity to criticism and being ultra-competitive: the two traits don't sit together well and both took a massive blow on *Strictly*. The judges' scathing comments hurt. They really went for me. Len Goodman, the nice guy on the panel, started gently: 'You came out with so much aggression and so much attack that you lost your finesse.' Bruno Tonioli added: 'You went to the Neanderthal approach to the cha-cha and you smashed it to the point of extinction . . . That was murder.' And Craig Revel Horwood stuck the knife in: 'I just say that's 21½ hours' training wasted, sadly. It was stompy, unrhythmic, it didn't work.' Only Darcy attempted to soften the blow with some kinder words. I took it all to heart.

I know it is just a bit of fun, a light entertainment show, but I hated losing so badly. While I didn't think we deserved to be in the bottom two, I tried to take it on the chin. As soon as I saw we were pitted against Jamelia, I thought, *That's us out.* The only way I was ever going to get better was for us to stay in the competition for as long as possible. Even to this day it stings when people remind me that I was the first to go; it haunts me as a failure.

The public mainly agreed that my dancing might not have been the worst, but sure wasn't anywhere near the best. More than the judges, though, they gave me credit for giving it a go and keeping a smile on my face.

A couple of years later, the public were most definitely not on my side. *The Island with Bear Grylls* was a survival show: celebrities were dumped on a tropical island and left to fend for themselves. It was known as the most gruelling celebrity show ever, and that wasn't wrong. It was tough beyond words; the isolation, the discomfort and the hunger. I, and most of the others lost a lot of weight (in my case, over 13 kg/2 stone) in the first two weeks on the island.

I loved the challenge of overcoming those obstacles and relished the experience – until I got home. My agent had warned me beforehand: 'They are going to expect you to be the alpha male, chopping down trees and doing all the manly stuff. Don't be afraid to show your sensitive side.' I tried, but it didn't matter what I did. Producers can edit the programme to paint someone however they want, and so for the first three or four weeks I was the pantomime villain: domineering, patronising and a misogynist.

Here's one example. When Sharron Davies left the island, I was interviewed and said: 'I thought she'd leave. It's got to be tough for a 54-year-old woman who has had three operations on her back and is worried about her daughter.' When the show went out, the audience saw me saying, 'I thought she'd leave. It's got to be tough for a 54-year-old woman.'

When the show was broadcast, I was stunned and angry. I watched open-mouthed; that wasn't how I remembered it. But this was Iwan Thomas: what a sexist pig! They even created a montage, mostly edited and taken out of context, of what I had said. All this so they could eventually show me crying on the beach, saying I want to go home – which I did. The alpha male had been broken by the island: that was the narrative. I had been so naïve.

There were headlines slamming me and a social media pile-on. I was helpless to respond. I couldn't deny that I had said those things, there I was on screen. I'd watch it over and scream, 'But it wasn't like that!' It was pointless. I'd totally misjudged the show. I saw it as an adventure series and not a *Big Brother* spy camera that captures every unguarded moment and edits them to suit the storyline. All I could do was hold my hands up. I even had to go on *Good Morning Britain* and account for my behaviour. It was a salutary experience.

And it left me doubting myself. Was I the decent person I thought I was? What had I meant when I said that? Sport and television – they are different entities and when they cross it can be entertaining for viewers, but not great for the sportsmen. Professional sportsmen and women are self-programmed for winning. That's all. A single-track mindset. To outsiders it can come across as self-centred and arrogant. Of course, most aren't like that in life, and are as lovely, sensitive and caring as the next person. But most have a game-on switch, and I had switched mine on. I did things, said things that I regret. They didn't need to edit things down to show me being bullish and blokish. I swore the next time that, as much as I wanted to win, the switch would be off.

It took me a while before I could face anything like that again and I knew I was taking a risk when I signed up for *Hunted* in 2022. I couldn't hide away from these things forever. *Hunted* is a game show where pairs of competitors go on the run around the country, trying to elude expert detectives, hunters and hackers. It looked exciting and I knew I would enjoy partnering paralympic athlete Richard Whitehead. We made for a good team: he was calm and methodical, I was energetic and impulsive.

The show wasn't gruelling like *The Island*, but it was tough in its own way. Having to stay one step ahead of the hunters grinds you down mentally. You're on edge, and the feeling of paranoia is constant. It was such fun, though. And the generosity of the public was a real eye-opener. It's easy to forget how open and helpful most people can be, but having to rely on the kindness of strangers really brought it home.

It's so funny how differently you can be seen on TV. This time I recognised myself: that bloke who was fidgety and made rash decisions. A bit cheeky, a bit vulnerable and wanting to see the best in people – that was me. And it was also me who eventually turned that switch on when it was needed. I knew Jordan Wylie, the hunter who was chasing me at the embarkation point. He was always ribbing me about how he could beat me in a race. Having to beat him to the helicopter took me back to my running days – and there was no way he was going to win.

*Hunted* turned out to be the antidote to *The Island*. It was reaffirming and made me feel so much better about myself. The feedback from the public was incredible and two years later, people still message me to say how much they enjoyed the series.

Being someone and being recognised as someone is important to me. Yes, maybe it is just vanity or covering my insecurities, but it is part of who I am and there's no point denying it. Athletics put me on a stage and I loved it; the nerves, the challenge, the success and the acclaim. I lost it and missed it desperately, but I got a chance at the next best thing.

Being recognised can throw up some awkward situations, though. One of my favourites happened in 2020. I had been hosting an annual athletics meeting at the Olympic Park since 2017 and turned up to the Holiday Inn on the day before as usual. A bit knackered, I thought I'd have a couple of hours' sleep before meeting the others for dinner. I stripped down to my tight white pants, lay on top of the bed and drifted off. It seemed like hours later when I was woken by the sound of a key card in the door. I sat up and saw an elderly gentleman enter the room.

'Whoah! Who are you?' I blurted.

'I'm Iwan Thomas,' he said.

'No, I'M IWAN THOMAS,' I spluttered.

'I know you is,' he replied in a strong Welsh accent. 'We love you on the *One Show*.' At which point he ushered in his wife.

'Look Maureen, it's Iwan Thomas in his pants.'

It turned out, the usual reservation had been changed that year and instead I was booked in at a hotel around the corner. This fella just had the same name and a room on the same day. What are the chances of that?

I chose to work in TV in much the same way I chose athletics. It just happened and I happened to be quite good at it. I never knew what to expect; TV seemed like a such a different world with all the comfy sofas and air-kissing, but it turned out there are plenty of similarities. There's a lot of hanging round for a start. Filming can be nerve-wracking and you put yourself and your credibility on the line. And it's pretty cut-throat; there might not be a stopwatch, but there are execs, producers and directors out there who'll cut you out without flinching.

I like working in TV.

# Sixteen

# EVERYTHING CHANGES

All I could do was stare at him and will him to fight for life. To somehow transfer my strength to him. And yet, all I could think was that I was watching him die. To think that I'd willingly put myself through such pain as an athlete and thought nothing of it, even enjoyed it, yet here I was broken by something so much worse than any physical pain: heartbreak. It was devastating.

Our baby, less than a day old, had a deadly infection and there was absolutely nothing I could do. His tiny body lay there almost motionless, tubes feeding into and out of him. I wanted to hold him close, protect him from whatever it was that was harming him and make him safe and healthy through pure love. I couldn't even do that.

Nothing prepared me for this moment. Being dumped at boarding school, big race defeats, career-ending injury, tabloid headlines, relationship breakdowns – they all fade into insignificance in the face of such trauma. It destroys all the Big Man stuff you carry around. Be strong, take control, shoulder the burden – all that is impossible when you are a quivering wreck, tortured by anxiety and impotence.

Teddy being born was the best thing that ever happened to me. I was the proudest person on the planet. As soon as I saw him appear, I burst into tears. I held him in my arms and was hit by an immediate immense feeling of pure love. Wow, I wasn't expecting that. It came like a huge wave of emotion sweeping me along.

'Mother and baby fine.' Those are the first words all new dads want to be able to say to friends and relations. I couldn't wait to ring to my parents, who were away on a cruise. And I did say those words – and tell them just how perfect our baby boy was. I left the hospital around four in the morning and got home, exhausted and exhilarated. I laid down on the bed. The image of Teddy being held by his mum was etched on the back of my eyes, and, with a huge smile on my face, I fell asleep.

It felt like I had been asleep for five minutes when I heard the phone ringing. Still half asleep, I grabbed it and answered. It was Anna calling me from hospital. She could barely get the words out. 'You need to come back to the hospital quickly. He's in intensive care.'

It made no sense. I glanced at the time. No, that can't be right. There must be some mix-up. I'd been home less than two hours.

'His breathing's not right. You have to come in now.'

In seconds, the bottom fell out of my world. The joy I had gone to sleep with was replaced with fear and panic. My mind was spinning. *This doesn't happen. It can't happen. What the hell is going on?*

By the time I got back to hospital, the baby I had left in his mother's arms was in intensive care. He was lying there motionless with tubes in his mouth and his nose. Still shell-shocked, I was told that a vigilant midwife had noticed his breathing wasn't normal. He was grunting and gasping for air. They took him away for scans and tests which revealed he had fluid on his lungs and he had pneumonia.

In intensive care there were rooms numbered One to Four. All were for babies in desperate situations. Room One was where the most critical cases were and Room Four the least severe, although even those tiny souls were still in serious danger. He was in Room One. Just him and one other baby. It was horrific. Most of the babies there were very premature and tiny. They looked weak and ill. Teddy was normal size and looked fine, were it not for the tubes. We were not allowed to touch him. He just lay there, a baby hanging on to life.

The doctors were not sure what was wrong. His breathing was obviously not right and he had contracted pneumonia, but until they had done all their tests they wouldn't know. They were just keeping him alive at this point.

I watched him through the glass of the incubator. There were tubes going everywhere and a scary loud hum of machines constantly punctuated by beeps and buzzes. I'd spent my whole life fixated on numbers on a stopwatch or a race scoreboard, but here I had no idea what the digital displays on these machines meant.

Every time there was a beep at Teddy's incubator or a number rose or fell, I panicked. 'What does that mean?' I shouted desperately each time, and each time was gently reassured.

Five minutes later the digital number changed again and I was pointing to it and asking: 'That's no good, is it?' I had no control and it was torture.

In the end a nurse had to calm me down. 'Just relax,' she said. 'We've got this under control.'

I stayed as late as they would allow before I had to leave Anna and go home. I went straight to bed and lay there thinking the worst. My boy was going to die or need who knows what kind of support to have any life and there was absolutely nothing I could do. 'Please, God, take me instead.' I've never been religious, but I prayed to swap places with him. I closed my eyes, but I could still hear the hum, the buzzes and beeps.

I went back the next morning and walked into Room One. The incubator where he had been was empty. My heart sank and time stood still as I stared at where he had been. Thoughts sped through my head, but I couldn't grasp any of them. The hospital staff saw me and, rushing over, said, 'Don't panic. He's had a really good night. He's been moved to Room Two.'

There, they told us that he now had a diagnosis. He had Strep B. Strep what? We'd never heard of it before. We had no idea how he'd caught it, how serious it was and if he would recover. Group B Strep, we soon discovered, is bacteria carried by 2-4 women in every 10 that causes infection. They carry the bacteria without symptoms. It's an issue only if it transfers to unborn or newborn babies. That doesn't always happen, but when it does, it can lead to meningitis, pneumonia and sepsis.

He was in the best possible hands. That was the only reassuring thought I could find. He was no longer in Room One and he was being monitored, having regular blood tests to determine the level of infection. The waiting for results was agonising, but he had stabilised. Briefly. Even that proved to be a cruel trick. On the third day, when the test results came in, four doctors who I'd not seen before came running in and said, 'We're really sorry, but we've got to take him away immediately.'

His blood infection scores had suddenly risen from 46 to over 130. He was now in a critical state and they needed our permission to do a lumbar puncture. They had to be sure it wasn't meningitis and that it hadn't gone into the spinal fluid or his brain. We just said, do what you have to do. That my baby, less than a week old, was having to go through this was just pitiful. I couldn't even watch them insert the needle and repeated to myself, 'He won't remember this . . . he won't remember this.'

Now was an even more torturous wait; 24 hours waiting to discover if our son had suffered brain damage. You can't help but run that through your head over and over again. *How badly will he be affected? What are we to do? How will we be able to help him?* You can try to tell yourself it might not happen, but constantly your mind finds its own way of coming back to the possibility.

It was such a relief when they told us that they had got to it in time. I'd been desperately trying to hold it together and to be a calming force. That was OK when there were others around, but when I went home I was distraught and useless. I was falling apart and had hardly eaten in days. I'm not sure I would have done if my friend's wife hadn't started leaving meals for me on the doorstep. Those acts of kindness mean so much.

On day 5, Anna's auntie came down from Northumberland. I knew her least of all her family, but for some reason seeing her was the impetus for me to break down in tears. I had tried so hard to be the brave strong guy in front of everyone and suddenly the façade crumbled. All I could do was take myself off to the family day room in the hospital to try to collect my thoughts. I walked in with tears streaming down my face, and instead of the empty room I was used to by now, it was packed. I could hardly find a seat. Despite that, it was silent, and everyone looked up at me as I went and sat down. Looking for any distraction I could find, I got my phone out. Straightaway a message came through on one of the social media networks.

'I don't want to bother you. I'm in the family room and just seen you come in. You look in distress and I thought you might just need a hug.'

Jesus, he was right. I looked around and saw a guy give me the thumbs up and come over. I asked him how things were for him and he told me his daughter was here and his wife was in intensive care as well and it wasn't the first time – they'd lost a daughter last year. I was staggered. We hugged and I immediately felt that he, I and the others there were all connected through intense emotion. There were all these people in the same boat as me – or one even worse. I looked around the room. We were all fighting our own internal battles. All trying to come to terms with anguish and heartbreak and looking for a glimpse of hope. That feeling of human spirit can be so uplifting when you are at rock bottom.

By day 10, after 8 days in intensive care, Teddy had most of his tubes removed. The antibiotics were working. Those doctors and nurses at the Princess Anne Hospital had performed a miracle. We were taking Teddy home. We well knew that he was not out of the woods yet. We watched him obsessively, for anything that might seem out of the ordinary. Anyone who's had a baby knows they are not ordinary; they cry for no apparent reason, can vomit for fun and do the strangest coloured poos. When you are on a knife edge, all these can seem like symptoms of another emergency.

By this time we also knew that one of the main things with Strep B is that he had a massive chance of developing cerebral palsy. Is that what the poor thing faced now? They said they wouldn't know for a year. A year! It would take that long for any symptoms to emerge. This nightmare seemed like it just wasn't going to end. For the next 12 months and more, we were watching his every move. When he began to crawl and later walk, I'd think, *Is his right leg turning in?* and immediately fear the worst.

Teddy is now five. He still suffers from the consequences of Strep B. With his immune system damaged, he picks up every virus going and he has some pretty bad respiratory issues. He's permanently on inhalers and steroid-based antibiotics and regularly has coughing fits that land him in hospital. Twice, he has been rushed there by ambulance when he has struggled to breathe. We'll never forget how lucky we have been, though. One in ten babies with Strep B die and many are left with brain damage or other serious health issues. I'm now in touch with many of them and completely understand their struggles.

With all he puts up with, the boy is a 100 per cent trooper and he won't let any of it stop him or slow him down. From 5.30 in the morning until way past bedtime, he goes at it 100 miles an hour and nothing wears him out. He's up for anything, charges around and is always running. He has no off-switch. And two gears: full gas or fast asleep. Add in his cheek and sense of mischief and he's me – that hyperactive boy charging around and forcing a reluctant smile from my teachers. I'm not calming him down, I know exactly what it's like.

'Daddy, I don't want to be sick any more,' he's said to me when things get tough. How do you deal with that from a toddler? Especially one who always wants to be up and about? I try to turn it into a positive. I explain to him that the reason he coughs is because he's a superhero and if he didn't cough it would be unfair on everyone else. He'd be so much faster and stronger than them that no one would have a chance.

When COVID lockdowns were imposed, my work opportunities dried up. It was a blessing in disguise because I found myself at home with Teddy. We spent so much time together and I loved every minute as he grew from being a miracle baby to a fabulous boy.

Three years after his birth, his brother Dougie came along. This time, there were plenty of precautions and safeguards, though thankfully none were needed. This time there was no fuss, but the end result was the same: a fabulous boy who consumed my heart which already felt full to bursting. Dougie is so different to his brother. He is quieter and more self-contained. Just like my brother was a contrast to me, he doesn't feel the need to go at 100 mph. He is so different and yet just as adorable. I've got plenty of love to go round when it comes to my family and they can take as much as they want.

Becoming a dad meant a massive adjustment in my lifestyle. For so long my life had been so self-centred. Being an athlete meant being single-minded. It was always about me, about getting the most out of my body in order to be the best that I could be. I've wrecked past relationships through that determination. I had that 'If you don't like it, you know where the door is' attitude. Even at the time I often knew I was behaving like a complete jerk, but it was the person I believed I had to be.

I eased off when the athletics finished, but TV and presenting work has its own demands. I have to be away for long periods of time or be in certain places at specific times. That doesn't happen without a partner who is willing to compromise or even sacrifice their own plans and even dreams.

Then came Teddy. Suddenly nothing was about me. If I was up all night with Teddy, that was what I wanted to do. If I had to reschedule a work meeting to take him to the park, I was only too happy. My day revolved around him and that was the way I liked it. I want to be the best dad ever: indulgent, involved, fun. I'm soft to the extent of being a pushover and find it hard to say no.

I'd never thought much about having children of my own. I enjoyed playing with my mate's kids, but being a father wasn't a role I'd dreamed about. Maybe I didn't want the responsibility or I'd just been too busy to think about it. And yet, when it happened, my God, it was like I'd found a key piece of the jigsaw in my life. The love, the caring and protecting and the fulfilment I get just being with them feels so natural.

I feel as if it was all meant to be; the athletics, the dark times, getting my feet back on the ground. It has all led to this point. Those boys have helped me to feel complete and find contentment. Whatever it was that drove me through the highs and lows – the *must win, must be loved, must push myself to the limits* impulses – have if not gone, then been massively diluted by fatherhood. It has made me slow down, appreciate there is more to life than me and given me a real purpose.

# Seventeen

# 100 MILES

The pain was unbearable. I'd been limping from the start thanks to my still injured foot, but by Mile 10 my good foot was hurting so much that I didn't even notice the bad one. As miles went by, cramp-like pain gripped my whole body. Each tiny stone I stepped on felt like broken glass.

'He might as well quit. He's not going to make it.' That's what the steward said as I left the checkpoint. 'Fuck off,' I responded breathlessly. I'd avoided the cut-off by four minutes and still had 30 miles to go, but I knew for sure that I'd make it – as long as my body didn't give out on me. I had a photo of Teddy in my pocket and the words 'For those less fortunate' marker-penned on my arm. Every time it hurt, I looked at my arm and my picture and they reminded me why I was there.

I knew I would never quit. I could take any amount of pain, I wouldn't stop. And this time I had an extra reason, the most compelling reason, to keep going. Teddy had almost died from Strep B. Now I had a great opportunity to publicise the campaign to raise awareness of the danger. I was no longer running for medals, for records or pride. It wasn't about me any more. I wanted to make sure no other baby or parents went through the same ordeal as us and I was willing to put myself through anything to achieve that.

I might have given up athletics in 2006, but I'd never stopped running. The competitions and sponsorship ran out, I couldn't get near the speeds I once ran even when I was taking it easy, but it was in the blood. I ran. In 2008, a couple of years after I had not retired, I did a piece for *The McCain Track and Field Show* on Channel 4. I was taking some athletes through the preparation for a perfect race. I'd warmed up with them and felt good, so I asked the producers if I could run the race too. They thought it was a great idea. Lane 8 was free and I settled in on the start line. Maybe it was because I'd been talking them through the race, but I was well up for it. I went off really fast, smiling and feeling great. I was thinking to myself: *Hey, I've still got it!* Then, after 300 metres, reality set in. Those old feelings reappeared: the empty tank, the aching muscles. I was hurting so badly but pressed on and finished. And vomited. Just like old times!

I'd run 48.02. Not bad. At 36, I now qualified as a veteran and it was an official British record for that age group. That was it, though. My 400 metres days were officially over. I decided to try a longer distance, like 26.2 miles. Just for fun and to help raise a bit of money for charity. In 2009, I ran the London Marathon for the first time, and did it again in later years whenever I had the chance. In total I ran it eight times – and every single one was a massive struggle.

Marathons are painful and exhausting, but the camaraderie of the runners and the crowd's enthusiasm keeps you going. I managed to come in under four hours on my first London Marathon, but my times slipped over the next few. I loved stopping to have a laugh with people on the way and even started a tradition of stopping to have a pint en route. Still, my last try in 2016 was my best ever: 3:58:15.

Distance was now my thing. I still loved, even needed, to run. If I went a while without running, I'd feel grumpy, like something was missing. My addiction to running was satisfied by park runs, half-marathons and 10Ks – all just for fun. I did the Great North Run a few times and the Great South Run.

For all the training I'd gone through, I was never going to be a great distance runner. Back in the woods we'd run only half a mile. I'm 98 kg (15½ stone). I was built to go from A to B in 44 seconds, not plod away at a steady pace for hour after hour. So many people never got it. They looked at me, a former professional athlete who looked in OK shape, and expected me to be up among the leaders. They'd overtake me, slap me on the back and yell, 'Come on, mate, you're an Olympic medallist, you should be blowing this lot away!'

I loved being among the endurance athlete crowd, though. They were my kind of people; they enjoyed the suffering and pain. I met Mel C, aka Sporty Spice, in 2011 when I interviewed her after she had completed a triathlon in London. She is true to her nickname: she was a 200 metres runner in her youth and carried on running even at the height of Spice Girl mania. I already liked the Spice Girls, so I was always a bit in awe of her. She'd invite me to their shows, so it always felt a bit weird running alongside someone I'd watched on stage in front of thousands of screaming fans, but we got on really well and became training buddies and friends.

I met Susie Chan when I was hosting the National Running Show in 2020. Susie is one of the best-known UK ultrarunners and is inspirational. She's run the Marathon des Sables – six days and 250 km (160 miles) across the Sahara – an incredible four times and can convince almost anyone to be an endurance runner.

Including me. I made a foolish boast that I was over marathons and was ready for something longer. 'What about an ultra – a 50-miler?' I proposed. A double marathon. Yep, that sounded doable – with a little training. Susie and Mike Seaman, CEO of the Show and himself an experienced ultrarunner, took me up on it. Then Susie called my bluff.

'If you did a 50-mile race, people would really respect you, but –' a pause – 'if you want to be known as a double-hard bastard, you need to do a centurion. You know you've got to.'

'For fuck's sake. 100 miles? Over hills? That's what – well over 24 hours' running?' I ran it through my mind. That's four marathons and I had struggled to complete one. I had no idea if my body could take it; I'd had so many injuries, there were joints, tendons, muscles all waiting to give out. It was utter, utter madness. 'Yeah, sure. I'll do that.'

So I agreed to do the South Downs Way Centurion, a trail of 100 miles (160 km) from Winchester to Eastbourne. With a total climb of 10,000 feet

(3050 metres), it's equivalent to going a third of the way up Everest. Why did I agree to do it? You're right, I'm an idiot, but more than that, I cannot resist a challenge – and this time I had an incentive.

With first-hand experience of the dangers of Strep B and an understanding of how preventable it can be, I wanted to help publicise the Group B Strep Support charity in any way I could. As a result of the interviews I had done around the subject, I had already been contacted by mothers who had been tested and discovered that they were a carrier in time and others who hadn't and had sadly lost their babies. This was a massive opportunity, not just to get the message out but to raise money too. And if I could just help one person, it was going to be worth the pain.

For the first time in my life, I was taking on something that I really doubted I could achieve. I hadn't run more than 5 miles (8 km) for at least a year. I was a complete ultrarunning novice with just eight months to prepare. My 5 miles a week run needed to get up to 50 miles (80 km) a week as soon as possible. The trouble was, despite Susie's help, I was already struggling with the motivation, the sheer effort required and the toll it was taking on my body. It was also peak COVID time and we were in lockdown, which restricted the time we could train together.

A month passed and we still had hardly even started on the serious miles. Shit. I seriously considered ditching the whole idea. Of course, that was impossible. Letting myself down was one thing, but this was for Teddy and the thousands of others who had suffered. I owed it to him and them. I had to carry on.

It was a struggle. I didn't progress at all in those early months. My body was still broken from the pressures I'd put on it through the years. It hurt every time I went out. I felt it resented what I was putting it through and was doing its best to thwart me. I was back to trying to pitch my mind against my body – and for once, I really wasn't sure which would triumph. Susie continued to be encouraging and optimistic, but I knew she had real doubts too.

Eventually, I got my head down and with Susie's help began to get on top of the training. It was hard graft, getting out in all weathers and putting in the miles, but it was making a difference. The ultrarunner mindset had replaced my sprinter instincts. Short of moving your legs, ultrarunning has nothing in common with sprinting. It's a totally different sport. The Centurion was the equivalent of four hundred 400 metres races: it was about pure survival.

I'm built for speed and power, not for slogging it out over hills for mile upon mile. Sprinting is all about big strides, pumping arms and high knee lifts; ultrarunning is all about conserving energy and pacing yourself. For someone who always has to try to stop themselves going off like an express train, deliberately running really slowly takes some doing. I learned to run all over again. I practised pacing myself, worked on getting in the right frame of mind for a run that goes on all day and discovered on-the-move nutrition. Learning to eat and drink while running was one of the most difficult things of all.

By December, things were beginning to look up – and then *bang*. Literally *bang*. My car was stuck on a small tailback on the slip road joining the M27 when it was shunted from behind by a car doing 80 km/h (50 mph). The car was written off and fortunately no one was badly hurt, but I was shaken up, battered and bruised. I injured my back, neck and shoulder and couldn't even run, let alone put in the miles required at this stage. This was a feeling I hadn't experienced for years: watching the days – three whole months – just slip by, when I should have been ratcheting up the miles.

It was March before I was out again, just three months before the run. Strangely, I was feeling good. I did a marathon and felt alright. *I might be months behind schedule,* I thought. *But, this might not be so bad, you know?* Then another surprise. The organisers wanted me to do a 50-mile (80-km) training run in April – twice as far as I'd ever run before – to prove I was up to the Centurion. It was no longer about doubts, bluster and blind faith. This was make or break.

The route was along the South Downs Way from Farnham to Portsmouth, following some of the course the Centurion would take. Susie and Mike were running with me and a few friends said they would join for sections (including Suzanne Shaw of Hear'Say – I do like girl group runners!), which at least meant I would get plenty of support. I was so nervous. I still felt nowhere near ready. I knew I had the conviction to see it through, but that wasn't enough. Would my body hold out?

The answer was brutal: no.

It was hilly and tough, but I was doing fine. Ten, fifteen miles (16–24 km) went past and I felt as good as I had since I began training. I passed the marathon distance. Incredibly, it had taken me only 3 hours 40 minutes – nearly 20 minutes faster than my personal best on the London Marathon. And this run had hills. My confidence was boosted. Sure, every part of my body was beginning to ache, but I could cope with that. *This is bloody great*, I finally allowed myself to think. *I can do this. It's going to be OK.*

Then, around Mile 35 (56 km), I felt a pain shoot through my left foot. A broken bone was my immediate thought. I couldn't run. It was as much as I could do to limp through the last 15 miles (24 km). Every step was accompanied by an agonising, shooting pain. It was the most punishing four hours ever, as I counted down every mile to the finish. Teddy was waiting for me when I crossed the line – nearly 11 hours since I'd started. I was so pleased to see him and I gave a big hug, but my next thought was, *That was 50, how the hell am I going to do 100 miles?*

I had proved myself. But at what cost? I was broken. My foot was swollen and throbbing, the top of it constantly painful. The next day I went to A & E thinking I must have broken bones, maybe the metatarsals. I was wrong. I'd damaged the ligaments and tendons – which may sound better, but it was going to take longer to heal and time was something I didn't have. My foot was seriously injured.

They gave me crutches.

'But . . . I've got a 100-mile race in seven weeks,' I explained, like it was the most obvious thing in the world.

'Well, you can forget about that. There's no way you'll be ready.' They were adamant that it was impossible.

Those weeks went by. First hobbling around on crutches and resting up, then gingerly hobbling around, but nowhere near training. The issues were mounting up. These were crucial weeks meant to be bringing me to peak fitness, and here I was struggling even to get in the car. Added to that, my foot hadn't recovered and still hurt when I put pressure on it. For how long would it hold out?

I'd had worries and fears all along, but this now was an avalanche of doubt. It was time for making a decision. On the one hand, I might find it physically impossible. Plus it was very possible that I could do serious damage to my foot.

On the other, I'd made a commitment to the charity. I didn't want to back down and defer for a year (and I couldn't face going through all that training again). Sure, it was going to be a trial of how much pain I could take, but what could I do? It was always going to hurt, now it would just hurt a little bit more.

The run was getting close now. In nearly seven weeks, I'd done no training, just rested. Susie said, 'You've got to decide. Are you going to do this or not?' A few days before the run, we met at Butser Hill, one of the hills on the route. I did a 3-mile (5-km) jog to test how my foot reacted. I had a week or so left and was still limping and in a lot of discomfort. I struggled through the few miles, but it's fair to say I failed the test. I was so anxious; I'd never been so unsure about a decision in my life. But there was no going back now: I was going to get to the start line and see how it went from there.

Between then and the Centurion another problem arose. The day of the race, 12 June, came smack in the middle of a heatwave. Not exactly perfect for a pasty-faced, natural redhead. In all my time as an athlete I never fared well under a blistering sun; now I faced running across open ground for every minute of what was virtually the longest day of the year. It was going to sap my energy and make every mile of the 100 that much more difficult.

Not only would I be applying gallons of sun cream, but hydration would be a major issue. I was going to have to consume well over a litre (1¾ pints) of water per hour if I wasn't going to dehydrate. I had a double-barrel hydration pack vest – one with just water and one with a diluted sugar or energy drink. Each had a tube to suck and I needed to remember to sip regularly.

Susie told me that it could get up to 28°C (82°F) during the run and that much of the South Downs Way was completely exposed. Apparently, when the temperatures rise that much the DNF (Did Not Finish) numbers double. Runners don't change their plans to account for the heat, and they pay the price. She told me to save my energy, keep my heart rate down and just to walk in the hottest parts of the day.

Those few days, I ran it over and over in my head: I was driving myself crazy. It came to a head when I had to do my packing on the eve of the run. Unlike athletics where all you need is your kit and spikes, you can't afford to forget anything. You need to carry everything you might need: salt tablets, sun cream,

221

electrolytes, sweets, cashew nuts, head torch (and spare batteries) for night running, painkillers, energy drinks, spare layers – all squeezed into a small vest sack. When I packed it all in, tried it on and felt how heavy it was, I panicked. *I'm going to carry this, and run for 30 hours in a heatwave – on one leg?*

I had to calm myself down. *I've said I'll give it a go and I will. Stick with the plan.* When I laid out all my equipment and packed my bag, I felt like a soldier. *This is what it is. I'm going into battle against my deepest fear: failure.*

The early morning start left little time for any more ruminating. I had to get myself to the start around 4 a.m. as I was due to set off soon after that. It's a staggered start with the expected faster finishers at the front, so I was well down the list. I had but one objective: finish. And there were only two things that could stop me. Quitting. Or missing one of the many timed cut-off points, stationed at intervals along the course and intended to help us make the finish line within 30 hours of starting – the final cut-off. I was fairly confident of making the early points, but knew I was going to have to stay alert and not let my pace drop too much later on in the run.

My mates Tim and Scott picked me up at 3 a.m. to take me to the run. While there was an exciting buzz around the start, it wasn't evident from me, from Susie or from Mike of the National Running Show, who was going to be my running partner on the run. They were both nervous too, which didn't make me feel any better. My anxiety had really kicked in, but it was time to be optimistic. I put on my Factor 50, smothered my feet in Vaseline and engaged my positive mindset.

The first few miles of the run were odd. We had to do three laps of this huge bomb hole in a field. Three times we passed Susie at the start line and each time she tentatively put her thumbs up and mouthed, 'Is it alright?' I kept quiet and just kept running. Eventually I said to Mike, 'My foot's not good.' He ignored it and I ignored it. I was just going to keep running until my foot fell off.

Those first 10 miles (16 km) on the course were quite busy. The atmosphere was friendly, but the heat was so strong – we were sweating buckets at 6 in the morning – that not many words passed between anyone. Everyone knew they had a battle to get to the end. We didn't say much, just gave each other a look that said, 'We're all in this together.' I remembered a few people as they went by, including a nice guy who gave me a big encouraging smile. There was one couple who really got on my nerves, though. Every time we came to a kissing gate they would stop to kiss. I thought, *We're here to run 100 miles and you're just interested in public affection.* By the third gate, I'd had enough and said out loud, 'Oh, come on!' I obviously wasn't feeling so bad.

By around Mile 20 (32 km) we had got to Butser Hill where I had done my fitness test. The route became confusing because there was another run around there on the same day. Mike and I were chatting and missed a turning on the left, which meant we ended up running up the biggest hill in the midday sun. We hadn't seen any other runners for about an hour. I felt uneasy, but Mike reassured me that we were on the right track. Then his phone rang. The organisers had noticed on their tracer that we had gone off course. We'd gone over a mile in the wrong direction – an hour and a half wasted. It wasn't Mike's fault we'd got lost, but by the time we got back on course I was so angry that we didn't talk for a while.

At Mile 25 (40 km), I met briefly with Anna and Teddy in a car park along the way. That cry of 'It's Daddy' when he saw me was so uplifting, but the feeling didn't last long. Teddy was coughing a lot and Anna was quiet; she didn't want to tell me how bad he was. There was time for a hug before I was on my way – now I had something to worry about other than myself.

It wasn't long before we got lost again. This time wasn't as bad, but it was demoralising. And it was the last straw for Mike. He stopped to rest. I felt awful leaving him, but he was adamant that I carried on without him. He made it halfway and dropped out, and he wasn't the only one: the trail was so exposed that sunstroke was claiming plenty of victims. I couldn't have been looking that good either: the guy who had given me a big smile earlier, who I now found out was named Hideo, stopped to give me an ice cream.

I was on my own now. I just couldn't quit, though. There were too many reasons to carry on. I had the photo of Teddy and the words on my arm, an oath I couldn't break. I had also brought along a small silver cylinder. In it were some ashes of my friend Aaron, who had died during COVID. I'd asked his girlfriend if I could take them with me to feel he was with me along the way. I knew the big man would get me round.

Thinking back, the whole experience was bizarre. I had to eat on the move, every 40 minutes: salt and vinegar crisps (I needed a lot of salt), loads of cashew nuts, cheese sandwiches, caffeine tablets. At the aid stations along the route, I'd grab what I could, but Susie made me stay off too much sweet stuff to avoid a sugar crash.

There were some periods when I'd shuffle along, my backpack wearing me down, and others when all I could manage was a brisk walk. My throat was bone dry: no matter how much I drank, I couldn't feel hydrated. I felt the sun beating down on my back, sucking the energy out of me; I could feel the blisters growing by the minute; and my joints and muscles took it in turns to remind me of the injuries and operations I'd been through. What goes through your head through the hours and hours on the move is scary. Memories, anxieties, random thoughts – you just have too much time.

Ultrarunning just doesn't seem natural. First of all, you have to stay awake for 30 hours. You also have to keep moving forward, uphill, as fast as possible. And people do this for fun.

I calculated I was doing fine on the cut-off times so far and Mile 50 (80 km) was now my goal. Not only did it mark halfway, but at that point, the rule allowed Susie to run alongside me for a while. As soon as she joined me, I asked: 'How's Teddy and Anna?'

'Yeah, all fine,' she replied.

They continued to play on my mind. After another few miles, I had to ask again. 'Something's not right. I know.'

'Anna didn't want you to know,' she began. 'Teddy is in hospital. He's having breathing problems.'

*Oh Jesus. Decision time again. Do I quit now and get a taxi to Southampton or make it to the finish line for him?* I told myself Teddy was OK and in the best hands. And on a ventilator in hospital. Every single bit of me wanted to quit, except the one bit making that decision.

Where was I going to get a cab from anyway? I was in the middle of nowhere. There was nothing I could do. Even if I got to the hospital, COVID regulations were in force and only one parent could attend. I looked at his photo and the words I'd scrawled along my arm and carried on. I felt powerless and distraught;

I just had to get through this and get back to him as soon as I could, and the only way now was getting to that finish line.

I was battered. It was 9 p.m. and night was closing in. I'd never run at night and here I was in the middle of nowhere, no other runners in sight. I constantly looked at my watch, counting the miles and willing them to come sooner. I scanned ahead searching for signs of life. Finally, I saw the lights of the station at Mile 60 (96 km). A few people were resting. They were taking their shoes off, drinking tea, eating cake and chatting! I'd been watching my cut-off times carefully and thought, *What! I haven't got time to talk. I've got 40 miles to go!* I had a few sips of Coke, grabbed some wine gums and carried on.

By the time the next day ticked over, I'd been running for around 17 hours and still faced another 12. Susie had warned me that nothing can prepare you for running at night. She was so right.

I was completely alone in the pitch black with just a headlamp lighting my way, and the dark played tricks on my exhausted mind. Shadows cast monstrous shapes, sticks took the form of snakes reaching out for me and I was terrified by screaming demons that hurt my ears. Only after experiencing hallucinations based on every horror film I've ever seen did I discover those were the squeals from a pig farm. It was torture.

I was at my lowest ebb. I hurt so badly. And now I began to lose my motivation. Whatever it was driving me on from the start had been ground down. *What am I doing this for? Why put myself through such agony?* I had absolutely nothing to prove. And then I'd remember. *It isn't about me now. Every plodding, excruciating lurch gets me closer to the finish line. Keep going, keep going.*

I needed food so desperately. I knew that Susie's husband, Shaun, was on his way and I could smell the Chicken McNuggets® before I could even see him. He brought a Quarter Pounder® with Cheese too! I resisted the urge to devour it and took it slowly. Even so, my mouth was too dry. I couldn't taste anything and couldn't chew. I ended up spitting it out and throwing it away. Anyone who knows me will tell you how much I love a burger; this must have been the only time ever I haven't finished one.

Around 5 a.m., the sun finally rose over the Downs. I had survived the night. It was such a relief. I still throbbed and ached and burned across my body, but to have got to this point, with the early morning sun shining across the Downs, felt almost spiritual. I felt like I was dying, my body about to surrender, but at the same time I felt so alive. A new day and I was still running. At that moment, I saw Hideo again. I hadn't noticed, but he had overtaken me sometime in the night. I put an extra effort in to catch him and he greeted me with: 'Oh my God! You're still going!'

This is known as the toughest Centurion in the country, and the heat and humidity just made it worse. People were dropping around every corner. Half the starters didn't finish the race. One bloke arrived at the checkpoint looking awful. I asked him if he was OK and he just said, 'No, I'm finished. That's me done.' I thought, *Yep, that's me. I could do that.* I saw another runner slumped on the ground. Had he collapsed? It certainly looked like it. When I got nearer, I said, 'Are you alright, mate?' He opened his eyes a little and said, 'Yeah, thanks, I'm just getting a bit of sleep.' I let him be.

I still had another 30 miles (48 km) left. If I was still in the run. When I got near to the checkpoint I thought: *I'm OK here, I've got 24 minutes left before the cut-off,* so I was surprised when the official shouted: 'Come on! You've only got four minutes to spare!' I had miscalculated my start time and had 20 minutes less than I thought. I'd get through this one OK, but I was in serious pain and couldn't imagine how I would make the next checkpoint in time. I was in real danger of not completing the race.

Susie told me I had to make up 20 seconds every mile from now on. That meant I needed to average 18-minute miles for the next 25 if I was going to finish. It really did feel impossible. I just couldn't run for long periods and I wasn't able to walk any faster. My head throbbed, marking every second that was ticking away. I cursed myself in fury, shame, embarrassment . . .

The writing on my arm was now illegible, worn away by sweat, but by now I knew exactly what it said and what it meant. I couldn't let all that training and the excruciating pain, heartbreak and physical effort of a whole day's running be in vain. When I heard the steward say: 'He might as well quit. He's not going to make it', I still had enough in me to rise to it. To see it as a challenge. Here was some kind of flashback to my racing days. *I'm not going out like this. I'm not going to let this race beat me. I never gave up in the 400 metres, never. This is not happening.* The Switch clicked.

This was what I did. I found something beyond the pain. Something stronger. This time it wasn't for a gold medal, for sponsorship deals or for a record time, it was for something that meant so much more to me. No amount of hurt was going to overcome that drive. It was an out-of-body experience – almost. (Oh, how I'd loved that to have been the case.) When the morning sunshine was interrupted by fog up in the hills, it was all too surreal.

I was counting every second and checking my pace. I was cutting it so fine, I didn't even stop to pee. I turned the 4 minutes to spare into 10 minutes, then into 15. By the time there were only 8 miles (13 km) to go, I had somehow managed to build for myself a 20-minute cushion. I ran the last 30 miles (48 km) more quickly than the first 30.

I emerged at the top of the hill to see Eastbourne, my destination, stretched out before me. The route, though, looked the most treacherous yet: a steep, single-file track down the hill, scarred by holes, stones and branches stretching across the path. I became paranoid, sure that injury, which had dogged my career, had one last cruel surprise for me. Convinced I was going to trip and break my ankle, I now took such care with my foot placing as I descended.

With 5 miles (8 km) to go, time was no longer a problem. But the paranoia crept over me. My body was still sending danger signals. I ached so much all over, it seemed every joint and muscle was on the verge of giving out. Then I made the weirdest calculation. *If I tear my hamstring or my knee pops out, can I crawl the rest of the way and still make it in time?* I had to cross that finish line one way or another.

I was 25 minutes clear of the end cut-off time when I reached the final mile. Hours and hours ago, running with Susie, I'd been chatting away to pass the time and going through all my jokes. I said to her, 'When we get to the final mile, I've got something to tell you.' She said, 'What is it? Come on. Tell me.' I fobbed her off, saying, 'Oh just a crap joke.' I put my secret away in my locker: it was one more thing to help me get through.

We were about half a mile from the finish when she said, 'Hey. What was that joke you promised to tell me?'

I looked her in the eye and said, 'Susie, I wanted you to be one of the first to know.'

'What? Know what?'

'I'm going to be a dad again!'

She started crying and that set me off. I'd known that wanting to tell her my secret would get me to the finish line – and now it almost had.

The final 400 metres of the 100 miles was a lap of the athletics track at Eastbourne. What an irony. This the slowest, most painful, most emotional 400 metres I had ever run. I was a complete mess, unable to control my thoughts and emotions. Swirling around my head were memories of Teddy in intensive care; the stories told to me by Strep B parents about their babies; the endless training; the car crash and injuries; the moments of despair in the race when I thought I wouldn't make it; the overwhelming pain that radiated through my body – and the relief and pride of having reached the finish. It took me three minutes to run that final lap – every second of them filled with tears.

I finally crossed the line, looked at my watch, smiled and said, 'Ah, I've got 25 minutes to spare. Piece of piss!' It got a good laugh from the organisers. I think I was second to last of those who managed to finish. I went and sat down because my foot was so bad. And at that point all the adrenaline drained away. I went white as a ghost and collapsed. They had to cut the socks off me; my blisters had ballooned, they were purple and covered half the side of my foot. Shaun and Mike (who had kindly waited for me to finish) carried me to the car. I don't remember the journey home, but when I arrived Anna and Teddy were still at the hospital. I knew they wouldn't be back until later that night, so I hobbled up the stairs and fell into bed.

I didn't get out of it for three days, I couldn't move.

It was by far the toughest thing I have ever done in my life. The trauma is unimaginable. The damage I did to my legs on that race means I might never be able to run again. But I will never regret having run it. The Centurion wasn't about me proving anything, looking for approval or having to be the best. Those days are long gone. I ran it when I was 47 years old. Running because I wanted to. Because I had a cause I believed in so badly.

As hard as it was, whenever someone asks me my personal best, I say: 29 hours, 35 minutes and 3 seconds. It is something I will never forget – and if I ever can, I will do it all over again.

# EPILOGUE

I'd never really considered writing an autobiography. It has been a quarter of a century since I was headline news on the sports pages. What was there to say? It turned out there was plenty. When things went well everything went so fast. I never had a chance to stop to consider what was happening. And when they stopped, it was too tough to see through the dark clouds.

Perspective is everything.

I know I was privileged. I was blessed in having parents who cared and supported me. I enjoyed a fantastic career in athletics. I had the best 400 metres coach in the world in Mike Smith, met great athletes, including the guys I won the gold medal with and still count as friends, and I got to race against (and beat!) the best 400 metre runner the world will ever see.

I know too what it is to suffer. To feel both physical pain and the black cloud of depression that seems like it will never leave. But even they don't come anywhere near to the heart-wrenching helplessness of seeing my newborn child lying in intensive care. My heart will forever go out to those facing that same agony and distress.

What I know about the present is that I am the most contented I have ever been in my life. Together, Anna and I have made a beautiful family that's made me feel complete. Every moment we spend together is worth more than a gold medal to me. By the time this book is published, I will have a third son. I can't wait. If only I could still run, we'd make a fabulous relay team.

I am also so grateful to be involved with athletics and television – a sport for which I have such a passion and a great career I never thought I'd have. Like many people, I still have times when I am down, but now I am able to share those feelings and I know they will pass. I've come to terms with myself. All my life I've desperately looked to prove myself and to earn affection – especially from those I love. Now, I feel I have all the love I need and only want to be the best father I can possibly be.

In May 2022, at the Diamond League athletics meeting in Eugene, Oregon, Matthew Hudson-Smith ran the 400 metres in 44.35 seconds. By one hundredth of a second, it broke the British record. A record that I had held for 25 years. Finally, it was over – and I was so relieved. I had been Iwan Thomas, the British record holder for too long. An honour I was once so proud to carry had become a burden, a chain that connected me to a part of my life that I had never fully been able to leave behind. Now, that was possible.

Finally I could admit what I had waited 15 years or more to say: I was an athlete – a really good athlete. And then I wasn't.

I am Iwan Thomas.

# ACKNOWLEDGEMENTS

I couldn't finish this book without thanking some really important people in my life.

Firstly, to everyone who has tried to keep my body in one piece when it kept breaking as an athlete. You know who you are, thank you for your help.

Mike, who sadly will never get to read these words: you are so special to me, way more than just a coach. Every day I'm grateful that we met. I'll always be in debt for your guidance and I realise I would not have accomplished anything in my career without you.

To my close circle of friends, old and new, thank you for being true. Really importantly, Sue, who has been a brilliant manager and has stuck by me through some, frankly, pretty tough times. Thank you for being there when times were good and bad, I will always be grateful to you.

To all my training group: cheers, lads, you truly helped shape me.

To Adrian, who has been a godsend, helping me put pen to paper. Thank you for your patience, and I'm sure both of us have learned a lot along this journey. I couldn't have done it without you.

To my parents, thank you for always being supportive. Quite frankly, I owe you everything.

My brother, Gareth: sorry I was such a little shit growing up.

Lastly, to Anna: thank you for putting up with me and giving me the three most amazing children I could wish for.

My boys, this book and everything I do is for you. Your daddy will always love you.

Iwan
Southampton, 2024